The Attack of Stonewall Jackson at Chancellorsville

by
Augustus C. Hamlin

Introduction by
Frank A. O'Reilly

SERGEANT KIRKLAND'S
Fredericksburg, Virginia

Copyright 1997

Published & Distributed by
Sergeant Kirkland's Museum
and Historical Society, Inc.
912 Lafayette Blvd., Fredericksburg, Virginia 22401-5617
Tel. (540) 899-5565; Fax: (540) 899-7643
E-mail: Civil-War@msn.com

Manufactured in the USA
The paper in this book meets the guidelines for permanence and durability
of the Committee on Production Guidelines for Book Longevity
of the Council on Library Resources, Inc.

Library of Congress Cataloging-in-Publication Data

Hamlin, Augustus C. (Augustus Choate), 1829-1905.
  [Battle of Chancellorsville]
  The attack of Stonewall Jackson at Chancellorsville / by Augustus
C. Hamlin; introduction by Frank A. O'Reilly.
      p.   cm.
  Originally published: The Battle of Chancellorsville. Bangor, ME:
A.C. Hamlin, 1896.

ISBN 1-887901-12-4 (alk. paper)

  1. Chancellorsville (Va.), Battle of, 1863. 2. Jackson, Stonewall,
1824-1863. I. Title.
E475.35.H22   1997
973.7'33—dc21   97-10127
                            CIP

Printed in the United States of America.

1 2 3 4 5 6 7 8 9 10

The Attack of Stonewall Jackson at

Chancellorsville

Contents

Introduction
By Frank O'Reilly

In the early morning of May 2, 1863, a small cavalcade of Federal horsemen galloped out the Orange Plank Road. At the head of the group, "...with the air of a king, very red in the face, but holding his big fat body very erect," rode the commander of the Army of the Potomac, Major General Joseph Hooker. Close behind him cantered the one-arm nascent leader of the Union Eleventh Corps, Major General Oliver Otis Howard. Merry staff officers bantered and teased while the generals glanced over their defenses. After a short look, Hooker voiced his satisfaction with the Eleventh Corps position and returned to Chancellorsville to consummate his mysterious plans for victory over Confederate General Robert E. Lee.[1]

Nine hours later, the soldiers of the Eleventh Corps sat stoically manning their trenches or cooking dinner and listening to the sweet refrains of musicians in the distance. They also heard rumors that the Confederates had abandoned the battlefield and now hurried to escape the Federals' clutches. "Unharness those horses, boys, give them a good feed of oats," laughed General O.O. Howard. "We will be off for Richmond at daylight." Suddenly, a startled deer bolted from the forest, barreling through the astonished soldiers. Other deer darted from the woods, pursued by rabbits, foxes and birds scurrying in every direction. All nature had gone awry. Driving the wildlife before them came the cadenced ranks of Lieutenant General Thomas J. "Stonewall" Jackson's Confederates. The gray-clad Southerners plowed into the Union defenses "...like a crash of thunder from the clear sky."[2]

---

[1] Baron Friedrick Otto von Fritsch, "A Modern Soldier of Fortune," memoir. Library of Congress (hereafter cited LC).

[2] Luther B. Mesnard, reminiscences. Civil War Miscellaneous Collection, United States Army Military History Institute (hereafter cited USAMHI).

The Rebels swarmed out of the woods and around the Federals' flank and rear. Almost all of the Northerners faced to the south, as did their earthworks, but Jackson's men charged from the west. Outnumbered Federals attempted to stand before the torrent but the Confederates lapped around their flanks and threatened to swallow them whole. Von Gilsa's brigade caved in, then McLean's. "No troops could have acted differently," empathized Confederate artillerist, Colonel Edward Porter Alexander. "All their fighting was of one brigade at a time against six." As these men fell back, the Rebels pressed after them and savaged their ranks. More and more Federals became caught up in the reeling nightmare. Soon confusion set in, and then panic. Jackson's Confederates routed a substantial part of the Eleventh Corps off the field. O.O. Howard exploded irrationally as his corps evaporated in turmoil. Waving a pistol with his one remaining hand he screamed at the survivors, "Halt! Halt! I'm ruined, I'm ruined; I'll shoot if you don't stop; I'm ruined, I'm ruined." One of his division commanders, Brigadier General Charles Devens had left the field, wounded in the foot. His replacement, Brigadier General Nathaniel McLean, had also fallen. Many Eleventh Corps line officers tumbled, killed or wounded in the first few minutes, and Howard despaired. Later he admitted, "I felt…that I wanted to die…. I did all in my power to remedy the mistake, and I sought death everywhere." The stream of soldiers ignored the humiliated commander and continued toward the safety of Chancellorsville. Everywhere the Federals turned, "…gray infantry flowed like a sea that nothing could push back." Nearly surrounded, the Northern soldiers scampered for safety. "And, why did we run?" queried a survivor. "Well, those who didn't run are there yet!"[3]

General Hooker sat relaxed on the front porch of the Chancellors' home when a staff officer pointed westward and exclaimed, "My God, here they come!" A raging deluge of bewildered, disheveled, and disorganized refugees roiled past the

---

[3] Edward Porter Alexander, *Military Memoirs of a Confederate*, (New York, Charles Scribner's Sons, 1907) p. 337; James H. Peabody, "Battle of Chancellorsville," *Grand Army of the Republic War Papers, Department of Ohio*, (Cincinnati, n.d.) Vol. I, p. 53; Ernest B. Furgurson, *Chancellorsville 1863*, (New York: Alfred A. Knopf, 1992) p. 181; William B. Southerton, reminiscences, Ohio Historical Society (hereafter cited as OHS).

westward to blunt the Confederate advance in the darkening forest. But Stonewall Jackson's men had already checked their rampage for the evening and Jackson himself soon fell victim to a lethal encounter before the night drew half past nine.[4]

The men of the Eleventh Corps had endured a terrible fright, but their battle was just beginning. A few hours of combat soon transformed itself into a lifetime struggle for dignity and justice. An Eleventh Corps soldier plaintively opined, "Could I have guessed the horrible disgrace my good Corps would have to endure later on," he would have insisted O.O. Howard personally reconnoiter the weak left flank.[5]

When the Federals abandoned Chancellorsville and retreated across the Rappahannock River on May 6, 1863, the rest of the Army of the Potomac blamed their misfortune exclusively on the Eleventh Corps. American-born soldiers with strong nativist Know-Nothing beliefs had eyed the Eleventh Corps suspiciously from the start, focusing on its cadre of Germans and German-Americans. American soldiers derided the Eleventh Corps soldiers as "foreigners," even though only 4,000 of the 12,000-man corps could be considered German or of German-descent. Many insisted that the Battle of Chancellorsville had been won until the feeble Dutch had fled (Americans derived "Dutch" inelegantly from the word "Deutsch," meaning "German"). The once-proud cry of "I fights mit Sigel" now carried a contemptuous coda: "and I runs mit Howard." These Germans had somehow snatched defeat from the hands of certain victory.[6]

"The Eleventh Corps was branded coward after that throughout the army," a Third Corps soldier reported. Captain John Barclay Fassitt, of Major General Daniel E. Sickles' staff, called the hapless soldiers "...the flying Dutch fools," and testified to their perfidy. "Posted as they were," he scrawled, "any beings with manly instincts should have held until the earth swallowed them up." An observant Second Corps staff officer noted that

[4] Augustus C. Hamlin, "Chancellorsville," *National Tribune*, July 13, 1893. (Unless otherwise noted, all references to the *National Tribune* are part of a series of articles Hamlin wrote in 1892-1893.)

[5] Von Fritsch, "A Modern Soldier of Fortune," LC.

[6] T.A. Meysenberg, "Reminiscences of Chancellorsville," *Military Order of the Loyal Legion of the United States — Missouri Commandery*, (n.p., 1892; Wilmington [N.C.], 1993) Vol. I, p. 306; Southerton, reminiscences, OHS.

everyone treated the Eleventh Corps with "a feeling of contempt." Henry N. Blake, of the 11th Massachusetts, recorded, "The Germans sought to escape the censure which the whole army justly bestowed upon them," but the rest of the army agreed that the Germans had failed utterly as soldiers and "...not the slightest sign was given of sympathy."[7]

The Army of the Potomac, forged in the 1862 Peninsula Campaign under Major General George B. McClellan's nurturing hand, classified the Eleventh Corps as outsiders and never accepted its soldiers into their close-knit fraternity. Their Germanic heritage only accentuated the fact that they did not share the same élan as the older corps. The obdurate army's suspicions now seemed justified. Northern newspapers labeled the Germans as "a worthless lot" and "ragged scums" and called for "shooting the whole corps." Factions inside the army begged Hooker to dismantle the corps. "The denunciation became extreme, and soon passed the bounds of decency," wrote the medical director of the Eleventh Corps, Doctor Augustus Choate Hamlin.[8]

"The Eleventh Corps was then considered as [the] lawful dumping-ground for errors and mistakes," lamented one soldier, "and all kinds of burdens and humiliations were heaped upon it." These external distractions influenced the view of many inside the maligned corps. "After the battle the entire corps was denounced...Americans, Germans, French, Italians, Hungarians, Swiss, Irish, and Welsh—were massed together as a worthless lot, and described as Dutchmen." Many attempted to disassociate themselves from the German element and echoed the criticisms already heaped on the Teutons. Oliver O. Howard led the initiative by blaming the lost battle on the "bad conduct of his corps". John Lewis, of the 17th Connecticut, regaled the folks back

---

[7] John B. Fassitt, letter dated May 9, 1863, Civil War Collection, West Virginia University (hereafter cited WVU); Francis A. Walker, *History of the Second Army Corps*, (New York, 1887) p. 229; John Bigelow, *The Campaign of Chancellorsville*, (New Haven, 1910) pp. 311-312; Henry N. Blake, *Three Years in the Army of the Potomac*, (Boston, Lee and Shepard, 1865) p. 180.

[8] *National Tribune*, August 3, 1893; *National Tribune*, June 29, 1893: Hamlin wrote, "When the corps joined the Army of the Potomac at Fredericksburg, it certainly did not meet with that cordial welcome which it expected.... On the contrary, there is abundant testimony to show the existence of a strong dislike and distrust, which was undeserved."

home: "You will no doubt hear that the 11th Corps broke and run which is so, but our Briggade [sic] stood firm till outnumbered." He concluded, "...the Dutchmen proved themselves cowards." Marlow D. Wells, of the 157th New York, noted that the Germans "ran like dogs." Darwin Dianthus Cody, of an Ohio battery wrote, "They run without firing a gun...I say dam [sic] the DUTCH." Even the Chief Surgeon of Barlow's brigade, with the truly Dutch name of Henry von Aernum, admitted, "...the Dutch part of it did behave like slinks in the fight...." Few Americans denied that the Germans panicked. Instead, they cautioned outsiders to be careful whom they called Germans.[9]

Morale collapsed in many units in the aftermath of Stonewall Jackson's surprise attack. A member of the 33rd Massachusetts wrote, in a letter from the battlefield, "Every body is cursing the 11th corps...We are now in disgrace." Dr. von Aernum agreed, informing his family, "Just now it is a reproach for a man to belong to the 11th Army Corps." "The 11th Corps has got a bad name now, and we were not to blame," declared Marlow Wells, "although we belong to the 11th and consequently have to bear the stigma that will be attached to it." Some of the soldiers tore the once-treasured corps badges from their uniforms rather than be associated with the Eleventh Corps. Some sneered that the corps donned "the Flying Half Moon" and others hissed at its bearers "...for the crescent was recognized as the insignia of a poltroon." A rumor even circulated that a colonel in the corps had blown his brains out rather than live with the disgrace.[10]

The officers and men of the corps argued that no troops under similar circumstances could have withstood Jackson's onslaught, but very few outside the corps listened or even cared. Brigadier General Alexander Schimmelfennig complained that, "...if the infamous lies uttered about us are not retracted," the

---

[9] *National Tribune*, August 10, 1893; *National Tribune*, August 3, 1893; John Lewis, letter dated May 14, 1863, Lewis Leigh Collection, USAMHI; Cazenovia [NY] *Republican*, May 20, 1863; Darwin D. Cody, letter dated May 9, 1863, possession of Mr. Roland Lowery, copy in collections at Fredericksburg & Spotsylvania National Military Park (hereafter cited Fred-Spot); Henry von Aernum, letter dated May 15, 1863, Von Aernum Papers, Fred-Spot.

[10] Edward Louis Edes, letter dated May 4, 1863, E.L. Edes Collection, Massachusetts Historical Society; Von Aernum letter, Fred-Spot; Cazenovia *Republican*, May 20, 1863; Blake, p. 180; Alexander Bird, "The Eleventh Corps at Chancellorsville," *National Tribune*, April 22, 1886.

morale of his men would be hopelessly destroyed. Some of the soldiers believed that the generals' official reports would cast some light on the true nature of their defense. "Suffice it to say," piped one such optimist, "official reports will vindicate us." Major General Carl Schurz also believed in this riposte. He demanded that all of his officers file their reports as soon as possible. He also encouraged them to circulate their reports so they could compare and dissect the events of May 2, 1863. Schurz closed his own report: "Being charged with such an enormous responsibility as the failure of a campaign involves, it would seem to me that every commander in this corps has a right to a fair investigation of his conduct...." He anxiously begged permission to publish his report to answer the Eleventh Corps' critics. When Hooker failed to respond, Schurz pressed the War Department for permission. General-in-Chief Henry W. Halleck, reputed to have "...had a mortal aversion of all foreigners desiring to serve in our armies," declined Schurz's plea, stiffly observing that "Publication of partial reports [are] not approved till the General commanding has time to make his report." Schurz remained powerless until Hooker filed his own version of events. Hooker never did file a report on Chancellorsville, thus thwarting Schurz's vindication.[11]

A month after the Chancellorsville debacle, the loyal Germans of New York held a mass meeting at the Cooper Institute to protest "the unjust treatment" of the Eleventh Corps. Speakers on behalf of the corps included the provost marshal of the army, Brigadier General Marsena R. Patrick, and Irish favorite, Brigadier General Thomas F. Meagher. The government refused to take any notice of their petitions. Denied a voice to expose the truth, the corps' ignominy became ingrained after the war as part of the rich, but random, tapestry of popular history. Several advocates of the corps tried to temper this fervor but endured blistering personal attacks, slurs, and gibes.[12]

---

[11] Samuel P. Bates, *History of Pennsylvania Volunteers*, (Harrisburg, B. Singerly, State printer, 1869) Vol. II, p. 896; Benjamin A. Willis, [Hempstead] *Queens County Sentinel*, May 21, 1863; Bigelow, p. 478; Von Aernum letter, Fred-Spot; *National Tribune*, June 29, 1893; Furgurson, p. 335.

[12] *National Tribune*, August 3, 1893; Adin B. Underwood, *The Three Years Service of the Thirty-Third Massachusetts Infantry Regiment*, (Boston: A. Williams & co., 1881) p. vii. The Cooper Institute meeting convened June 2, 1863.

Post-war writers and historians continued to blame the Chancellorsville fiasco on the recreant Germans right into recent times. One circumspect historian noted that "a victim was needed, and...the Eleventh Corps was made the scapegoat." Joseph Hooker became the first and most virile detractor. He constantly belittled the corps and particularly its commander. Often the subject of the Eleventh Corps lined his "bucket of abuse." In a letter to historian (and chief Hooker-protagonist) Samuel P. Bates, Hooker bitterly condemned Howard, believing "...the stampede of Howard's Corps, result[ed] solely from the imbecility and want of soldiership on the part of its commander." Hooker thought Howard acted like an old woman and "...if he was not born in petticoats, he ought to have been, and ought to wear them."[13]

Hooker's death, in 1879, sparked a renewed tirade against Howard and his unreliable corps. Regimental histories from Massachusetts and New Jersey perpetuated the stories of "shameful cowardice" and "frightened sheep" in the German corps. Their tales "...became household words in the land, and linger yet." James H. Peabody, of the 61st Ohio, cried, "The burning shame of that stigma had followed us for nearly twenty-eight years, and will follow us on to the grave, and still on to the end of time." Quietly, he confessed, "Many times I have hesitated to admit having been in the Eleventh Corps." An Eleventh Corps officer wryly noted that reunions among some New Jersey units "lacked inspiration" until a few faithful "Falstaffs" warmed the crowd with hilarious stories of wild Huns scrambling through the Wilderness. Eventually, other regimental histories promulgated the stories, "taking it for granted without investigation" that the Germans were not worthy of being called soldiers.[14]

A series of histories continued to bury the veterans of the corps still deeper in abuse. In 1888, Federal cavalryman Brigadier

[13] *National Tribune*, July 27, 1893; August 3, 1893; August 10, 1893; Joseph Hooker letter to Samuel P. Bates, dated December 24, 1878, Samuel P. Bates Papers, Pennsylvania State Archives; Hooker interview in San Francisco *Chronicle*, May 23, 1872. Hamlin generously glossed over Hooker's vituperation, observing, "it is certainly charitable to believe that Hooker's head was severely injured at the Chancellor House, as well as his back."
[14] Henry C. Ropes, 20th Massachusetts, quoted in Bigelow, p. 478; *National Tribune*, August 3, 1893; C.W. McKay, "Buschbeck's Brigade at Chancellorsville," *National Tribune*, March 12, 1891; Samuel E. Pittman, "The Operations of General Alpheus S. Williams and His Command in the Chancellorsville Campaign," *Military Order of the Loyal Legion of the United States – Michigan Commandery*, (Detroit, 1893) Vol. I, p. 10; Peabody, p. 57.

General Alfred Pleasonton penned a collection of self-serving and fantastic stories of single-handedly stopping the crush of Stonewall Jackson's Confederates, and saving the key ground of Hazel Grove amidst the chaos of panicked Germans overturning cannon and wagons until the debris piled many feet high. Pleasonton's imagination met with immediate acclaim and others rushed to incorporate his stories into their writings. James H. Stine, John Watts DePeyster, and the Comte de Paris uncritically accepted the story as fact. Abner Doubleday even embellished Pleasonton's toxic fiction with reputed quotes between the general and his officers. The artillerist John C. Tidball used this fantasy to claim that the Germans created so much confusion at Hazel Grove that the Union Third Corps lost one of its cannons. (Closer examination however, reveals that the Third Corps never reported any missing guns.) Augustus C. Hamlin classed Pleasonton as a "shallow braggart" and noted that his skewed memories "...have been printed in encyclopedias, in mushroom military works, in official and semi-official volumes, both in this country and Europe." Fiery Dan Sickles, leader of the Third Corps, continued to rail against the Germans, employing Pleasonton's account, well into the twentieth century. Even the most respected student of the battle, John Bigelow, criticized the Germans in his definitive study of the campaign. He acknowledged that no troops holding the Eleventh Corps' position could have staved off disaster, but he suggested that "...other men might have comported themselves with more dignity, or less ignominy, even while running for their lives."[15]

Hooker's death and Pleasonton's stories provoked several Eleventh Corps veterans to speak out in defense of the soldiers. Adin B. Underwood, colonel of the 33rd Massachusetts, tried to make "a full defence, which long since should have been done," in his regimental history. Theodore A. Dodge of the 119th New York also wrote a book on Chancellorsville and constantly lectured against "the remarkable romancing" of tainted history. Other writers took up their cudgels in the newsprint of the *National*

---

[15] *National Tribune*, December 12, 1892; Theodore A. Dodge, "The Romances of Chancellorsville," *Papers of the Military Historical Society of Massachusetts*, (Boston, 1903) p. 197 (hereafter cited *P.M.H.S.M.*); Bigelow, p. 479.

Tribune. Only one voice, however, rose above the clamor to argue for the dignity of the Eleventh Corps with authority.[16]

Doctor Augustus Choate Hamlin stood in a position to judge the merit of all the arguments for and against the beset corps. Born in Columbia, Maine, in 1829, Hamlin was the son of Elijah Livermore and Eliza Bradley (Choate) Hamlin, and the nephew of Abraham Lincoln's first vice president, Hannibal Hamlin. Young Augustus graduated from Bowdoin College in 1851 and studied medicine in Paris and then at Harvard, where he received his doctorate in 1854. Three years later, he married Helen A. Cutting of Bangor, who blessed him with two children: Helen Agnes, born at the outbreak of the Civil War; and Fred Cutting, born in 1873. When war erupted in 1861, the new father did not disappoint his vice-presidential uncle. He raised a company of volunteers at his own expense and went to war as the assistant surgeon of the 2nd Maine Volunteer Infantry. "Although numerically the second," documented the unit's history, "this was in fact the first regiment which left the State for the seat of war." After a rocky initiation to battle at Manassas on July 21, 1861, the doctor rose to brigade surgeon in April, 1862, and, eventually, became the Medical Director of the Union Eleventh Corps. Major General John C. Fremont commended Dr. Hamlin for being "...most worthy and efficient in his duties." In the summer of 1863, the army elevated Hamlin to medical inspector and sent him to Major General Quincy A. Gillmore's Department of the South, where he witnessed most of the operations around Battery Wagner and Charleston, South Carolina. Late in the war, he transferred to the staff of Major General George H. Thomas at Nashville. Hamlin finally mustered out of the army in November, 1865, and set up a private medical practice in Bangor, Maine.[17]

---

[16] Underwood, p. viii; Dodge, *P.M.H.S.M.*, p. 196.

[17] Simon Moulton Hamlin, *The Hamlins of New England*, (printed privately, 1936) p. 37; United States War Department, *War of the Rebellion: A Compilation of the Official Records of the Union and Confederate Armies*, 128 vols. (Washington D.C., 1880-1901) Vol. XII, p. 26 (hereafter cited *OR*); *OR* XXVIII, part 2, p. 6; *Who Was Who in America*, (Chicago, 1943) Vol. I, p. 512; William E.S. Whitman and Charles H. True, *Maine in the War for the Union*, (Lewiston [Me.], 1865) p. 37; James H. Mundy, *Second to None: The Story of the 2d Maine Volunteers*, (Scarborough, ME: Harp Pub., 1992) pp. 81-83; James Grant Wilson and John Fiske, eds., *Appleton's Cyclopedia of American Biography* (New York, 1888) Vol. III, p. 66. Mundy intimates that Hamlin left the field at First Manassas prematurely and the 2nd Maine never forgave him.

Augustus C. Hamlin continued to lead men in the post-war era. He served twice as the mayor of Bangor, assumed the position of department commander for the Maine Commandery of the Grand Army of the Republic, and chaired the pension commission on behalf of the national constituency of the G.A.R. His love of history led him to serve as Maine's commissioner to the Yorktown Centennial celebration in 1881. His civic and medical efforts drew international attention and, in 1878, the Czar of Russia made Hamlin a chevalier of the Order of Saint Anne.[18]

Hamlin was peculiarly suited to champion the Eleventh Corps' actions at Chancellorsville. The doctor not only offered a strong war record, familiar political connections, and a sterling post-war civic career, but he also loved to write. Augustus C. Hamlin thrived on the written word and authored a profusion of books and articles ranging from medical discoveries to gem collecting and trout fishing. His first published article, "Salmon toma," appeared in 1856. Ten years later, he started composing again and, by the 1870's, Hamlin had made a name for himself as an accomplished and prolific author. In 1873, he wrote an article on "Alimentation, Considered in its Relations to the Progress and Prosperity of the Nation," and concurrently released a book on gems titled *The Tourmaline*, which examined "beautiful and matchless crystals" found in Maine. The next year, Hamlin produced two medical articles on blood transfusion and tuberculosis. At the same time, he wrote a lengthy report, "On the Salmon of Maine" for the United States Commissioner of Fish and Fisheries. In 1875, he submitted an article on "Shall We Lance the Gums in the First Dentition?" and then settled in to exclusively writing books. In 1884, Hamlin published another tome on crystals, *Leisure Hours Among the Gems*, and, in 1895, he heralded Maine's hidden assets in *The History of Mount Mica of Maine*, which focused on the state's most significant deposit of tourmaline.[19]

As much as Hamlin enjoyed writing about health, crystals and fishing, he also published several pieces on the Civil War.

---

[18] *Who Was Who*, I, p. 512; *Appleton's Cyclopedia*, III, p. 66.
[19] *The National Union Catalog, Pre-1956 Imprints* (London: Mansell, 1972) Vol. 228, pp. 623-624; *American Book Publishing Record Cumulative 1876-1949: An American National Bibliography*, (New York, 1980) Vol. IV, p. 707.

Immediately after the war, he published a book called *Martyria; or Andersonville Prison,* which made a scathing indictment of the prison's conditions. Many considered this study as the seminal work on the prison's record. The book featured sketches drawn by Hamlin that reveal another dimension of this multi-talented man. Hamlin also did an analytical article for the Military Historical Society of Massachusetts, "Who Captured the Guns at Cedar Creek." The doctor showed himself to be a very clever and resourceful investigator; when Alfred Pleasonton wrote his tissue of lies on Chancellorsville, the historian Hamlin felt challenged to answer his exaggerations.[20]

Hamlin railed at a score of authors whose carelessness not only objurgated Howard's veterans but simply made poor history. He studied everything he could about Chancellorsville to answer the Eleventh Corps' detractors. Starting in 1889, Hamlin immersed himself in three years of research "...on behalf of the subordinate officers, and the rank and file of the condemned corps." After examining the published official reports for both armies, Hamlin fired his first salvo against Pleasonton and his protégés in the Boston *Journal* and the *National Tribune.*[21]

Hamlin claimed, in 1892, that his objective was genuinely "...to ascertain how much of the abuse so liberally heaped upon the Eleventh Corps,...is properly bestowed...[and] really worth consideration." He surgically unraveled all of the accounts and constructed a logical sequence of events for May 2, 1863. He discredited Pleasonton's memories as a mere fabrication for his vanity. Later Hamlin wrote, "The battle Pleasonton describes belongs to the pages of Baron Munchhausen."[22]

The doctor demonstrated that the so-called "German Corps" actually boasted twice as many "Americans" (those born in the United States) than immigrants (including naturalized citizens who had resided in the United States, in some cases for decades). Detailing the Confederate plans for Chancellorsville, Hamlin revealed their near-flawless execution. On the other side, many of

---

[20] *Appleton's Cyclopedia,* III, p. 66; Joseph Sabin, *A Dictionary of Books Relating to America,* (New York, 1877) p. 40; *National Union Catalog,* Vol. 228, p. 624.

[21] *National Tribune,* December 5, 1892; Boston *Journal* reference in Biglow, p. 296, n. 3.

[22] *National Tribune,* December 5, 1892; Mary Anna Jackson, *Memoirs of "Stonewall" Jackson,* (Louisville, KY: Prentice Press, 1895) p. 545.

the key Federal regimental, brigade, and division commanders fell within the first few moments of Jackson's attack. That, Hamlin theorized, crippled the corps' defense. Under the circumstances, Hamlin argued, the Eleventh Corps' battle "...was no longer a fight, but a massacre...and, had they stayed 10 minutes longer, the result would have been...annihilation." He likened the odds against the Eleventh Corps to the recent tragedy of George A. Custer on the Little Big Horn.[23]

Hamlin admitted that part of the corps had fled and the rout swept others from their commands, but he disputed the stories of Germans thronging through Hazel Grove, overturning cannons and careening wagons into a creek. Those blown loose from the Eleventh Corps ran toward Chancellorsville using the Plank Road, nearly a mile north of Hazel Grove. It made no sense, Hamlin contested, for distraught soldiers to abandon the swift escape route of a safe road to thrash through the bramble barriers of the Wilderness. At the same time, Hamlin rejoined that the Eleventh Corps rearguard fought well and deliberately, and fell back well over an hour after the initial routed portion flocked through Chancellorsville.[24]

Pleasonton insisted, and others maintained, that the harried Germans exploded through their lines with the Rebels screaming hot on their heels. Hamlin demonstrated, instead, that Buschbeck's brigade and Dilger's cannon withdrew after the Southern pressure had slackened. Hamlin searched to make sense of this conundrum and, eventually, proved that the Eleventh Corps had come and gone long before a small detachment of Stonewall Jackson's Confederates cautiously probed north of Hazel Grove. There they encountered and stampeded the wagon train and camp followers of the Union Third and Twelfth Corps. Ironically, the critics of the Eleventh Corps had lambasted the "shameful cowardice" of their own units. Hamlin sardonically noted that the Confederates had not frightened the Eleventh

---

23 *National Tribune*, July 6, 1893; July 27, 1893.
24 *National Tribune*, December 5, 1892.

Corps into Hazel Grove, but may have "frightened Pleasonton out of his wits."[25]

Augustus Hamlin's monograph in the *National Tribune* led many veterans of the Eleventh Corps to press for a book detailing all of the doctor's articulate arguments. The Eleventh Corps' veterans association designated Dr. Hamlin as their official historian and spokesman. This spurred Hamlin on to even more intensive study. "The evidence has not long been accessible to the public," Hamlin warned, "and until it could be collated and examined no one wished to encounter the storm of abuse" that would surely bedevil the corps' advocate.[26]

The doctor corresponded extensively with the survivors of Chancellorsville, both North and South, gleaning as much information as possible from all sides. He interviewed several of Stonewall Jackson's staff officers and acclaimed Jackson's guide, David Kyle, and his rendition of Jackson's last ride and wounding. Dr. Hamlin made at least three field trips to the battlefield at Chancellorsville and probably many more. Often he embarked on these trips accompanied by "the most prominent living actors" from the battle. On one such excursion, Hamlin gathered a group of officers from both sides to offer him "...the clear solution of many of the obscure and ambiguous accounts...." Among those touring the field with Hamlin came Brigadier General James H. Lane of North Carolina, Colonel William H. Palmer of A. P. Hill's staff, Captain William W. Blackford of J.E.B. Stuart's staff, and Captain Randolph J. Barton of the "Stonewall" Brigade, as well as other prominent Southerners. Representing the Federals on this junket Hamlin hosted Colonel Pennock Huey of the 8th Pennsylvania Cavalry, Lieutenant Colonel John T. Lockman of Krzyzanowski's brigade, and Captain Hubert Dilger—commander of an Eleventh Corps battery and a Medal of Honor recipient.[27]

Examining the topography gave Hamlin an invaluable insight into the battle that is not obvious by merely viewing maps.

---

[25] *National Tribune*, December 5, 1892; Fassitt letter, WVU; Milo M. Quaife, ed., *From the Cannon's Mouth: the Civil War Letters of General Alpheus S. Williams*, (Detroit: Wayne State University Press, 1959) p. 191; Bigelow, p. 478; Jackson, p. 545.

[26] *National Tribune*, June 29, 1893.

[27] *National Tribune*, June 29, 1893; Jackson, p. 550, 552; Alexander, p. 339., E. Porter Alexander stated that Hamlin "made many visits to the field."

Hamlin compared many maps of the area, including the field notes of Hooker's chief engineer, Brigadier General Gouverneur K. Warren, and another engineer named Major Nathaniel Michler. Hamlin believed that Warren's map misled readers by showing broad open fields where woods prevailed. Instead, Hamlin recommended Major Michler's maps to his readers. Composed several years after the battle, Michler's drawings revealed a much more precise and accurate picture. Hamlin documented the May 2 action at Chancellorsville in nine highly-detailed maps. "All the maps used in these papers," Hamlin enthused, "are based on Maj. Michler's surveys."[28]

With an overview from many different sources and an intimate familiarity with the battlefield, Dr. Hamlin set out to censure the Eleventh Corps' nay-sayers. He composed a list of well-publicized fallacies surrounding the Eleventh Corps' performance at Chancellorsville. Many of the arguments he had already touched on in his series of articles for the *National Tribune*. In some cases, Hamlin lifted large passages out of these articles and re-used them verbatim. Others showed more care and maturity than in his initial defense. Specifically, Augustus Hamlin hoped to address four primary issues:

1. Hooker claimed that he had warned Howard of the impending attack and ordered him to protect his right flank.

2. Stonewall Jackson's Confederates had completely surprised the Eleventh Corps as it prepared its supper.

3. The entire Eleventh Corps ran away on May 2.

4. The Eleventh Corps abandoned its strong positions and weapons without a fight.

Joseph Hooker's apologists pointed vehemently to an order sent at 9:30 a.m., May 2, alerting O. O. Howard of Stonewall Jackson's flank march and ordering the Eleventh Corps to take precautions against a surprise attack. Hamlin disproved this argument by showing that Hooker changed his mind about an impending danger during the day. By mid-afternoon, Hooker wired the left wing of his army that the Southern troops had

---

[28] *National Tribune*, June 22, 1893.

retreated and Sickles' Third Corps hounded their escape. When Sickles bogged down in a vicious fight around Charles C. Wellford's Catharine Furnace, he asked the neighboring corps for help. Lieutenant J. Ridgeway Moore, of Sickles' staff, approached Howard, seeking reinforcements. When Howard stated that he had none to offer, Moore turned to Hooker and obtained an order remanding one of Howard's brigades to Sickles. At 4:00 p.m., assured by Hooker that Robert E. Lee was on the run, Howard gave Moore Brigadier General Francis Barlow's 3,000-man brigade, the largest in the corps. Howard, and now Hamlin, believed that Moore's order taking Barlow's brigade rescinded the previous order, then six hours stale. To Hamlin, this showed "...positive evidence that at Hooker's Headquarters there were no apprehensions whatever of danger to the exposed Eleventh Corps."[29]

Persistent stories of the Germans' utter surprise piqued Dr. Hamlin. He documented that no less than fifteen warnings of the impending attack emanated from the Eleventh Corps itself. The old canard that the Eleventh Corps had no pickets fell apart as Hamlin unearthed time and again the good work of the pickets and patrols detecting Jackson's immense build-up on the right flank. Many junior officers broached the information to division, corps, and even the army's headquarters but no one acted on it. Hamlin attributed the lack of initiative not to the rank and file of the corps but to the hierarchy of the command. Brigadier General Charles Devens, commanding the westernmost division, exhibited "a remarkable fatuity" in Hamlin's eyes, and Howard appeared just as culpable. Hamlin traced Devens' and Howard's carelessness to "...the remarkable hypnotic effect coming from Headquarters of the Army at the Chancellor House." When the attack fell upon the right, Hamlin wrote, "Von Gilsa [was] ready to receive the attack." Unfortunately, his tiny command offered no match for the thousands descending on his position. The corps had not been surprised, only its high command.[30]

---

[29] Dodge, *P.M.H.S.M.*, p. 199; Hartwell Osborn, "On the Right at Chancellorsville," *Military Order of the Loyal Legion – Illinois Commandery*, (Chicago, 1907) Vol. IV, pp. 182-183; Oliver Otis Howard letter dated August 5, 1881, O. O. Howard Papers, Chicago Historical Society; *National Tribune*, July 13, 1893; July 20, 1893.

[30] *National Tribune*, July 20, 1893.

Aspersions that the entire corps broke at the first fire and stampeded fueled popular Know-Nothing hatred for the unreliable foreigners. Veterans of the Army of the Potomac dwelt on accounts of the Germans abandoning their weapons and frantically fleeing while sturdy American staff officers and soldiers tried to beat the loathsome "Dutchmen" back to their work. "Careful investigation," Hamlin revealed, "seems to show that the advance of the routed part of the corps was much exaggerated." Inspection records revealed very few soldiers lacking arms after the debacle. Hamlin also contended that the broken elements of the corps had to run more than three miles before reaching Chancellorsville; if they still showed the haste attributed to them after that distance, then "...they must have possessed wonderful strength and endurance." He concluded that the terrified mob jostling around Hooker's headquarters must have been the Third Corps and Twelfth Corps wagon trains and ancillary units frightened out of Hazel Grove and described in Alfred Pleasonton's picturesque natterings.[31]

Even the idea that the entire Eleventh Corps fled struck Hamlin as ludicrous. He computed that the corps contained 12,000 soldiers. Barlow took 3,000 with him to join Sickles, missing the shock of the flank attack and the indignity of the rout. The corps lost 2,500 in casualties trying to stave off disaster and, when darkness ended the fighting, an estimated 3,500 to 4,000 men stood in the defenses around Chancellorsville. To Hamlin's logic, that left only 3,000 men to join the confusion of a stampede—only a quarter of the corps at best, rather than the whole corps.[32]

Hamlin lastly addressed the opinion that the Germans refused to fight and abandoned their defenses without a contest. This troubled Hamlin for two reasons. First, the Army of the Potomac completely ignored the fact that the majority of the Eleventh Corps fought deliberately and heroically against Stonewall's famed legions for more than an hour without any reinforcements from the rest of the army. The stands made by Colonel Adolphus Buschbeck's brigade and Captain Hubert Dilger's Ohio battery displayed incredible bravery, but remained

---

[31] Pittman, pp. 10-11; *National Tribune*, August 3, 1893.
[32] *National Tribune*, August 3, 1893.

unnoticed amid the savage allegations of cowardice. The second misconception arose from an utter lack of respect for the Confederates' abilities. The rest of the Federal army trusted that it would have beaten the Southerners if it had held Howard's line.[33]

Hamlin had a fascination for the architect of the Eleventh Corps' demise. He voraciously studied Lieutenant General Thomas J. Stonewall Jackson. Hamlin dedicated a large portion of his book to chronicling Jackson's intents and execution and his tragic fall at the pinnacle of his career. The doctor admired Jackson as "one of the ablest soldiers of the age," and esteemed his "...intuitive genius of war, courage and endurance, qualities eminently requisite in a soldier." Hamlin's impartial judgment so impressed the general's widow, Mary Anna Jackson, that she allowed him to contribute an essay to her book, *The Memoirs of "Stonewall" Jackson*, published in 1895. Hamlin became one of only two historians to augment Anna Jackson's project and the only Yankee. Dr. Hamlin's admiration for his foe stood in marked contrast to intense political debates brewing between the North and South in the 1890's and served as a salve between aging warriors. Hamlin desired that "the history of to-day should cover both [sides] with equal fairness, and it should also respect the valor of the Confederate soldier." "As the mists of prejudice clear away and the true ideas of a national sentiment prevail," the doctor crusaded, "the wish to accord the Southern soldier the full measure of his merits in the Civil War grows." He thought of ex-Confederates as "national treasures" and proffered a compromise between old antagonists, writing, "Just and worthy praise to either one reflects its beams upon the other."[34]

Hamlin insisted that no troops could have stopped Jackson and his men. The results of the battle appear to have been predictable--not because the victims were German, but, rather, because the odds favored the vastly larger Confederate force at the point of combat. Any corps would have given way under those circumstances. The old soldier hoped that, someday, "...in

[33] *National Tribune*, July 27, 1893; Fassitt letter, WVU.

[34] Jackson, p. 559; *National Tribune*, December 5, 1892; June 22, 1893; Comer Vann Woodward, *Origins of the New South*, (Baton Rouge, LA: Louisiana State University Press, 1971) pp. 280-283. Woodward details the political clime of the 1890's with great insight and care.

the not far distant future…an intelligent and enlightened nation will erect common monuments to some of the leaders of our great Civil War." Hamlin's willingness to investigate and scrutinize the battle from both sides provided him with a balanced objectivity theretofore unknown in the written scholarship of the Civil War.[35]

"There is certainly reason to believe that there was a deliberate conspiracy to foist the errors of the battle upon the Eleventh Corps," Hamlin intimated with a ring of truth.[36] The Army of the Potomac needed to save face after Chancellorsville. Officers struggled to resuscitate flagging morale in the aftermath of another defeat in a precedent-setting string of losses.

They dismissed Chancellorsville as the shoddy work of outsiders, foreign to the United States and equally foreign to the core of the Army of the Potomac. This fostered the idea that the old army had not been degraded, only the pathetic Eleventh Corps, thus leaving the rest of the army unsacred and ready to redeem the embarrassment of a second-rate corps. Many years had passed between the urgency of a national crisis and Augustus C. Hamlin's study of the great Battle of Chancellorsville; Hamlin felt the time had come to look objectively at people and events. "The blame of the disaster at Chancellorsville was thrown upon the Eleventh Corps, and chiefly upon the German regiments," the doctor remembered, but the evidence disclosed a different conclusion:

> The investigator fails to find cause for blaming the Germans in the battle of Chancellorsville; on the contrary, he finds much worthy of praise, and that the denunciations against them are extremely unfair and unjust, and arose from ignorance or from malice or from prejudice.[37]

Augustus C. Hamlin completed his work in 1895. Members of the Eleventh Corps veterans organizations devoured its contents and endorsed it as the factual account of their record at Chancellorsville. The Society of the Officers and Soldiers of the Eleventh Army Corps convened in New York City for its annual meeting on December 19, 1895, and unanimously passed a

---

[35] Jackson, p. 560.
[36] *National Tribune*, June 29, 1893.
[37] *National Tribune*, August 3, 1893.

resolution giving their "earnest and hearty thanks" to the corps historian. The resolution declared, "Colonel Hamlin has fully vindicated the honor and courage of the soldiers of said Eleventh Corps, as appears at length in his able history of said battle...." The veterans further awarded him a golden loving cup as a token of their gratitude shortly before the doctor's death in 1905.[38]

Hamlin completed a preface in 1896 and then published the book in Bangor at his own expense. Hamlin released his masterpiece simultaneously in cloth-bound and paperback editions and selected a variety of cover art for his work. Purchasers could obtain the book with a blue cover stamped in black ink, or a yellow cover marked in black, blue, or red ink. The paperback edition came with a yellow cover printed in black. Starting in January, 1897, book catalogues listed the hardback edition at $1.00 and the paperback at 75¢. [39]

Oliver O. Howard received a copy of Hamlin's book at the annual meeting of the Eleventh Corps Association on December 15, 1896. Howard perused the book and resented Hamlin's implications that he and his division commanders permitted timely warnings to go unheeded. Howard's son preserved his father's enmity for Hamlin's opus by penciling marginal notes in the general's copy. At one point, Harry S. Howard's marginalia reveals: "...the author hurt Gen. Howard's feelings when the book appeared." O. O. Howard thought himself "condemned by faint praise" by Hamlin and the corps. On the other hand, Lieutenant Andrew B. Searles, of the 45th New York Volunteers, thought the book did not go far enough and wrote his own article for the Boston *Journal* that "...places the bravery and heroism of the old Eleventh Corps in even stronger light than Colonel Hamlin." Neither critic, however, disputed Hamlin's evidence.[40]

In spite of Howard's persecuted brooding and Searle's bluster, Hamlin's book met with near-universal approval. *The Nation* dedicated almost an entire page to applauding Hamlin's

[38] Augustus C. Hamlin, *The Battle of Chancellorsville*, (Bangor: Author, 1896) p. 175; *Who Was Who*, I, p. 512.

[39] R. R. Bowler, ed., *The American Catalogue, 1895-1900*, (New York: Publishers' Weekly, 1941) Vol. I, p. 202; *American Book Publishing Record Cumulative 1876-1949: An American National Bibliography*, (New York, 1980) Vol. X, p. 1926.

[40] Oliver O. Howard's copy of Hamlin, Curatorial Collections, Catalogue #503, Fred-Spot, p. 34; Boston *Journal*, n.d., copy in Fred-Spot.

work. The reviewer contended that "...if Dr. Hamlin was not the official historian of the corps, his book would still command attention by the ability with which he had arrayed the evidence." "The fourth chapter of the book, on the 'Personnel of the Eleventh Corps,'" the review read, "is itself a valuable contribution to the history of the Civil War." Michler's maps, he continued, "can hardly be improved..." and "they make, of themselves, a history of the field that is a model for work of the kind." The review concluded that "In every sense Dr. Hamlin's is a useful and welcome addition to the material for our military history," and that his work would place a "serious demand upon future writers of history to weigh with careful scrutiny and just balance."[41]

Hamlin's book did make demands on future historians and students of the war. Many hailed Augustus C. Hamlin as the paramount historian of the Battle of Chancellorsville. No one wrote about Chancellorsville without consulting Dr. Hamlin. Dr. Henry A. White, professor of history at Washington and Lee University, wrote a biography of Robert E. Lee in 1898 in which he relied on Hamlin's account to complete his Chancellorsville chapter. The widely published Confederate, E. Porter Alexander, lauded Hamlin's work on the May 2 assault as "...the fullest and most accurate account yet produced of the history of that evening, including the wounding of Stonewall Jackson, from either Confederate or Federal sources." Alexander encouraged his own readers to study Hamlin, as "No future student of this battle can afford to be ignorant of his story."[42]

Modern historians also relied on Hamlin's study of Chancellorsville. The authoritative John Bigelow depended largely on Hamlin to flesh out his chapter on Jackson's flank attack. In his notes, Bigelow confessed that he "...adopted...the dispositions given by Hamlin in his minute account of the battle...," and, in certain instances, he copied Hamlin "in large part verbatim." Captain Thomas W. Osborn's memoirs of the Third Corps artillery has recently been published with the editors using Hamlin for context, classifying the doctor as "...an authority on Chancellorsville and a leading source for John

---

[41] "The Eleventh Corps at Chancellorsville," *The Nation*, January 21, 1897.
[42] Henry A. White, *Robert E. Lee and the Southern Confederacy*, (New York, 1898) p. 269; Alexander, p. 334, 339.

Bigelow." Historian Robert K. Krick also recognized Augustus C. Hamlin's scholarship. In an essay on the fatal wounding of Stonewall Jackson, Krick appraised the nineteenth-century historian: "...though ardently polemical in northern outlook and primarily concerned with the Federal Eleventh Corps [he] devoted more careful attention to Jackson's foray than any other early student."[43]

Other battlefields stimulated historians. John B. Bachelder studied Gettysburg and Ezra A. Carman ruminated on Antietam. Chancellorsville fortunately, inspired Augustus Choate Hamlin. Thanks to the dedication of Ronald R. Seagrave and Sergeant Kirkland's Museum and Historical Society, Inc., Hamlin's beautiful history, *The Battle of Chancellorsville* is available again for the first time in more than a century. Students and scholars will appreciate the meticulous care and study that Dr. Augustus C. Hamlin invested in dissecting one of America's most confusing and celebrated battles, an event that created Southern legends, foreign scapegoats, and years of heated debate and controversy.

Frank A. O'Reilly
Guinea, Virginia
May, 1997

[43] Bigelow, p. 286, n. 1, 288, 309, n. 2; Herb S. Crumb and Katherine Dhalle, eds., *Thomas Ward Osborn: Letters From the Field*, (Hamilton [NY]: Edmonston Pub., 1993) p. 137; Robert K. Krick, "The Smoothbore Volley That Doomed the Confederacy," in Gary W. Gallagher, ed., *Chancellorsville: The Battle and Its Aftermath*, (Chapel Hill, NC: University of North Carolina Press, 1996) p. 119.

"He who does not speak the truth fully is a betrayer of the truth."—*Horace.*

THE BATTLE OF
CHANCELLORSVILLE

*THE ATTACK OF STONEWALL JACKSON AND HIS ARMY UPON
THE RIGHT FLANK OF THE ARMY OF THE POTOMAC
AT CHANCELLORSVILLE, VIRGINIA, ON SAT-
URDAY AFTERNOON, MAY 2, 1863*

By AUGUSTUS CHOATE HAMLIN

*Formerly Lieutenant Colonel and Medical Inspector, U. S. Army
Historian Eleventh Army Corps*

BANGOR, MAINE
PUBLISHED BY THE AUTHOR
1896

PREFACE.

I N THIS inquiry into the events of the battle of Chancellorsville, occurring on the second day of May, 1863, the
narrator at first was simply actuated by a curiosity to
ascertain the truth of the particulars of the action which
was said to have taken place at Hazel Grove. And the
unlooked-for results, which were so much at variance with
the official reports and accepted tradition, determined him to
ascertain, if possible, the actual condition of things as they
occurred during that eventful afternoon and evening. In
this long and laborious inquiry, he has endeavored to bear
in mind the counsel of Cicero, that ''it is the first law of
history that the writer should neither dare to advance what
is false, nor suppress what is true ; that he should relate the
facts with strict impartiality, free from illwill or favor.''
This search for exact information has occupied most of the
past five years, and during this period the official reports of
both armies have been again and again carefully analyzed
and compared with all information accessible or known to
the collections of our military history. Three visits to the
battlefield have been made in successive years, in company
with officers of both armies who were actively connected with
the events of the day. All accessible maps, official and
unofficial, relating to the territory, have been consulted, and
with their aid, strengthened with new surveys, a series of
maps has been constructed, showing the position of the
various bodies of troops at brief intervals of time, to demon-
strate the correctness of the narrative. The task has been
entirely voluntary, and of exceeding difficulty, mingled with

much unpleasantness. But the reward has been ample, in the conviction that the labor has resulted in clearing up a great wrong in our military history. Why this injustice was shown to the Eleventh Corps at the time, and why it has remained so long uncorrected, will be apparent to the student of our history. Machiavelli well says: "When you would discover who is the author of a crime, consider who had an interest to commit it."

In the preparation of these papers, the author has been assisted by a great number of officers and soldiers of both armies, who have shown a laudable desire to ascertain the exact truth concerning the events occurring on Saturday, May 2d, 1863. To the late Gen. A. B. Underwood, and to Col. Theo. A. Dodge, the first writers of the battle on the Federal side, many thanks are due. To the late Col. W. L. Candler, of Hooker's staff; Col. Pennoch Huey, of the Eighth Pennsylvania Cavalry; Capt. J. H. Huntington, of the artillery of the Third Corps, and to many officers and soldiers of other corps, he is under great obligations. To many officers and soldiers of the Confederate army the thanks of the writer and the country are due. In fact, without their assistance, the narrative could not have been accomplished. Many thanks are due to Gen. James H. Lane; Col. W. H. Palmer, of Gen. A. P. Hill's staff; to Col. Kyd Douglas and Maj. Jed. Hotchkiss, of Jackson's staff; to Col. Eugene Blackford; Capt. Randolph Barton, of the Stonewall Brigade; to Ves Chancellor, and especially to Jackson's couriers, James M. Talley and Dave Kyle.

AUGUSTUS C. HAMLIN.

BANGOR, MAINE,
February, 1896.

CHANCELLORSVILLE.

May 2d, 1863.

CHAPTER I.

The Armies and Preliminary Movements.

CHANCELLORSVILLE seems to have been a tragedy of errors, and the terrible losses and sacrifices did not result in decided or satisfactory results on either side. The populous and powerful North could easily replace its loss in artillery, in equipment and in men, but with the South, already enfeebled and overstrained, it was far different. The gain in cannon, in prisoners and in morale was great, it is true, but it was fearfully paid for by the victorious army. It may be said, with some truth, that the campaign was Lee's masterpiece in audacity and celerity, but his victory was like that won in ancient times by Pyrrhus, for it was indeed a mortal blow to the vitality of the Army of Northern Virginia. And it may also be affirmed, that when the shot-torn flags of Jackson's Corps were planted in triumph on the crest of Fairview at 9 o'clock on Sunday morning, May 2d, 1863, the culminating point of its daring and its strength had passed, never to return. The South could not replace the host of dauntless men who went down in the determined and desperate struggle.

Both armies moved to the front with great confidence. The Federal army felt secure and strong in its superior numbers, its splendid equipment, its devotion and its enthusiasm. The Confederate army, strengthened by the conscription act, and stimulated by the long winter's rest, also felt invincible under the guidance of its trusty leaders. Moreover, the rebels believed that their knowledge of the topography of the country, their skill in bushcraft and marksmanship, gave them a decided advantage over their opponents. Besides all these considerations, there was a determined resolution on the part of the Southrons to hurl the invader back at all hazards.

The rebel Army of Northern Virginia at this time was a remarkable and powerful body of men, led by one of the ablest soldiers of the age. It was skilled in the use of arms, hardened in service, animated in a high degree with the enthusiasm of their cause and the desperate courage of self-defense. The convictions of most of the Southern army were, that they were right in their views, and their stubbornness in defending them, and the privations endured in the defense, is ample evidence of their sincerity. The glorious Army of the Potomac, which fought 60 per cent. of the battles of the war, can afford to bestow deserving praise on that determined and resolute body of soldiers who, although deficient in equipment and comforts of military life, and inferior in numbers, yet with a devotion, skill and tenacity worthy of the highest cause, kept them at bay for four long years, and struck down on the field of battle 182,000 of its numbers—killed and wounded. Just and worthy praise to either one reflects its beams upon the other. Both armies will descend to posterity with military records of the highest rank, and history, with its impartial pen, will not discriminate to the credit or discredit of either.

This Army of Northern Virginia was composed of the best and the bravest men in the South, and they believed and boasted that they carried with them not only the flag, but the glory and the very life, of the Confederacy. The South considered this army as the bulwark of secession, and sent to it selected bodies of their best men to represent them. Among them were the famous Washington Artillery, of New Orleans; the Louisiana Tigers, the renowned riflemen of Mississippi; selected infantry of Alabama, Georgia and Tennessee, and the hardy descendants of the mountaineers of North and South Carolina who fought with Marion and Morgan in Revolutionary times.

It is eminently proper for the Northern soldiers to consider the character and the qualifications of their antagonists. At this time—1863—most of the Army of Virginia were volunteers, and comprised the best men of the South. Many, if not the most, of them had been Union men and strongly opposed to secession, but the first shot at Fort Sumter brought back to light all those pernicious views of state rights which had slumbered like the germs of a fatal pestilence for nearly a century, and with some show of reluctance they obeyed the commands of their respective states. The plantations were soon left to the care of the women and the slaves; the colleges and academies were closed, for the professors and pupils had marched away at the call of the drum; and, in fact, nearly all of the men of the South not required for the civil service or the direction of the important industries enrolled themselves with enthusiasm under the fascinating banner of secession. Many of the excessive ideas of state rights and extravagant state pride owed their origin to the times as far back as the stormy period of the early days of the Revolution of 1775, and some of the states openly considered their rights as superior to those of the North, or the country in general. The men of North Carolina had not forgotten that the first contest between England and the colonists took place there, and that the Declaration of Independence at Mecklenburg preceded that of Philadelphia by a year or more. The Virginians were excessively proud of the traditions which came to them from the earliest colonial times, and they recalled the immortal efforts of their ancestors in building up the structure of the great Republic, and the fiery and matchless eloquence of Patrick Henry, which aroused the patriotic mind with the force of actual conflict. In estimating the stamina of the Army of Northern Virginia, it is proper to allude to all the influences that gave it form, or lent it strength, and with propriety we may say that the

most of these men of the old colonial states, when they
marched to resist the invasion of their territory and the
advance of the Federal troops, considered themselves as
sincere patriots and as ardently attached to the principles
of freedom as the men of the North.

> "Treason never prospers; for when it does,
> None dare call it treason."

The crossing of the Rappahannock River does not seem
to have been much of a surprise to Lee, as the country had
been carefully surveyed in anticipation of this crossing, and
in the plans of defense, the Wilderness and broken territory
had been regarded in the nature of natural fortifications, in
which the rebel soldier would have superior advantages over
his opponent.   It is doubtful if Lee intended to offer any
serious resistance to Hooker's crossing, any more than he did
to Grant a year later.   The Wilderness, with its almost im-
penetrable thickets, was a great and natural fortress for the
lightly armed and lightly clad Confederates.   And the circumstances of the conflict recall the remarks made at the time
of the Revolution of 1775, when it was said in England, that
"The old system of tactics is out of place, nor could the
capacity of the Americans for resistance be determined by
any known rule of war.   They will long shun an open field,
every thicket will be an ambuscade of partisans, every stone
wall a hiding place for sharp-shooters, every swamp a fortress, the boundless woods an impracticable barrier."

And so it proved, for the rebel in his faded uniform was
almost invisible in the woods, and his skill as a marksman,
his knowledge in bushcraft, certainly compensated largely
for a considerable inequality in numbers, and in the thickets
of Chancellorsville, and later, in the Wilderness, the rebel
soldier was certainly superior to his antagonist, man for man,
courage reckoned as equal.

So confident was Lee in the strength of his army and
his position at this time, that he had sent Longstreet, with
two of his divisions, away down to southeastern Virginia,
leaving at his disposal but sixty thousand men, which he

deemed ample to meet any movement made by the Army of the Potomac, with double its number of men.

At the time of the battle of Chancellorsville, the rebel critics state that General Lee found himself at the head of an army unsurpassed in discipline and all the hardy virtues of the soldier, strengthened by the additions of the winter, and the enforcement of the conscript act, and numbering about sixty thousand men, according to the statements of General Taylor and Major Hotchkiss, of Lee's and Jackson's staffs, and others. This estimate does not include the forces which had gone off with Longstreet, south of Richmond, and which were not available in the approaching conflict. General Taylor, who was the Adjutant General of the Army of Northern Virginia, states that General Lee moved towards Chancellorsville with forty-eight thousand men, and, keeping Anderson's and McLaw's Divisions with him—less than fourteen thousand men—he hurled Jackson with the rest upon the flank and rear of the Federal army—or thirty-four thousand men. Later, Taylor qualifies his remarks by saying that Jackson had twenty-six thousand infantry, six thousand cavalry and sixteen hundred artillery, or a total of thirty-three thousand six hundred men. Major Jed Hotchkiss, of Jackson's staff, has stated that Jackson's Corps increased in three months before the battle from twenty-five thousand to thirty-three thousand muskets, but from this estimate must be taken Early's Division, which remained at Fredericksburg to confront Sedgwick and his forces. There were one hundred and two guns attached to Jackson's Corps, with twenty-two hundred men, but how many of these were actually in action, it is difficult now to ascertain. Besides these, the four batteries of Stuart's horse artillery must be added, and also the four or more regiments of cavalry, which screened the movements of the rebel infantry and effectually picketed all the roads. A few days after the battle, and after the death of General Jackson, General Lee stated to the War Department at Richmond that each of the two corps had then thirty thousand men, and were too many men for one man to handle, and asked to have the two corps divided into three.

Hooker had, with great celerity, moved the bulk of his army across the Rapidan and the Rappahannock Rivers, and on Friday morning, May 1st, was moving down the Plank and Turnpike roads towards Fredericksburg. About two miles from Chancellor's his advance was checked, and Hooker then discovered that Lee was entrenched across his path, with a line of earthworks extending from the Rappahannock River southward to the Massaponax stream, and more than three miles in length.

At eleven o'clock, May 1st, Jackson arrived at the front, stopped all work on the earthworks, and prepared to hurl fifty thousand men upon the three columns of Hooker's army, then attempting to debouch from the thickets and rugged country in which the Union army was entangled. At two o'clock, or later, Jackson had turned the right flank of the Twelfth Corps near Aldrich Farm, on the Plank Road, had turned both flanks of Sykes' Regulars on the Turnpike, and menaced the column of the Fifth Corps, under Griffin, on the River Road. Sykes, at this moment, found himself confronted by a vastly superior force, with Griffin, of the Fifth Corps, on the bank of the river three miles distant, with a broken and almost impassable country between; the Twelfth Corps a mile to his right, southward, and unconnected, and watching Posey's and Wright's Brigades marching steadily along the unfinished railroad to gain the rear of the Union army.

The Eleventh Corps was on the Plank Road near Chancellor's, a mile or more in rear, while the Third Corps was still farther in the rear, between the White House and the river, two or three miles distant.

Hooker had no alternative but to fight under great disadvantage, or retreat. The broad open fields Hooker's enemies so strongly allude to were about three miles away, and between them were strong entrenchments, and behind them Jackson, with fifty thousand men fresh and eager for the fray.   The broad fields which appear on Warren's map, and others, were mostly covered with forests then, and are to-day.   Major Michler's map, made with great care three or four years after the battle, indicates that this statement is correct, and to this map the reader is referred as to all movements connected with the battle of Chancellorsville. All the maps used in this paper are based on Major Michler's surveys.

About two o'clock Friday afternoon, May 1st, Hooker ordered his advanced forces to return to the selected position near Chancellor's to entrench and remain on the defensive.   From documents extant, it is clear that Hooker determined to remain on the defensive, and wait the effect of the strategic movements of his second army under Sedgwick, and his cavalry under Stoneman and Averill.   And so confident was he of his success, that he promised victory to his men, defying even Divine interference.   Had Hooker adhered to this resolve to remain strictly on the defensive, and withstood the brilliant temptations held out to him in the fatal movement in the fancied pursuit of Lee's column below the Welford Furnace, to the southward, the results of the campaign undoubtedly would have been different.   Certainly the Eleventh Corps would not have been deprived of its strong reserve, nor its officers hypnotized with the fallacious statement that Lee and his entire army was retreating with great haste towards Gordonsville.   Certainly the line of defenses would have been kept unbroken, and more than twenty thousand men would have been available for the support of the attacked and outflanked and weakened Eleventh Corps.

Late in the evening, Jackson met Lee in the woods near the Plank Road, a little over one mile south of the Chancellor House, and held a council of war.   The Confederate engineers reported upon the strength of the position to which Hooker had retired, and adversely to any attack upon it from the eastward.   It was then determined to attempt a flank movement, and endeavor to reach the right flank and rear of Hooker's army, and get possession of the roads leading from Chancellorsville to the Ely and United States Fords. The movement was entrusted to Jackson, and more than thirty thousand men received orders to move at daybreak, or sooner, in the direction of the Wilderness Tavern. Jackson was the trusty lieutenant of Lee, and all details of a campaign were fully entrusted to him. Between these officers there was a steady friendship and a sincere mutual regard, and in all military matters there was much of that complete harmony and adjustment which gave an immortal luster to Marlborough and Prince Eugene. Jackson had that great quality so necessary in desperate actions—moral courage and invincible determination. He was perseverance itself. Nothing could shake his resolution. His early appearance in the war gave no promise of his powers, and Johnson's definition of genius might then be applied to him: "Genius is nothing but strong natural parts accidentally turned in one direction," and in his movements the Federal soldier might have applied to him the remark made by the Hungarian officer about Napoleon at Lodi: "He knows nothing of the regular rules of war; he is sometimes in our front, sometimes on our flank, sometimes in the rear. There is no supporting such gross violations of rules."—*See Map No. 1.*

Jackson started promptly with his men, and moved forward with that reckless abandon that he had previously exhibited in his flank movements in the Shenandoah Valley, and in the later campaign, which drove Pope and the Federal army back to the shelter of Washington. At this time he had twenty-eight regiments under A. P. Hill, twenty-two under Rodes, twenty under Colston, or seventy regiments of infantry in all, and also many guns in the artillery battalions, under Colonels Crutchfield, Walker, Carter, Jones and McIntosh, etc., besides the four batteries of the horse artillery, under Major Beckham, and four regiments of cavalry under General Stuart. The columns of this great force filled all the roads and paths leading through the forest towards the west. They passed along the front of the Federal army in plain sight of the Third Corps and the Eleventh Corps, a mile or more to the soutward. For several hours the procession moved in sight of and within reach of the guns of the Federal army, seemingly in contempt of their foes. Birney reported the movement to Sickles, and Sickles to Hooker. Finally Birney received permission to try the range of his guns upon the column marching past the Welford Furnace, about half a mile south of his front, at Hazel Grove. A few shots from Clark's rifled guns dispersed that portion of the enemy's column then in sight, and caused it to seek another route farther to the south, out of reach of the Federal guns, and out of sight of the Federal scouts.

Berdan's sharpshooters, well supported, then advanced to the Furnace, and afterwards to the unfinished railroad, still farther south, where they captured most of the Twenty-Third Georgia Regiment, which was acting as rear guard to Jackson's fighting trains. From these captures and these operations sprang the fatal notion that General Lee and his entire army were retreating in dismay. This strange impression was spread rapidly through the army, then halted about Chancellorsville, and was soon magnified into a positive certainty, and generally believed. However, in the Eleventh Corps there were many men who had fought Jackson in two of his flank marches before, and were not so easily deceived, who refused to believe the rumor, and were soon assured of its falsity, but they failed to convince the higher officers of the corps of the fact, and the impending danger, even at the last moment.

At this time, Jackson's collection of fighters, trudging along the woods and its by-paths, would certainly have presented a curious appearance to a martinet critic of any of the military schools of Europe. The first sight of the commander, in his dingy clothes, with ragged cap perched over his brow, astride Old Sorrel; the tattered flags—worthless as material, but priceless to the hearts who carried them— the strange appearance of the men, in ragged and rusty

2—B. C.

clothes, marching along carelessly, and at will, might have suggested Falstaff and his ragamuffins.   But a closer and keener look would have soon convinced him that outward appearances do not always indicate the true measure of the soldier, and he would soon have seen that this shabby-look‧ ing and apparently undisciplined rabble would, at a signal from their trusty leader, be transformed into a resolute army, more than a match for any equal number of the best troops of the European armies in the singular contest about to com‧ mence.   And it may be affirmed that thirty thousand of these European troops would have been as helpless before them in the tangled thickets of this wilderness as Braddock and his British regulars were before the French and unseen Indians in the woods near Fort Duquesne, in colonial times.   The scene might also have recalled the remark the British offi‧ cer, Ferguson—second only to Tarleton—made when he noticed the mountaineers about to attack him at King's Mountain, in the old Revolution, and who soon cleaned him out, in spite of his regulars and his superior arms.   In this very column could be found many of the descendants of the men whom Ferguson affected to despise as "dirty mongrels," and they were the sons of Scottish Covenanters, French Huguenots and English sea rovers—the choicest of fighting material.   But the majority came from the descendants of the people who emigrated during a period of more than a hundred years from Scotland and the north of Ireland, and who made England repent bitterly of the oppressions that drove them across the ocean to the wilds of America.   The influence of the descendants of those people, both north and south, in the late civil war, was very marked.   The Cavalier and the Puritan may have supplied the poetic strain, but it was the Scotch and the Scotch-Irish, the Irish and the Ger‧ man blood, that furnished the sturdy stamina on either side.

   At about noon Jackson arrived at a point on the Plank Road about two miles south of the Talley Farm, where he met General Fitz Lee, who took him to the top of the eleva‧ tion at the Burton Farm, which gave him a view of the troops of the Eleventh Corps at the Dowdall Clearing, about a mile distant.   The Federal forces were at rest, as was most of the Federal army along the line, at that time.   Most of the Eleventh Corps were in sight, at the Talley and Dowdall Farms, and part of those at the Hawkins Farm, about half a mile in the rear, but a part of Devens' Division was concealed in the woods, and the whole of Von Gilsa's Brigade, forming the extreme right, was in the woods, half a mile from the Talley House, and could not be seen by Jackson from this position.   Von Gilsa was not discovered until the middle of the afternoon, when a party of cavalry and scouts dashed up the Turnpike, and unmasked their fire and their position.

The story that Von Gilsa's men were seen by Jackson playing cards and carousing, is a mistake, as the entire body of men were enveloped by the dense woods, and could not be seen, either from the Burton Hill or the Luckett Farm, on the Turnpike on the west.   Not only the Eleventh Corps, but the whole army, was in bivouac at this time, with the exception of Birney, exploring the vicinity of the Welford Furnace.

It was Jackson's intention to attack the Eleventh Corps from the Plank Road, and that part of the Federal force in position between the Dowdall and the Talley Farms, but as he viewed the position from the Burton Hill, he changed his mind and ordered the Stonewall Brigade, under Paxton, to remain on the Plank Road about one mile and a-half from the Wilderness Church, and four regiments of cavalry were to take position at the Burton Farm, only one mile and one-eighth from the Dowdall Tavern, the headquarters of the doomed corps.   The rest of the army was ordered to continue its march to the westward, until the Luckett Farm was reached, on the old Turnpike, two miles west of the Dowdall Tavern.

The day was hot and dusty, but the columns pressed steadily onward, hurried along by their impetuous leader, and at three P. M. Jackson, then at the Luckett Farm, sent his last dispatch to Lee. This dispatch is now in the State Library at Richmond, and reads: "NEAR 3 P. M., *May 2d, 1863.*—GEN. R. E. LEE: The leading division is up, and the other two appear to be well closed.—T. J. J." Rodes' Division was at once placed in line of battle, and had a long rest of ‑over two hours before called into action. As the rest of his army came up, it was placed in position, and at five P. M. most of it was ready for action.—*See Map No. 2.*

According to Jackson's staff officers, the attacking force was formed in three lines of battle, with Rodes' Division forming the front line, with Colston's Division as the second line, about one hundred paces in rear of the first. The third line was formed by Hill's Division, a part of which was deployed, the other part remaining on the Pike ready to be deployed to the right or left, as circumstances might require. The two front lines presented a front of two miles in length, and extended more than a mile north of the Pike, and to the rear of the Eleventh Corps, then facing south. The skirmish line of Rodes' Division was composed of selected riflemen, and was led by Colonel Willis, of the Twelfth Georgia, and so well did he perform his duty that Jackson spoke highly of him in his last moments. Another part of the skirmish line was commanded by Colonel Blackford, and Jackson's orders were carried out so accurately by these men that, although over ten thousand men rested on their arms for two hours or more within a mile of the right flank of the Army of the Potomac, not a man deserted or escaped to give warning of the coming storm.

At five P. M. all was ready for the movement which promised to wreck the unsuspecting Federal army. It seems incredible that an army of thirty thousand men could be moved directly past the front of a much larger force, and arrange itself in three lines of battle, within half a mile of the force to be attacked!

Treachery could not have placed the faithful, obedient and patient Army of the Potomac in a more unfortunate and perilous position than that in which it found itself at this moment, when Sickles and a selected force of the Federal army was about to attack Lee's "retreating and dismayed" men, supposed to be at or near the Welford House; and Hooker, completely blinded by the brilliant reports coming from the front, sent word to Sedgwick that Lee was in full retreat, and Sickles was among his retreating trains.

Most of the attention of the Federal army around Chancellorsville was then directed to this movement in front, below the Furnace. But Jackson, with his seventy regiments, and his artillery, and his cavalry, had long ago marched away past the front, and had completely vanished from the sight and hearing of Sickles' columns, and was then resting quietly in the dense forests in the rear of the Federal army, four miles in a direct line from the Welford House, and about to hurl his thunderbolts with almost irresistible force. Jackson, as he looked over the forests from the Luckett Farm, and noted the columns of smoke of the numerous camp-fires arising in the calm evening air, along the extended line of the encamped Federal army, might well have quoted to himself, in his silent prayer, that significant line of the ancients: "*Quos Deus vult perdere, prius dementat*"—"Whom the gods wish to destroy, they first make fools."

Jackson was in the best of feelings when he ordered Rodes to advance. He saw that his men, though fatigued, were full of enthusiasm and fight, and also, that the way was apparently clear for the destruction of a large part of the Federal army. Jackson's orders were explicit: To advance steadily without halting, and, regardless of all obstacles, seize the position beyond Talley's Farm. The two lines of battle, extending with a front of two miles, were expected to envelop and crush both Devens' and Schurz's Divisions, and it would probably have been done, but for the singular conduct of Colquitt, commanding the right brigade of Rodes' Division, at the decisive moment.

It has been stated that Jackson did not have any artillery in his column of attack on Saturday afternoon and evening; but, on the contrary, he had both Breathed's and McGregor's batteries of four guns, each following on the Pike, and keeping pace with the front line of attack, or in advance of it, and these batteries were followed by Moorman's battery of four guns, ready to assist if occasion required. A little distance in rear of these guns might have been seen the artillery battalions of Carter and Crutchfield, with many cannon. Jackson's attacking force was well equipped with cannon, but six only of the many pieces available were called into action, and these were worked so constantly and so rapidly that the gunners became exhausted at times, and were replaced with fresh men from the companies in the rear. These six guns were of Stuart's horse artillery, and were those which the gallant boy Major John Pelham had so often taken into action, and in so fearless a manner as to win for him the highest praises from Stuart, from Jackson, and from Lee. After Fredericksburg, Lee exclaimed to Jackson: "You ought to have a Pelham on each of your flanks." But the Marceau of the Southern army was no longer here. A fatal bullet of the Federal cavalry, a few days before, in a fight on the Rappahannock, had cut short his daring career. His men and his guns, however, were here, and fearfully did they avenge the loss of their beloved and youthful leader. Two of the guns at a time galloped to the front line and poured their shot into the confused masses of the Eleventh Corps, and these in turn were replaced by the sections in the rear, and so a constant fire was kept up until Dowdall's was reached, an hour and a-half after the action commenced, and here they were complimented by Jackson in person, and relieved from duty by Colonel Carter, as the men or horses had not been fed for forty-eight hours.

CHAPTER II.

Responsibility for the Disaster.

THE position of the Federal army at Chancellorsville, on Saturday morning, was as follows (*see Map No. 1.*): The Fifth Corps was strongly entrenched along a line extending southerly from the Rappahannock River to the White House, a distance of more than two miles, and facing to the east. The Second Corps was in position, extending southerly and easterly from near the White House to a point on the Turnpike about three-fourths of a mile east of the Chancellor House. The Twelfth Corps was entrenched about one-third of a mile south of Chancellor's, connecting on the left with the Second Corps, and on the right with Birney's Division of the Third Corps, which occupied earthworks at the edge of the woods on the north side of the Hazel Farm, and connecting on its right with the Eleventh Corps at Dowdall Tavern. In the rear of Birney, Williams' Division of the Twelfth Corps was stationed behind strong log works half a mile in length, and extending diagonally from the Hazel Grove ravine northerly to the Plank Road, and entirely in the woods. Berry's and Whipple's Divisions of the Third Corps were both bivouacked in the rear of Chancellor's House. A mile to the northwest of the Chancellor House, on the Ely Ford road, was stationed the division of regulars under Sykes. The Eleventh Corps formed the extreme right of the army, and occupied the line extending from Dowdall's to more than half a mile beyond Talley's, and covering a distance of more than a mile facing south, parallel with the turnpike. In front of the Fifth Corps, at this time, were the Third and Fourth Virginia Confederate Cavalry, picketing the paths and roads, and having as supports a small force of infantry stationed on the south side of Mott's Run, more than a mile distant from the Federal lines. In front of the Second and Twelfth Corps, and chiefly along the Turnpike and the Plank Road, Anderson's and McLaws' Divisions of the rebel army, with artillery, were deployed in a manner to exaggerate their actual strength as much as possible.

Adjutant General Taylor, of Lee's army, gives this strength as less than fourteen thousand men, but there is reason to believe that it was somewhat larger, and not far from seventeen thousand men. All the rest of the rebel army was then moving rapidly with Jackson to the west of Dowdall's, with the intention of getting possession of the roads leading to the Ely and United States Fords, on the rear and flank of the Federal army, then concentrated on the Chancellor fields, and acting on the defensive. And it was the intention of Lee to attack the Federal army in front of him, with Anderson's and McLaws' Divisions, as soon as he heard the sound of Jackson's guns in the Federal rear, and crush the disordered columns of the Federal army between them. These were the instructions given to Jackson before his departure, but fortunately for Sickles' forces, stretched out along the Furnace road, Lee did not hear Jackson's guns at all, owing to the peculiar condition of the atmosphere.

After Hooker returned to his headquarters from his inspection of the line of the Eleventh Corps, accompanied by many of his staff, on Saturday morning, and on being informed by Sickles that a movement of troops was passing his front towards his flank, he issued the 9.30 order, directed to both Howard and Slocum :

"I am directed by the Major General commanding to say, that the disposition you have made of your corps has been with a view to a front attack by the enemy. If he should throw himself upon your flank, he wishes you to examine the ground and determine upon the positions you will take in that event, in order that you may be prepared for him in whatever direction he advances. He suggests that you have heavy reserves well in hand to meet this contingency. The right of your line does not appear to be strong enough. No artificial defenses worth naming have been thrown up, and there appears a scarcity of troops at that point, and not, in the General's opinion, as favorably posted as might be. We have good reason to suppose that the enemy is moving to our right. Please advance your pickets, for purposes of observation, as far as may be safe, in order to obtain timely information of their approach."

This explicit and important order was received at the Eleventh Corps headquarters by General Schurz, who had assumed command while General Howard was resting from fatigue in the tavern. The order was opened by Schurz, and by him read to the commander of the corps, and with him discussed. Schurz, convinced that the attack would come from the west, was then strongly in favor of withdrawing Devens' Division and part of his own from the Talley and Hawkins Farms and the woods beyond, which he regarded as faulty and untenable in case of attack from the direction of the Pike on the west, and placing them in position on a line extending from a point east of the junction of the Plank and Pike roads, directly north, past the front of the little Church along the eastern edge of the little stream known as Hunting Run, facing directly to the west. This new position would have afforded some opportunity for Devens' Division to make a better defense, and given the artillery a chance to command both roads and to sweep with a broad fire the fields of the Hawkins Farm, where the left of Jackson's army debouched in such strong force. But his advice was not accepted.

A glance at the map, showing the positions of the troops at this time, will explain to the observer the strength of the proposed position far better than any description by means of words. The commander of the corps, however, saw no need of any change, and none was made of any moment, save the changing of front of some of the regiments on the Hawkins Farm, which was done by Schurz of his own volition. If anything else was done in accordance with this direct order, it does not appear clear to the investigator. The sending of two companies of the Thirty-third Massachusetts a mile to the north of Dowdall's, to picket the site of the old mill on a path to the Ely Ford, and the construction in the forenoon of the shallow rifle pits on the Dowdall Farm, facing west, may have been done and accounted for in the message sent to Hooker, as alleged, at eleven A. M., stating: "I am taking measures to resist an attack on the right." On the exposed flank, which Devens occupied, there seems to have been nothing done whatever, and the defenses there hardly merited the name of rifle pits or earthworks, and were trivial compared to those made by the Second, Third, Fifth and Twelfth Corps, remains of which are visible to-day. In fact, there were no rifle pits in front of Von Gilsa's men; nothing but the slight protection afforded by the slashing of trees, forming a slight abatis. To whose neglect this defect in the means of protection is due, is not very clear, but Warren and Comstock were the engineers in charge of all defenses, and Warren had been told of the movements of Jackson's men after the capture of the Twenty-third Georgia by the Berdan Sharpshooters. It is in evidence that the West Point officers did not believe that the enemy could march in force through the thickets on the right flank. However, the Federal army was slowly learning the art of war, and soon found, to its discomfiture, that the disdained rebel rabble could march through the woods in two lines of battle, with a front of two miles, and in sufficient form to attack promptly!

The Eleventh Corps at this time was formed of a large part of the forces that had previously served under Fremont and Sigel in Western Virginia and the Shenandoah Valley, and known as the Mountain Department, or later as the First Corps of Virginia. The veteran part of it had been engaged in contests in Western Virginia, in the Shenandoah, and in those of the campaign under Pope, ending at the second battle of Bull Run. It arrived at Fredericksburg too late to take part in that assault, and went into winter quarters at Stafford Court House, under the command of Sigel. At this time the corps consisted of twenty-seven regiments of infantry and six batteries. Sixteen of these regiments were veteran, and the other eleven were new. We will review briefly the composition of this corps, and see whether it was entitled, or not, to any confidence whatever by its new associates in the Army of the Potomac; and also whether the contemptuous expressions of worthlessness so freely bestowed upon it were properly placed.

When the corps joined the Army of the Potomac at Fredericksburg, it certainly did not meet with that cordial welcome which it expected and was clearly entitled to. On the contrary, there is abundant testimony to show the existence of a strong dislike and distrust, which was undeserved. It was spoken of as the foreign contingent, and hardly worthy of marching in line with the veterans of the old army. The historian of the Second Corps plainly stated the facts, when he wrote that "a feeling of contempt, doubtless undeserved, had been generally entertained by the older corps of the Army of the Potomac toward the Eleventh Corps ever since it came up in the rear after Fredericksburg. To 'fight mit Sigel' had so long been a current jest and proverb, that the troops were hardly disposed to do justice to the many excellent regiments which were incorporated in this command." He also intimates that the corps had not taken part in any hard fighting, such as the Army of the Potomac had seen on the peninsula; yet, if he had looked over the returns of the battle of the second Bull Run, he would have seen that the body of men which afterwards formed the Eleventh Corps did see some hard fighting, and fully as severe as the Second Corps saw at the battle of Fair Oaks, or in the seven days' battles about Richmond; and if mortality is evidence, they saw harder fighting than did the Second Corps at these times. There is abundant evidence to show the existence of a feeling of hostility throughout the army against the Eleventh Corps, and with no more foundation than that General Walker has mentioned.

Hooker was strongly urged to break up the corps, after the battle, and humiliate it still further by destroying its organizations, and it was admitted before Congress that it was largely due to the high price of gold, and the fear of its effects upon the anticipated draft, which prevented him from

doing it.   There is certainly reason to believe that there was
a deliberate conspiracy to shift the errors of the battle upon
the Eleventh Corps, and the statements of Hooker, Sickles,
Warren and Birney furnish sufficient proof of the intent.
Those who were the most implicated in the wild goose chase
below the Furnace, and who are the authors of the misfor-
tunes of the army, are the foulest in abuse and loudest in
falsehood.

The origin of this unjust feeling, and the fostering care
which sustained it, is still involved in some doubt.   But it
is certain that the chief of staff of our armies—whom Lincoln declared to be utterly destitute of friends—had a mortal
aversion to all foreigners desiring to serve in our armies.
How far this disposition at the War Department affected the
well being and efficiency of the Eleventh Corps may not
easily or soon be determined, but it will not be forgotten
that all supplications of the officers of the corps to speak in
their defense after the battle of Chancellorsville were sternly
refused.

It is often asked why the investigation concerning the
Eleventh Corps at Chancellorsville has been so long delayed,
when so many of its members and its accusers are dead.
The reasons are ample and proper.   The evidence has not
long been accessible to the public, and until it could be collated and examined, no one wished to encounter the storm
of abuse which has greeted those who have attempted or
desired to say a word of explanation or extenuation for the
unfortunate corps.

There were other bodies of excellent troops besides the
Eleventh Corps in our armies who were made scape-goats
and objects of undeserved derision, and who remained under
ban for a long time before the truth became known.   For
twenty years the excellent division of General Prentiss was
overwhelmed with disgrace for neglect of duty at the battle
of Shiloh, but in 1883 General Prentiss branded the statements as false and unjust, and proved them to be so by
ample documentary proof, which has been lately corrobo-

rated by General Shoup, Chief of Artillery of Hardee's Corps of the Confederate army. General Lew Wallace, who was under reproach for neglect of duty at the same battle, proved at a public meeting at Tipton, in Indiana, in 1883, that he acted from first to last by direction of General Grant, and that when he was ordered to march, it was then too late.

Military history has many examples of misplaced praise and blame, and even the last English campaign in Egypt affords a marked instance. The division of General Hamley, at Tel-el-Kebir, made the final attack at night and defeated the Egyptian army. But in the reports of the campaign, the part General Hamley and his division had taken was studiously ignored, and the men he recommended to favor for bravery and gallant service were not even mentioned in the general report. Hamley, in defending his men and claiming for them some of the honors of success, was forced to retire from the army in which he was regarded as one of its ablest officers.

The Republic has become too great and too magnanimous to allow gross errors to remain inscribed in its archives to aggrandize a few guilty and incompetent officers by the unjust treatment of many thousand worthy soldiers. The volunteers of 1861 and 1862, who left their workshops, their schools and their homes to defend the distressed Republic for a trifling pittance, and did their duty, or attempted to do their duty, to the best of their ability, are certainly entitled to the protection and the thanks of this government, and to the respect and sympathy of their fellow soldiers. In fact, the flag at this period of time covers alike all its volunteer defenders, whether Jew or Gentile, or whether descendant of the Mayflower or of the followers of William Penn.

CHAPTER III.

Germans in the Eleventh Corps.

THE German troops of the Eleventh Corps, or what were classed as Germans, were largely composed of the veterans who offered their services at the commencement of the war, and after the first Bull Run —where they stood firm—had later been consolidated with other German organizations, and under Blenker sent into Western Virginia, where they reported to Fremont. Not long after their arrival, Fremont ordered a close inspection of their condition, in consequence of their complaints of destitution and neglect. The Inspector, somewhat biased against the composition of the division, found to his surprise an admirable body of men, many if not most of them American citizens by adoption or birth, well instructed as soldiers, and officered by men of ability, some of whom were officers of distinction, who had seen service in foreign wars and in the Mexican War. The forlorn and neglected condition of the men was plainly apparent to the Inspector.

Gen. James Shields, in this very campaign, said, June 7th, 1862, to his soldiers in the Luray Valley, when complaining of the want of shoes, clothing, etc.: "The Germans are not half as well off as you are, but they hang on the enemy without respite."

The men who had left their families and their occupations to serve the country for the paltry sum of eleven or thirteen dollars a month were certainly deserving of the best treatment from the authorities at Washington, and this they evidently had not received. Rosecrans, while on his way to the Army of the Cumberland, led this division from the Shenandoah over the mountains to Fremont, and was much disturbed at the neglect shown to it by the officials at Washington, and sharply questioned Stahel about the want of shoes and other things which his brigade required. Stahel assured him of his frequent requisitions in behalf of his men, and the ignoring of them by the officials in charge, which the Inspector found afterwards to be true. The Inspector found the division destitute of many things required for the comfort of the soldier, and that requisitions made for these wants were not honored, or were not promptly filled. The men justly complained of their treatment, and also of the abuse bestowed upon them during their march across the Shenandoah Valley for alleged acts of pillage on the way. From what the Inspector saw, he was of the opinion that the stories had been over-estimated, and he has since thought that the Second Corps put in the breastworks at the North Anna more valuables, in the shape of pianos, scientific apparatus and choice furniture, than Blenker's Division stole or destroyed during their march over the mountains to Northern Virginia. Their booty and destruction, even as exaggerated, was infinitesimal, as compared to that of the Army of the Potomac at the capture of Fredericksburg.

The Eleventh Corps was generally supposed to be formed of Germans, or foreigners, and it was sometimes called the foreign contingent of the Army of the Potomac. Investigation shows that the corps—probably three-fifths of it—was formed of American citizens by birth, and that many of the remainder were naturalized citizens, and were entitled to the respect due to the adopted citizen. The commander of the corps sent to the War Department in May, 1863, a list of eleven regiments as exclusively German, amounting to four thousand men, but investigation shows, or seems to show, that not one of these regiments was exclusively German. The De Kalb, or Forty-first New York, which was regarded as the most exclusive, really contained several Yankees in its ranks, and the others contained many native-born soldiers, who were classed as foreigners because they spoke German or French. In fact, there were a very large number of soldiers in this corps wrongfully classed because of their names, when they were really as much citizens of the country as Admiral Ammen or Generals Rosecrans, Custer, Hartranft, Heintzelman, Wister, Mendenhall, Pennypacker, Hoffman, Roebling, and hosts of others, whose fathers and grandfathers were born in this country, and entitled to any honor that might be claimed by the descendants of the Mayflower.

At the time of the rebellion there were in the North many foreign-born but naturalized soldiers who had been educated in the armies and the military schools of Europe, and they promptly offered their services in many ways to our distressed government. Some of these men, it is true, had rank and title attached to their names, but for this offensive stain of aristocratic birth they were not responsible, as the honors came from inheritance, and could not be dropped any more than in the case of Baron Steuben, of whom Washington thought so much. But few of these officers, however, were of high title, and the chief of these, the Prince Salm-Salm, was deserving of military praise. The death of this officer, when he fell at the head of the Fourth Royal Prussian Guards, at the bloody battle of Gravelotte, in the French and German war, was a fitting close to his restless ambition.

The people applauded heartily the martial bearing and patriotic offers of these men, when they marched promptly to the front, from New York or Philadelphia, under Von Schack, Von Weber, Blenker, Bohlen, and others. At this time, in the early days of the rebellion, when treason was seductive and danger was imminent, there was no distinction under the flag between the naturalized and the native-born citizen; all were welcome, and all stood on the same footing. But as the pressing danger grew less, the expressions of welcome at Washington changed also, and soon there was a marked contrast in the War Department to that hearty reception Washington gave to the French and German officers in the dark days of the Revolution. The country rejoiced with great joy when it became known that the entire German population of the North rallied without hesitation to the support of the endangered Republic. The support was magnificent, and deserving of the highest gratitude of the country. It is also remarkable that all of the revolutionists then in this country, and who had followed Kossuth, Garibaldi, Sigel and Hecker, should offer their services to the United States. It was, indeed, a grand sight, when the entire mass of German-speaking and German-born people rose as one man and stood firmly by the flag of the Republic. What would have been the fate of Missouri, Illinois and Indiana, at the commencement of the war, had it not been for the patriotic efforts of Sigel, Osterhaus, Schurz and Hecker, and their resolute German followers? Has the country yet recognized the importance and the full weight of these facts? Missouri certainly would have drifted away with the southern tide, had it not been for the influence and resistance of these gallant men. The Germans were the first to take up arms and attempt to save the state. The first three loyal regiments raised in St. Louis were Germans almost to a man, and when the Home Guards of Missouri were first formed, none but Germans joined them. This movement on the part of the Germans and other soldiers of foreign birth and other nationalities was of vast aid to the northern cause, and contributed greatly to its final success, and its influence and its value cannot be estimated with the gold of the nation. What was the cause of this remarkable support and unanimity on the part of the Germans? The influences which gave rise to this happy result may be traced back to the days and the effect of the Revolution of 1775, and they may be reckoned as among the blessings derived from that distant struggle.

Let us go back for a moment to Colonial times, and see how the influence of the Germans affected the condition of the revolted colonists. Before the blow in 1775 was struck, the German officer, De Kalb, rendered important aid to the cause of the revolutionists. This able officer was sent by the French Minister Choiseul to investigate the relations between Great Britain and her disaffected colonies, and his inspection was of vast importance in shaping the later policy of France under Vergennes, when Lafayette was sent with material and effective aid to the assistance of the sorely beset revolutionists. De Kalb's influence in this report, though indirect, was probably a more powerful factor in shaping the views of the French government than the world is aware of. It is certain, however, that the love of liberty had but little to do with it, and that the movement was in revenge for the disasters of the seven years' war. It was more of a thrust at the vitals of England—the hereditary foe—than an honest support of the efforts for freedom in the English Colonies. But the United States, after the declaration of peace, derived aid and strength from an unexpected quarter, and this came from the much abused Hessians.

England, during the revolt of her American colonists, hired about twenty thousand men from the German princes on the Rhine to help fight her battles, and this act, which was extremely offensive to the revolutionists, led to important benefits and results to the Republic before a century had passed. After hostilities ceased, many of these troops from the Rhenish Provinces remained behind to become citizens of the new Republic, and many more also returned soon after from Germany to settle here. There were many Germans in the French army with Lafayette, and between the two armies, quite eleven thousand men remained behind to become citizens of the new Republic. Germany, it is said, derived much benefit from the experience of her soldiers in the expeditions to America, made at the expense of Great Britain. And the lessons the German soldier learned in the American Revolution were carried home and spread broadcast over the Fatherland. And under Gneisenau and others they bore substantial fruit in the great struggle for German liberty in the times of Napoleon. It was largely due to these impressions, germinating for nearly a century, that the great majority of the people of the German nation supported the Union cause in the civil war.

At the time of the rebellion, there were many Germans

and families of German ancestry throughout the United States. In 1862 it was computed by competent authority that there were over one million people of German descent in the state of Pennsylvania, eight hundred thousand in New York, six hundred thousand in Ohio, over one hundred thousand in Missouri, and about thirty thousand in New England. The great Northwest was also full of people of German origin, but no estimate of their numbers was given at this time. In the state of Maryland there were one hundred and twenty-five thousand people of German birth or descent, and it was largely due to their influence that the state of Maryland remained in the Union, and it was also largely due to their loyal feeling that General Lee received so few recruits when he invaded Maryland in the Antietam and Gettysburg campaigns.

It has also been estimated by excellent authority that nearly one hundred and ninety thousand soldiers of German birth—most of whom were naturalized citizens—were enlisted in the Federal armies. Besides these, there was a vast number of men of German ancestry, who spoke the language of their ancestors, but were classed as Germans by mistake. In the South, there were also many soldiers of German descent, who gave the Confederacy much trouble with their strong attachment to the old Republic, before they yielded to the demands and seductions of secession. During the war but few soldiers of German birth were attracted from the Fatherland to aid the southern cause, and although they were able and active men, like Heros Von Borcke and Estvan, they did not influence the Fatherland in the least against the Union cause.

The soldiers of the Eleventh Corps, especially the German troops, after Chancellorsville were hooted at on all sides and called in derision Dutchmen—Flying Dutchmen— as though the name expressed a low degree of courage. The term of reproach exhibited at the same time the animosity, the ignorance and the malice of the revilers, for the Dutch, known in ancient times as Batavians, were considered the

bravest and most warlike of all the nations of northern
Europe. And in modern times, infantry never stood firmer
than did the Dutch at the battle of Malplaquet, or fought
with more heroism and defiance of death than did the defenders of the trenches of Berg-op-Zoom, or Ostend. And
the sailors who swept the seas with Van Reuter and Van
Tromp were never surpassed in tenacious courage, save by
the boldest of the English sea rovers. To call a coward
a Dutchman in contempt is a serious mistake, for it invests
him with historic praise. A little more of the derided Dutch
character infused into our armies might have shortened the
days of the rebellion. The German character needs no apol-
ogy to the student of history for lack of martial virtues.
Since the days of the Cæsars, its unquenchable warlike spirit
has never been denied or questioned. The German nation
from the earliest periods has been rich in patriotic feeling and love of liberty. From it sprang the noble ideas
of ancient and modern chivalry, as well as respect for women
and veneration for old age. In brief, civilization owes more
of its high degree of excellence and strength to the descendants of the savages of the Hercynian forests than to the del-
icate morals of the effete Roman Empire. Truly did Carlyle
and Montesquieu say that the British Constitution came out
of the woods of Germany. Truly did another of the greatest
of modern historians say, that the fatherland of English-
speaking people is not England, but Germany. Napoleon
was wont to point with pride and with universal consent
to one of his marshals as the "Bravest of the Brave"—
Michael Ney, a German by blood.

In the western armies, the German soldier met with
little or no opposition, and some of their regiments, composed of Germans, or men of German descent, were regarded
as the choicest and most reliable of all the troops in the
West. The Ninth Ohio, composed entirely of Germans, or
those of German descent, with the exception of one man—
its brave commander, the gallant Robert L. McCook—probably had no superior in the western armies. In the western

armies, however, the volunteer element asserted itself, and maintained its influence and its rights. In the Army of the Potomac it was somewhat different. West Point shaped all things to the interest and the wishes of its faction, and it may truthfully be said that in the management of this army patriotism was often subservient to cold ambition, and that selfishness sometimes proved stronger than sense of honor; that "faults passed for virtues and rashness was regarded as proof of superior genius." As we strip away the veil of obscurity that hangs over the Army of the Potomac, and examine the ferment of jealousy, the concealed ambition, the rank suspicion, and the favoritism of its leaders, the picture is not pleasant to contemplate or to consider. But beneath this dismal revelation appears the glorious array of the rank and file and subordinate officers of the army, standing out in bold and clear relief, firm as its lines of steel, unsurpassed in the world's history in courage, devotion, intelligence and patriotism. And it also recalls to mind the fable which says: "An army of sheep commanded by lions is better than an army of lions commanded by sheep."

The Army of the Potomac was drawn from the best life blood of the North, embodying its intelligence and its patriotism, and though it had not the steady superiority, the obstinate obedience of Roman discipline, its courage and its devotion was no less sublime, and amid all, and in spite of all its reckless and stupid leadership, its sadly torn ranks stood firm and undaunted to the last.

CHAPTER IV.

Personnel of the Eleventh Corps.

NONE of the corps of the army were so diversified in their personnel as the Eleventh—none had so romantic or so extended a career. Commencing its history at the battle of McDowell, in Western Virginia, or still earlier in the war, with Blenker's Brigade at Manassas, fighting its way down the Shenandoah Valley and over the mountains to the second Manassas, taking a part at Chancellorsville and Gettysburg, and from thence across the country to the relief of Chattanooga, the attack on Lookout Mountain, the relief of Knoxville, and the famous march with Sherman to the sea, none suffered so severely and so unjustly the "slings and arrows of outrageous fortune." No better proof of its good qualities can be offered than the fact that it did survive the calumnies of Chancellorsville and Gettysburg, and far away with Sherman, in the heart of the Confederacy, showed that it contained among its survivors valiant spirits, worthy of the highest commendation.

Sigel, in April, had asked for release, and Howard had been assigned to the command. The one-armed soldier was received with kindness and attention. His frank, open countenance and pleasant manners, and empty sleeve, strengthened his position. But nevertheless, behind this, there was a silent feeling, or suspicion, that was not easily appeased. The exuberant religious manifestations of the new commander were not pleasing to the corps. Although there were among them many devout Christians, the great mass of the corps were untrammeled in their religious views, and they believed that fortune came to the big battalions, and that victory was the result of audacity, courage and vigilance, and was not deduced from auspices or assisted by incantations.

Shortly before the battle, the intrepid Barlow had been sent to the corps, at the request of Howard, and assigned to the brigade commanded by Col. Orland Smith. The displacement was not called for, and the advent of Barlow did not increase the feeling of contentment or confidence in the brigade. Col. Orland Smith was not a whit inferior in the many qualifications that make the successful soldier, and his career proved it. Nine days before the battle, General Devens appeared and was assigned to the First Division, then commanded by General McLean, who had been associated with troops of the command for a long time, and was entitled to all the honors attached thereto. Devens had been taken by Hooker from a division of the Sixth Corps and expressly ordered to the command of a division in the Eleventh Corps. The advent of Devens returned General McLean to his brigade, and Colonel Lee, then in charge of the brigade, returned to his regiment, the Fifty-fifth Ohio.

The change was unfortunate, and led to disaster. It created considerable feeling among the troops, as McLean had been in command for a long time, and was familiar with the men. McLean was a veteran of long service, and his ability had never been questioned. Lincoln's maxim, ''never swap horses while crossing a stream,'' was forcibly illustrated in this instance. Had McLean remained in place, Jackson never would have surprised the flank of Hooker's army, for he had fought Jackson in his two former flank movements, and was aware of his manner of fighting.

At this time the Eleventh Corps numbered about twelve thousand effectives, which is the estimate of General Howard and also that of Colonel Fox, but General Hooker stated before Congress that it was but eleven thousand men, and this is the estimate given by General Underwood, who made a careful study of the battle after the close of the war. The left wing of the corps, composed of the two brigades of Buschbeck and Barlow, and under the command of General Steinwehr, was stationed along the Dowdall Farm, with Buschbeck's Brigade strongly entrenched on the crest of the southern border of the farm and facing south, and supported by Weidrick's Battery of six guns. North of the Dowdall House, Barlow's Brigade was placed in reserve for the corps, and in the morning had constructed a shallow rifle pit, extending diagonally across the open field from the rear of Dowdall's to the woods in rear of the little Church, and facing west. In the same field, on its eastern edge, the reserve artillery of three batteries was parked. To the right of Buschbeck's, four regiments of Schurz's Division were interposed along the road facing south as far as Devens' Division at the Talley Farm, while the remaining five regiments were bivouacked on the Hawkins Farm, directly in the rear. Prolonging the right of Schurz, and extending for more than half a mile, were five of the regiments of Devens' Division, standing in the road and facing south. On the extreme right of this line were two regiments, deflected at a right angle from the pike, facing west and covering the approach from that direction. In the angle of the line, and in the road, were placed two of Dickman's guns, nine hundred and sixty yards from the Talley House. The other four guns were placed east of Talley's, facing south, to command the Plank Road. The remaining regiments, the Twenty-fifth and the Seventy-fifth Ohio, were held in reserve, formed in double column, and placed in the woods in rear of the Fifty-fifth and One Hundred and Seventh Ohio, facing south. Along the front of the five regiments of Devens' Division there were no defences of strength. The fences had been thrown down along the southern side of the road, and piled up, with a little dirt thrown over them, and in the woods the timber had been slashed in front of the Forty-first and Forty-fifth New York, the two guns in the road and the two deflected regiments, the One Hundred and Fifty-third Pennsylvania, and Fifty-fourth New York. The rest of Devens' Division was without protection of any kind, and, in fact, all the redoubts thrown up for the protection of the corps were rendered utterly useless by the attack of Jackson, far in their rear, excepting the trivial rifle pit east of the Dowdall Tavern, and the reports of the corps abandoning strong earthworks at the first fire are entirely erroneous. The only earthwork whatever that could furnish the least protection, and a chance to rally, to the broken regiments of Devens' and Schurz' Divisions, was the shallow and incompleted rifle pit in the field east of the Church and the Dowdall Tavern, and this could only afford shelter to a thin line of infantry lying down or kneeling behind it. It was so trivial in its construction that all traces of it have now disappeared.

The two deflected regiments of Von Gilsa, on whom fell the first blow of Jackson's army, were the One Hundred and Fifty-third Pennsylvania, a regiment of nine months men, mostly American citizens by birth. The other was the Fifty-fourth New York, an old regiment, few in numbers (about two hundred and fifty men), and composed mostly of Germans, or men of German descent. It was placed a little in rear of the right flank of the One Hundred and Fifty-third Pennsylvania, and in echelon. Neither of these regiments had any protection whatever, except what was afforded by the slashing of the timber in their front, and which delayed the onset of the enemy but a few moments. The nearest support to these two regiments was the Seventy-fifth Ohio, in double column, facing south, and seven hundred yards distant, while the regiments on the Hawkins Farm were over half a mile distant, far to the rear of their right flank.

The Eleventh Corps at Chancellorsville, as previously stated, consisted of twenty-seven regiments, of which eleven were new, while the remaining sixteen were old organizations, and had been tested in the campaigns of West Virginia, the Shenandoah Valley, and the second Bull Run, under Pope. The history of the veteran regiments certainly entitles them to the fullest confidence of their new associates in the Army of the Potomac. Concerning the personnel of the new regiments, much can be said in their praise. In the review of the Army of the Potomac by President Lincoln, in April, just before the battle of Chancellorsville, the Eleventh Corps made a most excellent appearance, and the division commanded by General Schurz impressed the presidential party as the best drilled and the most soldierly of all of the Army of the Potomac that passed before them.

Among the new troops in this corps, New England had two of its best regiments, the Seventeenth Connecticut and the Thirty-third Massachusetts. The Seventeenth Connecticut was well selected in its rank and file, and most of its officers had seen service in other organizations, one of whom was the brave Swede, Lieutenant Colonel Walter, who lost his life in this contest. Among the rank and file were the noted inventor, Elias Howe, and his son, and besides these there were many others of skill and talent, who had enlisted from a high sense of duty and patriotism. The Thirty-third Massachusetts was composed of the best soldiers of that patriotic Commonwealth, and New England had no better troops in the service than these under the command of Col. A. B. Underwood. From the far West, the Twenty-sixth Wisconsin claims special notice. It was classed as a German regiment, but with them there were mixed many other nationalities, as Scandinavians, Swiss and Americans. In this fight it won distinction, and afterwards became a noted body of troops, and was rightly reckoned by General Cogswell as one of the finest military organizations in the Army of the United States. The Eighty-second Illinois was also largely composed of Germans, mixed with Swiss and Americans. Among the Swiss was a youth of the name of Emil Frey, who was a student in Switzerland at the time of the outbreak, but who promptly left the university, with others, and offered his humble services to the Republic. He first enlisted as a private in the Twenty-eighth Illinois, but when Hecker called for volunteers, Frey raised a company of his own, joined Hecker, and served with distinction until June, 1865. This is the same youth whom Switzerland sent as its Minister to this country many years afterwards, and who is regarded to-day as one of its most eminent citizens. Besides this Swiss student, there were many others of ability in the corps, who left their universities, or their positions in the armies of Europe, to give their assistance to the Republic.

In this regiment was a company of Jews, and to provide for the wants of these men and their families, the Jews of Chicago generously raised a large sum of money. At the head of the regiment stood a citizen and man of sterling worth, whose name will always be remembered in the history of the West and the cause of human liberty with respect and reverence. The ability, patriotism and noble qualities of this grand man—Frederick Hecker—had been well established in the revolution in Baden in 1848, and to his newly adopted country he offered all he had. This regiment gained a great and deserving reputation in the war, and here at Chancellorsville the attempts it made to stop Jackson's surging masses show that it did have valiant men in its ranks, who were worthy of the highest praise.

The One Hundred and Nineteenth New York was formed largely of Germans or men of German descent, and its colonel was Elias Peisner. Peisner had been a revolutionist in Germany, but was a naturalized citizen and a professor at Union College, at Schenectady, New York, and a man held in the highest esteem. At the mention of his name at the great mass meeting held at Cooper Institute in 1863, in New York city, the entire audience rose to their feet in honor of the man. He was a bold and resolute officer, and had deployed his men safely, and was resisting the onslaught of the rebels after Devens had been compelled to retreat. At the first attack, Peisner fell beside his men, pierced with two balls.

The One Hundred and Fifty-third Pennsylvania was reckoned as an American regiment, although there were many names indicating German lineage, and it was regarded as an excellent body of men. The One Hundred and Thirty-fourth, the One Hundred and Thirty-sixth, the One Hundred and Fifty-fourth and the One Hundred and Fifty-seventh New York were all new regiments, composed of Americans, and well officered and worthy of confidence. The One Hundred and Thirty-fourth was commanded by Col. Charles R.

Coster, the One Hundred and Thirty-sixth by Col. James Wood, Jr., the One Hundred and Fifty-fourth by Col. Patrick H. Jones, and the One Hundred and Fifty-seventh by Col. Philip P. Brown, Jr.

Among the veteran regiments, there were six from the state of Ohio, nearly all American citizens, and equal in courage, intelligence and patriotism to any in the armies of the United States. Their reputation had been fully established long before the battle of Chancellorsville, in the campaigns of Western Virginia and at Cross Keys, and in the battle of the second Manassas, where the most of them won especial praise. They were the Twenty-fifth, the Fifty-fifth, the Sixty-first, the Seventy-third, the Seventy-fifth and the Eighty-second, all of which were commanded by American officers of acknowledged ability and courage. No words of praise are necessary for Colonel Richardson, of the Twenty-fifth, for Colonel Lee, of the Fifty-fifth, for Col. Stephen McGroarty, of the Sixty-first, for Col. Orland Smith, of the Seventy-third, for Col. Robert Riley, of the Seventy-fifth, or for that noble man and officer, Col. James S. Robinson, of the Eighty-second Ohio Regiment.

All of these regiments excepting the Seventy-third, then detached with Barlow, were in the fight, and attempted to do their duty, and did do it, at a terrible sacrifice of their men, for which adequate praise has not been given. It would be difficult to find six trustier regiments in all the armies of the United States than these. The Sixty-first Ohio was commanded by that sterling Irishman, Col. Stephen J. McGroarty, and his regiment seemed to be largely of Irishmen or men of Irish descent, so strong was the individuality of the commander. No one ever questioned McGroarty's courage or ability, and at the close of the war, he could have exclaimed with Marius: "My wounds are the proof of my nobility." The report of this gallant officer is not to be found, and its absence is a serious loss to the history of the fight around Dowdall's and at the Church. It is certain, however, that the brave officer who held his regiment as rear guard until midnight on the deserted field of the second Bull Run did all that one man could do in arresting disaster in the face of ruin, or what appeared to be ruin.

The Sixty-first was drawn up in line facing the west, waiting for the enemy, when the wrecks of Devens' Division, rushing down the road to escape the withering fire of Jackson's men, overran them and destroyed their formation, and carried a part of it away with them in the crowd, which continued on towards the Chancellor House. Parts of the broken regiment joined the line by the Church, and later on fell back to the Buschbeck line and fought there. Two of the companies attached themselves to Dilger's Battery, and stuck to him in the retreat, and followed him to his position in the line of artillery at Fairview, where they remained until morning.

The Forty-first New York, known as the De Kalb Regiment, was reduced by fighting and hardship to about three hundred men. It was formed by Von Gilsa, and it was said to have contained at first several hundred soldiers who had served with Von Gilsa in the Prussian army, and were well instructed men. The Forty-fifth New York was also a veteran regiment under Colonel Von Arnsberg, and although much reduced in numbers by campaigning, it contained a few more men than the Forty-first. These two regiments of about seven hundred men were placed in the road behind the two guns, on picket, and were attacked by the enemy in flank and rear, and were justified in retreating as they did. As the reports of this brigade are all missing and the commanders are dead, it is difficult to ascertain how much fighting these soldiers really did; but there is no doubt, from the personnel of these regiments, that they would have made a determined resistance if they had been in a proper position, and had had any chance whatever to fight.

The Seventy-third Pennsylvania was organized at Philadelphia in June, 1861, by Col. John A. Koltes, who was a gallant German soldier of distinction, who had served in the Mexican war, and had also been a soldier in the regular army. He was a citizen of this country, and employed in the U. S. Mint at the time of the civil war. His regiment was considered an excellent one, but at the time of Chancellorsville it had become much reduced in numbers, as it had suffered severely at the second Bull Run, where it lost both Koltes, who acted as brigade commander, and Bruenecker, who commanded the regiment in that sanguinary contest.

The Seventy-fifth Pennsylvania, a veteran regiment, but greatly reduced in numbers by two years of honorable service, was placed on picket south of the Dowdall Farm, and there it remained until it was too late to join the brigade at the Hawkins Farm. The men had seen, during the day, the movements of troops south of them and within range of their guns, but were ordered to remain quiet and not provoke a combat. When Doles' Brigade passed between them and the Dowdall House, there was no way of escape but by the woods to the southward, as the enemy in strong force prevented returning by way of the Plank Road or the path from Dowdall's. The regiment was rallied, and remained for some time spectators of the battle in rear of them, until the troops held back by Colquitt, now coming up in their rear, front and right flank, compelled them to retire. There were but two hundred and fifty men in the regiment on that day, and of these sixty had been detailed to service at the Hawkins Farm, leaving but two hundred men to perform picket duty south of Dowdall's. Here they were attacked by Colquitt's or Ramseur's men, and were soon dispersed, with a loss of fifty-nine killed, wounded and missing. The remainder of the regiment, reduced to one hundred and thirty men, crossed the stream to the southeast of Dowdall's, then in possession of the enemy, and escaped by following Scott's Run until they reached the southern edge of Hazel Grove, where they took the road or path leading from the Furnace to Fairview. They brought up the rear—not the front—of the grand skedaddle which Pleasanton has described, and when they reached the position where the artillery was placed in battery, they fell in behind Dilger's Battery, having retained their arms, and there they remained until ordered to the rear of the Chancellor House, late in the evening. This was General Bohlen's old regiment, and was formed largely of volunteers from men of German birth or of German ancestry, but among them there were many Americans of excellent qualities. The personnel of this regiment was of superior character, and it is doubtful if Philadelphia sent any better troops to the war.

General Bohlen, who raised the regiment largely at his own expense, was a distinguished soldier long before the rebellion. At the age of twenty-one he was, on the recommendation of General Lafayette, appointed on the staff of General Gerard, and served with him during the siege of Antwerp. He also served on the staff of General Worth in the Mexican war, and took part in several engagements. During the Crimean war he served in the French army, and was well versed in the art of war. Although born in Germany, he was intensely an American citizen, and when the rebellion threatened the liberties of his adopted country, he left the scenes of pleasure which his great wealth and social position gave him in Europe, and hastened at once to perform his part. The men whom he called around him in forming the Seventy-fifth Pennsylvania were of a superior class, and their standing should not be reckoned according to the monthly pittance received for their services. In fact, the volunteers of 1861 and 1862 were from the best class of citizens throughout the country, east or west, and were probably never surpassed in intelligence or patriotism in any of the civil revolutions of history. General Bohlen was killed in one of the fights preceding the second Bull Run.

The First Division was commanded by Gen. Charles Devens, who had been sent to the corps by Hooker and assigned to the division. Devens was an officer of ability and courage, who had taken part in the terrible ambuscade at Ball's Bluff, and had served with distinction on the Peninsula ; but his displacement of McLean, and the austerity of his manners, did not add strength to the corps, and it is useless to deny that his introduction into the corps was costly to Howard and fatal to the Army of the Potomac.

The Second Division was under the command of General Von Steinwehr, who was a man of great distinction, and a notable trained and veteran soldier. He came from a distinguished military family in Germany, and was well educated in the military schools of that country. He came to this country and served as an officer in an Alabama regiment during the Mexican war. Afterwards he became a farmer in Connecticut, and was a citizen of that state when the rebellion called for his services. He came to New York, assisted in forming the Twenty-ninth New York Regiment, was chosen its colonel, and commanded it with credit at the first Bull Run battle. Steinwehr's military reputation ranked high with all who knew him, his ability was never questioned, and he was deserving of the greatest confidence.

The Third Division was under the direction of Gen. Carl Schurz, who, though not educated as a soldier, was well versed in military matters, and served with ability. He was a noted leader in the Revolution of 1848 in Germany, but escaped and came to the United States in 1852, and soon became a citizen of the Republic. He promptly offered his services to the government in 1861, soon rose to be a major general, and commanded a division with ability at the second Bull Run. His rare intellectual gifts assisted him greatly in his military career, and the record of his services in the war is an honorable one.

The brigade commanders in the First Division were McLean and Von Gilsa. McLean was a son of Justice McLean, was one of the early volunteers of Ohio, and had won his way along the military path by sturdy fighting. He had recently been appointed brigadier general and put in command of the division, but was displaced by Devens and returned to his brigade. McLean was an officer of discretion and firmness, but did not possess that courage which dares do the correct thing when the commander is clearly at fault. His strict obedience to his superior officer was military, but it was fatal to his men.

Von Gilsa was another example of the typical German soldier. He had been an officer of the rank of major in the Schleswig-Holstein war, and soon afterwards came to this country and became a citizen. He was a school teacher when the rebellion broke out, when he came to the front at once and organized the De Kalb Regiment, which contained a large number of trained German soldiers who had served with him in Holstein. Von Gilsa served with credit wherever he was, was wounded at Cross Keys, and although he had served as commander of brigade and division, yet he was mustered out in 1864 as a colonel, the same rank he was given in April, 1861. He was a marked example of the neglect of the War Department in the distribution of its favors and its obligations. It was his misfortune to be placed on the extreme right, and to be left alone to face the full force of Jackson's first blow, and because he could not fight an overwhelming force of the enemy in his front and both flanks at the same time, he bore the blame of others, and the sting of injustice carried him to an early grave.

The two brigade commanders in the Second Division were Buschbeck and Barlow. Adolph Buschbeck was the son of a German officer, and was educated as a soldier in the military schools of Germany, and at one time was an instructor in the Cadet School of Potsdam. About ten years before the rebellion he came to this country, and became a citizen and a school teacher in Philadelphia. He assisted largely in forming the Twenty-seventh Pennsylvania Regiment, and was soon afterwards chosen its colonel, becoming general of brigade and division. The records show that he was a man of high soldierly qualities, and was well thought of by General Hooker and General Sherman. Gen. Francis Barlow was a new comer in the corps, and was but little known to its members. His ways were too abrupt and his views too much those of the martinet to please his brigade, but they soon discovered that he was as intrepid as Decatur, and as fond of a fight as the naval hero of earlier times.

The commander of the First Brigade of the Third Division was Brig. Gen. Alexander Schimmelpfennig, who had been an officer in the Prussian army. He came to this country and became a citizen, publishing soon after a history of the war between Russia and Turkey. At the outbreak he assisted in raising the Seventy-fourth Pennsylvania Regiment, and remained in service during the war. He is said to have come from the celebrated family of that name in Europe, and was considered one of the best read officers in military science to be found in the army. He was a man of slight figure but of great military ability and undaunted courage and resolution. He felt keenly the unjust imputation of Chancellorsville, and chagrin hastened his death soon after the war closed.

The commander of the Second Brigade, Third Division, was Col. Wladimir Kryzanowski, who had been exiled from Poland by the Revolution of 1846, and had become a citizen of the United States and a civil engineer by profession. But when Sumter was attacked, he promptly cancelled all his engagements and assisted in raising the Fifty-eighth New York Regiment, of which he became the colonel.

Major Ernst F. Hoffman, the chief engineer of the corps—a Prussian by birth and military education—was an officer of distinction at the age of twenty-four years, when he was decorated with the Order of the Red Eagle by the King of Prussia. Hoffman was a man of superior education, and more than the peer of the chivalric Heros Von Borcke, whom Generals Lee and Stuart thought so highly of in the rebel army. His life had been adventurous and romantic, and he had seen service with distinction with the Prussian army in Denmark, with the English army in the Crimea, and in Africa, and also on the staff of Garibaldi, in Italy. At the time of the war he was serving on the staff of General de la Marmora, in Italy, as major of engineers, and was sent by our Minister, George P. Marsh, to our government, with letters of the highest character. An eloquent tribute to the ability and the noble qualities of this sterling soldier may be found in the columns of the *National Tribune* of March 5th, 1885, from the pen of his distinguished and true friend, Maj. Gen. James H. Wilson, of the U. S. Army.

CHAPTER V.

Sickles' Fatal Reconnaissance.

THE fatal reconnaissance toward the Furnace by Birney increased in proportions as he descended the road southward and beyond the Furnace. Whipple's Division was then added to Birney's, and later Sickles called for Williams' Division of the Twelfth Corps, which was detached from its fortifications and added to the attacking force. Sickles also called for Berry's Division to support his movement, but Hooker refused to permit it to leave its position, and sent instead Barlow's Brigade of the Eleventh Corps. Barlow's Brigade of nearly three thousand men was taken from its position as reserve to the Eleventh Corps at between four and five P. M. and sent to Sickles, increasing his column of attack to quite twenty thousand men. The taking of Barlow's Brigade by Captain Moore, of Hooker's staff, may be regarded as a rescinding of the order of Van Allen at 9.30 A. M., and also as positive evidence that at Hooker's headquarters there were no apprehensions whatever of danger to the exposed Eleventh Corps.

This expedition to the Welford Furnace and below is clearly the cause of the failure of the campaign. It is difficult to place the authorship of this ill-timed movement on documentary proof, but up to ten A. M. it certainly cannot be ascribed to Hooker. The late General Underwood, who was one of the participators in its glories and a sufferer in its shame, declares that Sickles is responsible for it; that he planned the expedition, and persuaded Hooker to allow him to make it, and is the person of all others accountable for the forlorn condition in which the Eleventh Corps was left when Jackson's blow came. After depriving the Eleventh Corps of its reserves, and assuring it that Lee and the rebel army was retreating and far away on the road to Gordonsville, it seems incredible that Hooker, Birney, Sickles and others should attempt to lay all the blame on the defenseless and friendless corps.   Such appear to be the facts, and more-over, there seems to have been a conspiracy on the part of the guilty ones to shift all blame and error upon the unfor-tunate corps, to divert attention from the real causes.   It was stated to Congress that there was a conspiracy in the Army of the Potomac against Hooker, and there is certainly suffi-cient evidence to warrant the assertion that there was also a conspiracy in that army to wreck the reputation of the Elev-enth Corps.

Hooker's orders all indicate a determined resolution to remain on the defensive, and his words of caution to Sickles when he went down to the Furnace with Birney's Division were not to bring on a battle ; yet he permitted twenty thou-sand men to be detached from the entrenched lines of de-fense and moved forward two or three miles in a dense for-est, leaving a gap of three miles between Von Gilsa's de-flected force on the right flank and Berry's Division, the nearest available force in reserve.   Late in the afternoon, Sickles was about to attack the retreating enemy, and had called for Pleasanton and his cavalry to follow up the effec-tive blow.   The leaders of this unfortunate expedition seemed to have been as ignorant of Jackson's whereabouts at this time as General Knyphausen, of the Hessians, was of our Revolutionary fathers, when he inquired of the captain of the ship if he had not sailed past in the night the place called America, where the rebels were.   At this time or a little later, there was no enemy between Birney's extreme front and the Ohio River.   Posey and Wright and their brigades were con-cealed on his left flank in the woods, listening for the sounds of Jackson's guns as the signal to attack.   From his front Archer had long ago withdrawn his Tennesseeans, and was following the trail of Jackson's column, leaving the road free for Barlow's Brigade of the Eleventh Corps to march three miles south of the unfinished railroad, vainly seeking connec-tion with Birney's advanced force, and signs of the enemy.

At this hour, past five P. M., Hooker, Sickles, Warren, and most of the other general officers, excepting perhaps Slocum, believed that the rebels were in full retreat, and that the glorious opportuuity of capturing a large part of their force, with cannon and trains, was rapidly passing away. So completely did this idea take possession of their understanding, that they did not entertain or discuss even a suspicion that Jackson, instead of seeking flight, was marching for their unguarded rear. Sickles, away down in the woods below the Furnace, was so saturated with this notion of Lee's flight, that he refused to listen to the staff officer who brought him the information that the Eleventh Corps, less than two miles in his rear, had been fighting for more than half an hour and was being overpowered by greatly superior forces. Not until after the second officer arrived, bringing details of danger and disaster, could he realize the absurdity of his expedition and the extreme peril in which his troops were then placed. A more ridiculous and stupid surprise did not occur in the history of the civil war. It seems incredible that, when word came from Sickles to Hooker that he was among the rebel trains, Jackson was actually three miles almost directly in his rear, and was about to hurl the most of his thirty thousand men upon the feeble obstacles in his front, comprising only the forlorn Eleventh Corps, then deprived of its reserve brigade. It is still more incredible that, when Birney was preparing to bivouac with his powerful division below the Welford House, two miles below the Plank Road, wondering what had become of the enemy, he was not aware that Jackson had been pulverizing the deserted and depleted Eleventh Corps of nine thousand men for more than an hour.

Between the battle of Chancellorsville and that of Jena, where Napoleon struck down the Prussian monarchy almost by a single blow, there may be found some unpleasant points of resemblance. The Prussian army, like that of the Potomac, was pronounced by its leaders the first on the planet, and invincible, with its inherited maxims of Frederick the Great. But its leaders were as stupidly confident as were Hooker and his lieutenants, and they exhibited alike the same professional prejudices, blind self conceit and ignorance of what the enemy was doing, and where he was. Prince Hohenlohe, like Hooker, sent a dispatch to his reserves in the rear, ''I am whipping the enemy at every point;'' yet shortly after he took to his heels and ran sixty miles before he thought himself safe from pursuit, far eclipsing the famous retrograde record of Frederick the Great at the battle of Mollwitz.

It is certainly very singular that Birney, or Sickles, or Hooker did not suspect that Jackson's movement was to reach the rear of the Federal army. All the marching of trains and troops was in that direction, and the information derived from soldiers taken with the Twenty-third Georgia Regiment distinctly pointed in that direction, and when Lieutenant Thorp brought these men, who had been captured by the Berdan sharpshooters, to the rear and passed General Sickles somewhere in the vicinity of the Furnace, he said to Sickles that Jackson's Corps was moving to the rear. Warren, it is said, was informed of it also, but fatuity was the order of the day, not only at the extreme front, but in the rear and in the center of the army. And so the entire day passed, and all about the Chancellor House was in blissfull serenity. Pleasanton, with his calvary, instead of scouting on the exposed right flank, and developing the concealed enemy, clung to the shadow of headquarters, where he inundated Hooker with his vain advice. Well may the Confederate soldier exclaim, '' *Quem Deus vult perdere.* '' Hooker sat upon the porch of the Chancellor House, enjoying the calm spring evening, and listening to the sounds of the distant cannon, which were undoubtedly from Hardaway's artillery, only about one mile distant to the south or southeast of where he sat with Captains Candler and Russell. It was about half past six, or near that time, when Russell stepped out in front of the house, and, on looking down the road with his glass, exclaimed : ''My God, here they come !'' Hooker and both of his officers sprang upon their horses, rode a little distance down the road, and met the advance of the Eleventh Corps stragglers coming up the road, and from them he first learned of Jackson's attack.   Not a sound had he or his staff heard of the conflict, which had been going on for nearly an hour.   Not an officer had come to him from the front to give him warning, and this disaster came upon him with stunning effect.   Although Buschbeck and Schurz were then fighting with all the force they could muster, it was evident to Hooker at a glance that his army was in extreme peril, and well he might quail with dismay at the situation.

Sickles was at this moment miles away in the depths of the forest with twenty thousand of his best troops, and his destruction or capture seemed certain.   Turning to Candler, Hooker bade him seek the First Corps, then supposed to be in position behind the White House, barely half a mile away, and bring it in person to the Fairview field in front of him. Candler galloped rapidly away towards the north, and had almost reached the White House; when Russell overtook him with orders to return instantly to Hooker.   The commander had found out since the dispatch of Candler that the First Corps was not where he supposed it was, and had been ordered to be, but was still beyond the Rappahannock River, and was not available until midnight or morning. Candler then proceeded with new instructions to bring the First Corps with all haste, and to take other artillery on the road to assist the corps.   Candler did so, and personally led the First Corps into a position on the Ely Ford Road, a mile northwest of Chancellor's, and reported to Hooker at midnight that the corps was in position.   Then Hooker took a longer breath, but the blow had been too severe and too sudden, and the commander did not recover from it until after the campaign was over, if he did then.

At the Dowdall Tavern, the headquarters of the Eleventh Corps, at four P. M., all was serene, and no fear of the approach of the enemy was entertained ; in fact, there was nothing to disturb the calmness of the afternoon but the solicitude that General Lee might escape from the eager clutches of the

Army of the Potomac. The reports from the menaced outer lines were unheeded, and it is possible that the important and positive reports of Colonels Lee and Richardson never passed their division commanders. It has been strongly asserted by members of General McLean's staff that the important and positive reports of Colonels Lee and Richardson were never sent to the corps headquarters, and, moreover, Howard's staff assert that they never reached there. And they also maintain that the only information they had to consider was the widely spread and widely believed statement, coming from Sickles to Hooker, and which was to the positive effect that Lee was retreating, and that his fleeing troops were being captured in large numbers. This impression at the Dowdall Tavern was strengthened to a positive certainty when Captain Moore, of Hooker's staff, came and demanded Barlow's Brigade, between the hours of four and five P. M., to go to the Furnace to join Sickles' bold and brilliant movement, and assist Birney, then supposed to have a firm grip on the rear of Lee's fugitive columns.

There was no objection on the part of Barlow or Howard to the removing of this force in reserve—the biggest brigade in the corps—which separated it from the corps and removed it from its important position. The brigade was ordered under arms, and started in the path which led directly south from Dowdall's. The commander of the corps was in the best of spirits at this time, being completely hypnotized by the assertion that Lee was retreating, and he exclaimed gaily to the men shouldering their arms that they were going to join Birney and capture some regiments. No thought or suspicion of danger is apparent at Dowdall's Tavern at this time, and yet there were more than fifteen thousand rebels resting on their arms within one mile of the right flank of the corps, and whose presence could have been determined in thirty minutes by a single company or a regiment of men.

With Barlow went about three thousand men—or, to be exact, 2,950 men—and the last hope of a successful resistance by the Eleventh Corps. Generals Howard and Steinwehr, and Major Howard and Captain Moore, of Hooker's staff, accompanied the troops down to the Furnace and some distance beyond.   When they returned the net had been cast, the storm had burst, and the scene was enough to startle the stoutest heart.   The roar of the battle which had enveloped and destroyed Devens' Division, and the yells of the lines of infantry from the depths of the forest extending two miles in front, indicated that the whole of the rebel army were gathered there for a mighty blow.   Barlow was then three miles away, and Berry and his division, the nearest force in reserve, was over two miles distant in rear of the Chancellor House, in bivouac.   Hooker was sitting on the porch of the Chancellor House as oblivious of danger as General Buell was at the battle of Perryville, when he lay in his tent and did not hear a sound of the conflict which almost wrecked his army, only two-and-a-half miles distant.

Let us review briefly the condition of affairs in the Eleventh Corps at this time, and see if there is any reliable evidence to show that the situation was understood, and whether the officers of the exposed corps were negligent of their duty, and whether they are deserving of any praise or sympathy whatever.

CHAPTER VI.

Warnings of Danger Unheeded.

IT was not known that Jackson was moving past our flank, either to escape or to attack, until Saturday morning; but between midnight of Friday and early Saturday morning Lieutenant Colonel Carmichael, of the One Hundred and Fifty-seventh New York, was in charge of a portion of the picket line. Hearing the sounds of moving trains past his front, he in the morning reported the same at headquarters, and was told for his pains that new troops were easily frightened. At ten A. M. some of the officers of McLean's Brigade, who were keenly on the alert, observed troops moving in the southeast and south towards their flank, and called McLean's attention to it. With the aid of the old man, Hatch, living on the Talley Farm, a diagram was made showing how the rebels could reach their flank by the routes they were then pursuing. McLean promised to inform General Devens, and did so later in the day, and Devens reported it to Howard, who had noticed it before. Colonel Friend, the officer of the day of Devens' Division, reported to Devens that a large force of the enemy was passing to his rear, but Devens refused to give credit to the report. Friend then went to the headquarters of the corps, where he was rebuked for his statement, and warned not to bring on a panic.

General Schurz, commanding the division in the center, having observed the rebel troops marching from east to west, and being convinced that the flank attack would come, ordered Captain Dilger, in charge of the battery attached to his division, to look over the territory in rear of the established line, and be prepared to meet an attack from the rear. This battery, which was known as Independent Battery I, of Ohio, was equally composed of Americans and Germans.

and was regarded as the best in the corps. It was a veteran battery, and had been well tested in Western Virginia, the Shenandoah Valley and the campaign of Pope. It was commanded by Capt. Hubert Dilger, familiarly known in the army as "Leather Breeches," from the texture of his pantaloons. Dilger had been an officer in the Baden Mounted Artillery, but resigned to take part in our civil war. He had been thoroughly educated in the military schools of his native country, and was regarded as one of the best artillery officers to be found in our armies. Although he took part in many of the battles of the war, and served with distinction, and was recommended for promotion several times by distinguished officers of the Army of the Potomac and the West, even by Gen. George H. Thomas, he had the marked honor of remaining a plain captain until the close of the war. And so did McDougal, of the navy, whose splendid exploit with the frigate Wyoming in Japan equaled that of the dauntless Decatur with the pirates in Tripoli in 1804. None ever knew Capt. Hubert Dilger but to admire, love and respect his manly qualities, and to such rare men, brevets and mere words of praise are superfluous. Dilger followed the advice of Schurz, and examined the fields about the Dowdall and Hawkins Farms with the view of repelling an attack from the right flank and rear.

Early in the afternoon he determined to ride out on the exposed flank and see for himself what truth there might be in the rumors that had reached his ear that the enemy had appeared there in force. Mounting a trusty horse, and taking an orderly with him, he proceeded up the Pike to the extreme right, where he found Von Gilsa greatly disturbed at the situation, and who earnestly begged him not to venture farther, as the enemy were in force in his front, and he would run great risk of being taken prisoner. Dilger promised to exercise great caution, and proceeded slowly until he reached a place north of the Luckett Farm, a little more than a mile from where he left Von Gilsa. Here he ran into the rebel army, then advancing, and was cut off from his line of retreat and pursued by a force of cavalry, narrowly escaping capture. After wandering around among the many by-paths in the woods, he finally found a road which led him out to the U. S. Ford Road and to the rear of the Chancellor House. It was late in the afternoon when he reached the headquarters of General Hooker, and he felt it his duty to make known the result of his reconnaissance. He approached a long-legged major of cavalry, apparently an officer of the staff, and told him briefly what he had seen, and that he believed a large force of the enemy was collecting in our rear. The major of cavalry coolly advised him to proceed to his own corps and tell his yarn there. Dilger, feeling keenly the insulting manner of this officer, went with all speed to the headquarters of the Eleventh Corps and reported his adventure there, and to his disgust and indignation, his remarks were received without the slightest confidence, and in such a manner as to give him the impresssion that he had no business scouting out on the flank, and he was furthermore positively informed that General Lee was retreating — in full retreat — and that Barlow's Brigade, with the commander of the corps, had gone south to fall upon the rear of the enemy. Poor Dilger, crestfallen and tired, rode to his battery near the Church, and prepared for the storm which he was sure was soon to come. So confident was he of the approaching attack that he refused to allow his horses to be taken to water, and had hardly got his battery in order before the distant rifle shots announced the driving in of the pickets.

General Devens was repeatedly warned by his officers of the movements of Jackson, and the evidence is too strong to be denied. The statements of Colonel Lee are well fortified by the testimony of living witnesses. Colonel Lee was the commander of the Fifty-fifth Ohio, and until the untimely arrival of General Devens had been in command of the brigade for months. After the battle, Lee was so mortified by his treatment by Devens (it is so stated) that he resigned, and did not return again to the corps. He afterwards became the Lieutenant Governor of Ohio, and at the time of

his death was one of the most respected -citizens of that
state. His papers, sent to the compiler shortly before his
death, clearly describe the situation of things at the time,
and show plainly that the division had ample time, even after
the pickets were attacked, to change front and make a more
satisfactory resistance, if they had been permitted to do so.
Colonel Lee states that he ordered Captain Rollins, commander of the picket line in his front, to ascertain the truth of
the rumor of the approach of the enemy and report to him.

"At one o'clock a messenger came, and at two another messenger came, with information that the enemy were moving with infantry
and artillery across our front to our right flank." He also states
that "an hour afterwards another messenger came, and with him,
as I had done with each of the preceeding messengers, I went to
the headquarters of Generals McLean and Devens (both in the same
house), and put them in possession of all the information that I was
receiving, and from it I insisted that the evidence was satisfactory
that we must expect the enemy on our right flank, and an attack
upon that right flank. General McLean said but little on either
occasion. General Devens seemed to attach very little importance
to it, and to distrust the reliability of the report made, and to dis-
sent from the conclusions that I insisted should be drawn from it,
namely, that the enemy was moving to our right flank. He insisted
that he had no information to that effect from headquarters, and
that if such was the fact he certainly would receive it from corps
headquarters. He did not direct any of his staff, nor did he go himself, to communicate to headquarters the information that I had
borne to him. When the third messenger was with me at General
Devens' headquarters, and I was urgent that disposition should be
made to meet such an emergency, he said to me that it was 'not
worth while to be scared before we were hurt.' He then turned to
his chief of staff and directed him to go to corps headquarters and
ascertain whether there was any information there that the enemy
was probably passing across our front to our right flank. He did
not direct that any information that I had carried to him should be
given to the corps headquarters. I then left, and did not return
again to his headquarters. This was perhaps in the neighborhood
of four o'clock in the afternoon.

"I kept the commanders of my own brigade informed of the
information that I was from time to time receiving from the front,
and they shared with me in the belief that the enemy was passing
to and massing on our right flank, and also, of course, shared in
the anxieties we all naturally had as to the effect of it. I think they
each and all made such dispositions as are usual in anticipation of
a conflict that afternoon. We sent all our non-combatant material
to the rear. The opinion throughout our brigade was general that

we would soon be attacked from our right flank. Our picket line across our front to the southward was undisturbed, and not a shot heard in that direction, Shortly after the squadron of cavalry had reported, we began to hear firing of small arms on the extreme right flank. The road ran nearly westward, with heavy timber and woods on each side. This firing gradually increased in volume, and I rode rapidly out to the right flank of the army, which was only a distance of one division, and there I saw coming up the road a few of the enemy's cavalry, followed closely by a battery. I immediately went back to my position and awaited the result. Soon the men and officers on our right flank began to give way, and to retreat to the eastward in our rear in a disorganized form. The battery that had run up so close to us began to deliver grape and canister right along the road, and was very destructive to our line, which occupied the south side of the road, with a slight barricade made out of fence rails, with earth thrown upon them. Our line still fronted to the south. I immediately put my horse to his highest speed, and went eastward in the rear of the line to where I found Generals Devens and McLean, and informed them of the firing on our right flank, and that the enemy overlapped our rear, that our picket line in front was undisturbed, and inquired whether I should not change front so as to be able to meet the enemy. General Devens gave me no answer, and General McLean replied, 'Not yet.' I immediately returned to my position, and while I was gone, so destructive had been the fire upon my line that Lieutenant Colonel Gambee had withdrawn the line to the north side of the road and under cover of the timber, and thus put it out of the raking fire. I again returned with all possible speed to Generals Devens and McLean, and informed them that our soldiers on the right were giving way and retreating, and that there was no enemy in front, and again awaited instructions, but receiving none, received from General McLean the dismissing signal, and I again returned to my regiment. The enemy were slowly approaching with constant firing, and we were unable to deliver a shot.

" In the meanwhile, in the rear of our brigade, the Twenty-fifth and Seventy-fifth had deployed looking toward the enemy, and the Seventy-fifth had gone forward somewhat, but without any support or any connection on its right or left, and were engaging the enemy, but without stopping his onward movement."

At this time Colonel Lee was dashed to the ground and disabled by the wounding of his horse by grape shot, and when he recovered himself he found his regiment gone, and the division ruined. Lee, with a number of his brigade, rallied at the Buschbeck line and again vainly attempted to resist the progress of Jackson's men.

Colonel Richardson, of the Twenty-fifth Ohio, after the return of his scouts, went to Devens and McLean and stated to them that there were large bodies of the enemy on the right flank, and apparently resting, but Devens replied sharply that General Lee was retreating, and that he knew it, and then with decided asperity told General McLean to order Colonel Richardson back to his regiment, as he was unnecessarily scared.

Colonel Schimmelpfennig, of Schurz's Division, sent out Major Schlieter, of the Seventy-fourth Pennsylvania, to reconnoitre at about three P. M. The Major soon returned, and informed his superior officers that he found the enemy in great force, and heard the orders of the rebel officers as they massed their line of attack. Major Schleiter then reported the same at corps headquarters, and was laughed at for his views, and told not to get alarmed, for the corps commander has already departed with the reserves to join Birney and capture some regiments. Late in the afternoon a squadron of cavalry went out on the Pike, but soon returned, and the captain reported to Devens, in front of the Talley House, that he could go but a little ways, as he met a large body of infantry. Devens replied impatiently: "I wish I could get some one who could make a reconnaissance for me." The captain of the cavalry squad firmly replied: "General, I can go further, but I cannot promise to return." The cavalry were ordered to bivouac, and shortly afterward the attack came. Captain Culp, of McLean's staff, who was present when Richardson made his report and was sharply rebuked, says that there is no proof on record that any attempt was made to ascertain the truth or falsity of the reports. The assertion, coming from Hooker's headquarters, that Lee was retreating was too positive to be questioned by the humbler officers of the Eleventh Corps, but nevertheless, those who had fought Jackson in his two former flank movements in the Valley and at Manassas were not so easily convinced that the forces on their flank were simply a corps of diversion or observation, and refused to believe it. They were also cautioned against circulating the rumors of Jackson's movements, and warned of the liability of causing a panic among the men.

There were other warnings sent back from the lines from time to time, but all in vain to arouse a sense of danger. There is ample proof from men now living that not only did Von Gilsa and McLean have their pickets well out to the front, but that they were warned from time to time of the massing of the forces of the enemy. On the Pike, full a thousand yards west of the two guns of Von Gilsa, stationed in the road, were two bodies of sharpshooters. The one on the left of the road was under the command of Lieutenant Searles, and the other on the north of the Pike was under Lieutenant Boecke. These officers say that they sent in warnings to Von Gilsa, who sent them to his superior officers without avail. Act. Maj. Owen Rice, of the One Hundred and Fifty-third Pennsylvania, in command of the picket line, sent to Von Gilsa at 2.45 P. M. the following message : "A large body of the enemy is massing in my front. For God's sake make dispositions to receive him." Von Gilsa informed Rice the next day that he reported this dispatch personally at corps headquarters, and was repulsed with taunts. This statement may be found in publications of the Loyal Legion of Ohio of 1888. As early as five P. M., the pickets of both sides were exchanging shots, but the remarkable condition of the atmosphere prevented the sounds from being heard excepting at a short distance. The foliage of the woods was so far developed at this time that it was quite impossible for the pickets to see but a short distance in front of them. Von Gilsa, it is said, asked to be allowed to testify with Major Rice to the Committee of Congress on the Conduct of the War, but was refused. The often repeated statements of the want of a picket line are not sustained, as there is abundant proof of a picket line well established, and on the alert, and nowhere were the men completely surprised, as there was still time for all of the men of the Eleventh Corps to take their arms and offer some resistance to the foe, unless it was a company on the right of the Fifty-fourth New York, far in the forest. None of the corps left their arms in stack, and there were but few of the corps wanting arms the next day,

5—B. C.

according to the report of the officer making the inspection. It was also stated in the mass meeting held in New York a month later, in protest to the abuse of the Germans without investigation, that Von Gilsa's Brigade lacked but seventeen muskets and Schimmelpfennig's Brigade but fifteen.

In spite of all these warnings there was a remarkable fatuity existing with Devens and at corps headquarters, which can only be explained by the hypnotic effect coming from headquarters of the army at the Chancellor House.

There is abundant evidence to show that the commanding officers of the regiments of Devens' Division were aware of Jackson's presence and the danger of attack, and were deeply offended by Devens' refusal to listen to their advice and their warnings.   About half an hour before the attack, three of the colonels of McLean's Brigade rode with Colonel Reily, of the Seventy-fifth Ohio, out to the front and consulted with Von Gilsa, whom they found ready for the attack. On their return, Colonel Reily called his men together and said to them with great feeling that a great battle was pending, in which many lives would be lost.   "Some of us will not see another sun rise.   If there is a man in the ranks who is not ready to die for his country, let him come to me and I will give him a pass to go to the rear, for I want no half-hearted, unwilling soldiers or cowards in the ranks to-night. We need every man we have to fight the enemy.   If a comrade falls, do not stop to take him away or care for him, but fight for the soil on which he falls, and save him by victory." This speech of Spartan firmness has been preserved by one of the officers who heard it, Captain E. R. Montfort.   The colonel then told his men to lie down and rest, but not to leave their guns.

Most of the regimental officers of the division were aware of the danger, and kept their men close to their position, and would have been in a far better condition to fight if Devens had permitted them to change front at the first alarm.   But Devens refused to allow the change of position, as he was expecting an attack in front, which, however, did not come,

in consequence of Colquitt's stupidity ; and there is no evidence to be found as yet that he gave any orders to change
front at all, unless it was to the Seventeenth Connecticut at
the last moment.

CHAPTER VII.

Jackson Strikes the Eleventh Corps.

(See Map No. 3.)

A T FIVE o'clock Jackson said to General Rodes, at the Luckett Farm : "Are you ready?" "Yes," replied Rodes, who then nodded to Major Blackford, commanding a part of the advanced line. Shortly after the troops advanced, but soon halted for a few moments to allow the left wing to advance in the deep woods on the left. At 5.15 the signal was given in earnest, and Willis' riflemen struck the Eleventh Corps sharpshooters under Lieutenants Searles and Boecke, on either side of the turnpike. The bugles rang out clearly in the evening air, and a mighty roar of human voices shook the forest for a mile on the right and the left of the Pike, startling the deer and other animals from their lairs in the thickets. The Federal sharpshooters fell back before Willis' and Blackford's riflemen, firing as they retreated, and giving the alarm to the forces in the rear. Two pieces of Stuart's horse artillery galloped past the riflemen on the Pike, fired two solid shots down the road, raking the Pike and finally striking the ground in front of the Talley House, a mile distant, where Devens was lying down for rest at the time, having been injured in the leg the day before by his horse running into a tree. One of the shots bounded through the tree in the front yard, where some of McLean's staff were resting. The alarm was instantly given, and the troops, which were at ease, resting or eating, had ample time to seize their arms and take their places in position.

Colonel Lee, commanding the Fifty-fifth Ohio, then drawn up in line on the Pike just beyond the Talley House, mounted his horse and galloped to the front, where he found Von Gilsa ready to receive the attack, but not anticipating an attack far in his rear. Colonel Lee then rode back to the

Talley House, and found Devens and McLean mounted, and uncertain what to do, and asked permission to change front with his regiment, as there was no enemy in the direct front. "Not yet," was the reply, and Colonel Lee galloped back to the right of his regiment, where he found his regiment raked by the fire in his rear from the artillery and infantry coming down on and beside the Pike. The two regiments of Von Gilsa in the road, exposed to the same fire in their rear and without any chance to reply without a change of front, began to break and cross the road or come in confusion down the road. Lee again rode at the top of his speed to Devens and asked permission to change front, as his regiment was then suffering from the severe fire in the rear, and as yet there was no enemy in sight on the front. After some time, a sign of dismissal with the hand was all the response Lee received.

In the meantime the enemy had marched steadily down the road, and in the woods had captured the two guns on picket, were enveloping Von Gilsa, and were then pouring a hot fire into the men on the Pike attempting to change front. The two pieces of artillery stationed in the road were fired several times into the masses of the Confederates advancing up the road, and in the woods beside it, but the officer in command soon saw that further resistance was useless, and ordered his men to limber up their guns and retreat. Before they could escape out of range, the men of the Fourth Georgia Infantry shot down the horses and captured the artillery. The two small regiments in the road facing south, the Forty-first and Forty-fifth New York, were exposed to a withering fire both in flank and rear, and soon broke up, unable to return a shot to the enemy's attack. About three hundred of them crossed to the north side of the road and joined the rear of the One Hundred and Fifty-third Pennsylvania, and formed with their thin line the only force then presenting a front to Jackson's overwhelming army. With these men added to the One Hundred and Fifty-third Pennsylvania and the Fifty-fourth New York, Von Gilsa had only about one thousand men to meet Jackson's three lines of battle advancing against him, and extending a mile beyond either flank. The brave and sturdy Teuton bade his men to stand firm, and they poured a volley into the foe so effectually that the first line of Rodes' Division was severely staggered, and stopped, so that the second line of Colston's Division advanced and attacked Von Gilsa, but Von Gilsa's line on both flanks had been turned by the first line of Rodes' Division, and there was no alternative for the Federal troops but flight or surrender. Not until his troops had fired three rounds did Von Gilsa order them to retire, and then both of his staff officers were shot down while giving the order to retreat.— *See Map No. 4.*

Von Gilsa and the wrecks of his line of battle fell back through the woods on the north of the Pike until they came to the Seventy-fifth Ohio, drawn up in line in the woods north of the Pike four hundred yards in the rear. A few of Von Gilsa's men halted and joined the Seventy-fifth, which now attempted, without support, to resist the attack of two full brigades of the enemy. The Seventy-fifth Ohio had been stationed as a reserve near the Talley House, but as soon as the attack on Von Gilsa commenced, about seven hundred yards distant, the brave Colonel Reily ordered his regiment to change front, and without orders advanced through the woods to assist Von Gilsa, but on passing about two hundred yards beyond the Ely Ford path, he met the wrecks of the First Brigade returning, some of whom rallied with him. A moment after they were attacked in front and on both flanks by the regiments of two brigades, while two of Stuart's guns on the Pike raked them with canister. For ten minutes this brave regiment, with its few rallied supports, attempted to breast the attack, so as to give the division time to deploy in their rear, but in this short space of time, and in spite of a sturdy resistance, the regiment was utterly wrecked. The colonel was killed, the adjutant wounded, and one hundred and fifty of the rank and file struck down while firing three rounds. No troops in the world could fight and live in such a position.

The survivors of this brief conflict retreated five hundred yards in the rear, to the line then hastily formed in front of the Talley House. This new line of resistance was formed by the Twenty-fifth Ohio, which had been held as a reserve in front of the Talley House, and which had changed front and had been reinforced by some of the men of Von Gilsa's Brigade, and the two regiments stationed on the road facing south, who had been driven out of their position by the flanking fire along the Pike. Across the road and behind the Talley House the Seventeenth Connecticut was deployed, and attempted to cover that flank, but Jackson's artillery moved down the Pike, and poured out a rapid canister fire at short range, and three Confederate brigades enveloped both front and flanks. It was no longer a fight, but a massacre. The Federal troops had no better chance for resistance than had Custer and his men before the concentric fire of the Sioux Indians, and had they remained ten minutes longer the result would have been the same — annihilation. After a desultory struggle of ten or fifteen minutes, every mounted officer was struck down, and the fragments of the Federal line broke in confusion and retreated rapidly and tumultuously towards the Church, where General Schurz was forming or had formed the regiments of his division in the second position of defense of the corps. Flight or destruction were the only alternatives to the remnants of Devens' Division, and as they rushed down the road to escape the pitiless Confederate fire they broke through the lines of two of Schurz's best veteran regiments while changing front, and carried away with them some of the old soldiers of known bravery. A large part of these men rushed up the road, and were the men who greeted Howard's view, in front of the Dowdall Tavern, when he seized the colors of one of the broken regiments, and attempted to check the disorder. Many of them, from want of confidence in their commanders, refused to halt, and continued their retreat to the Chancellor House, two miles distant. However, a large number of them did rally on the Schurz and Buschbeck lines, and showed that they were made of sterner stuff. — *See Map No. 5.*

In thirty minutes Jackson had wrecked Devens' splendid division of nearly four thousand men, and rendered it almost useless for further resistance, and at six P. M. he had control of the Talley plateau, and ordered his victorious column to push forward without delay.   But where were the seventeen regiments of his right wing, who had been ordered to march along the Plank Road, and should have been in contact with the forces at the Dowdall Tavern at this very moment?   They had been detained by the fatuity of General Colquitt, who commanded the right brigade of Rodes' first line of battle, and were not even in sight when Jackson reached the Talley Mansion.   The remarkable delay of this great force was due to a trivial circumstance, and illustrates the remark that the fate of a campaign may depend, as it were, upon a single hair, as Napoleon was wont to say.   Colquitt, as he advanced in the woods, and had almost reached the Talley and Burton Farms, struck a determined picket line, composed largely of men of the Fifty-fifth Ohio Regiment, and as he saw some cavalry dressed in the Federal uniform near the Burton Farm, he conceived the strange idea that his flank was threatened by Federal troops advancing from the direction of Welford's Furnace.   He recalled the Sixth Georgia Regiment, which had almost reached the Talley Farm, halted his entire brigade, changed front to the south, and compelled Ramseur, who commanded the brigade in his rear, to do the same, and also to march some distance to the south in the woods in search of the enemy, but without finding a "solitary Yankee."   In the meantime the four regiments of cavalry under Stuart, and the five regiments of infantry of the Stonewall Brigade, then halted on the Plank Road near the Burton Farm, were compelled to remain quiet until Colquitt resumed his march, as he had the right of way, and the unmasking of the line of battle on that flank.   So by this singular act of stupidity seventeen regiments were held back forty to sixty minutes, and when they did arrive on the field

of battle, the wrecks of the First and Third Divisions of the
Eleventh Corps had escaped from almost certain and complete destruction or capture.

While Devens' troops were being destroyed, the brigades of Jackson's left wing were retarded in the dense
thickets through which they were obliged to march, and did
not come in contact with the Federal forces of the Third
Division, stationed at the Hawkins Farm, until some time
after Von Gilsa was attacked.   In fact, the Twenty-sixth
Wisconin and the Fifty-eighth New York were more than
half a mile in rear of Von Gilsa, and had ample time to prepare for the enemy.

General Schurz was impressed early in the day with the
weakness of his position in case the attack was made from
the westward, and several times expressed a desire to form
his division on the line indicated by the little stream known
as Hunting Run, flowing directly north from the Church to
the river.   His position then would have extended from the
Plank Road near the Church to the ruins of the old mill on
Hunting Run, a mile to the north, and is apparently the line
of defense indicated in the orders given to Howard and Slocum, May 1st, 4.45 P. M.   The military advantages of this
position over the one adopted are very apparent, but Schurz
was refused permission to make the change.   However,
Schurz did, of his own volition, change the front of the
Twenty-sixth Wisconsin and the Fifty-eighth New York, and
moved them to the edge of the Hawkins Farm, facing
westerly, and also placed the Eighty-second Illinois to support them.   The attack on Von Gilsa was soon observed,
and the regiments of the Third Division had ample time to
take arms and position, for the left brigades of Rodes and
Colston became entangled in the dense forest, and moved
slower than those of the right of the Confederate line, and it
was some time after Von Gilsa had been routed before the
rebel skirmish line struck the Federal pickets, well advanced
in the woods west of the Hawkins Farm.   When the attack
on the pickets began, and it became evident that a great

force of the enemy was present, and that their lines extended far to the north of the Federal position, the two regiments were ordered back a short distance near the Hawkins House, where they made a stand, with the Eighty-second Illinois on their left, and the three regiments calmly awaited the onset of four powerful Confederate brigades. This line was attacked with great energy and the Federal regiments fought with resolution, but were forced back towards the woods in their rear, and, with the One Hundred and Nineteenth New York, Sixty-eighth New York, Eighty-second Ohio and One Hundred and Fifty-seventh New York, and parts of the Sixty-first Ohio and Seventy-fourth Pennsylvania, near the Pike, formed a line of battle extending from below the junction of the Plank Road and Pike, along in front of the little Church, to the edge of the woods on the north of the Hawkins Farm. This second attempt at resistance was strengthened by some of the soldiers rallied from Devens' broken division, and numbered in all, perhaps, about five thousand men. Its left flank was protected by Dilger's Battery and a part of Weidrick's, and one of the reserve batteries some distance in the rear threw its shot over the heads of the infantry at the masses of the enemy adjusting their lines on the westerly fields of the Hawkins Farm, half a mile or more distant. The Twenty-sixth Wisconsin held their position as guarding the right flank with great obstinacy, and kept the enemy at bay for some twenty minutes of hard fighting, but were forced back into the woods, being flanked, and formed the right of the last position, or what is known as the Buschbeck line. Near the Pike, the Sixty-first Ohio, Seventy-fourth Pennsylvania, One Hundred and Nineteenth New York and Sixty-eighth New York formed that part of the line in front of the Church, but were much disorganized by the wrecks of Devens' Division rushing wildly through them and carrying off in the rush many of the men, especially in the Sixty-first Ohio and Seventy-fourth Pennsylvania, which were regarded as among the best troops of the corps. The One Hundred and Nineteenth New York was in front of Dilger's guns, and stood their ground for twenty minutes or more. It was a new regiment, and is entitled to much praise for remaining firm when its colonel was shot dead at almost the first fire, and its ranks were somewhat broken by the disorganized masses of Devens' Division rushing past on the Pike, or through its ranks. The men fired about twenty rounds, and fought bravely until they were overpowered and forced back to the rifle pit east of Dowdall's Tavern, where they were rallied by their youthful commander, Lieutenant Colonel Lockman, whose bravery was especially noticed at the time by General Schurz.

Captain Dilger, shortly after the attack commenced, rode up the road to the Talley Farm to see if he could find a good position for his guns. But on arriving at the farm he became aware of the magnitude of the attack. He saw the breaking of the troops in the road exposed to the fire in their rear, and also that there was neither opportunity nor time to advance his battery. The captain thereupon galloped back to the Church, brought his entire battery across the road to the western edge of the Dowdall Farm, and thus left the road free for the retreat of the disordered remnants of Devens' Division.

As soon as Devens' Division fell back from the Talley field and left the road exposed in front of the Talley House and beyond, Dilger opened fire from his six guns at the enemy, then debouching from the Pike more than a thousand yards distant. The grove of trees in front of him was not tall enough then to obstruct the view, and over their tops Dilger poured in a rapid fire of shell. A few moments after Hill came with his battery in position on the left of Dilger, and opened fire from three-inch Rodmans upon the enemy as they appeared on the Talley fields south of the Pike. Another of the reserve batteries, supposed to have been Wheeler's, also opened fire from their position in rear of the rifle pit, north of the Dowdall Tavern. This battery did not open fire until the Fifty-eighth New York and the Twenty-sixth Wisconsin had fallen back from the western field of the Hawkins Farm, and then it actively shelled the rebels emerging from the woods apparently in masses. This was all the artillery in action at this time. Weidrick's Battery did not open until the rebels had turned the flank of the Talley Farm, and approached along the ravine and under cover of the thickets, reaching the flank and rear of Dilger's position and rendering it untenable. For more than half an hour Dilger maintained his position, and as the rebels crept up to the cover of the thickets in front of him he changed to a lively canister fire, which seemed to arrest their progress slightly in his direct front. Hill, at this time, having no shot for close range, was obliged to withdraw his battery, and it was ordered to the Chancellor field. Up to this time no force had appeared on the Plank Road from the southward, owing to the fatuity of Colquitt, and our pickets were still in position south of Dowdall's, and witnesses of the battle which was raging in plain sight and to the north of them, and which deprived them of an avenue of escape in that direction. Here they (the Seventy-fifth Pennsylvania) remained until Colquitt's forces came and attacked them, losing about fifty, killed, wounded and prisoners. The balance of the regiment retreated by way of the ravine and south of Hazel Grove.

In front of Dilger, or to his right, the Sixty-eighth and One Hundred and Nineteenth New York Regiments were placed in line of battle, and over their heads Dilger engaged the enemy in sight on the Pike or the Talley fields, but as the rebels crept closer by means of the ravines and the thickets, these two regiments were obliged to retire to the rifle pit in the rear. Dilger then swept his entire front with charges and double charges of canister, but the rebels with great determination and enthusiasm pressed steadily forward, and soon convinced the artillery officer that a few moments' delay would sacrifice his guns. Reluctantly he gave the order to retire, but it was too late to save the entire battery. Five of the pieces were withdrawn safely, but the sixth, with two of its horses dead and two more wounded, was abandoned to the enemy, after a vain attempt to drag it away. Dilger himself was thrown to the ground by the death of his horse, and did not succeed in extricating himself from the dead animal until Rodes' men were close upon him, demanding his surrender. Dilger declined to listen to their terms of surrender, and ran to the rear as rapidly as he could, escaping the shots of his pursuers. He had run about one hundred yards when relief unexpectedly came to him. A little boy by the name of Ackley, who was greatly attached to Dilger, missed him as his battery passed by the Dowdall House, and, seizing a horse, rode directly into the front of the enemy in search of him. On finding his dear friend almost in the clutches of the enemy, he sprang from the horse and assisted him to mount, and both managed to escape. Dilger, ever grateful for this act of courage and love, has always described it as one of the bravest he ever saw. Dilger overtook the remains of his battery in the rear of the rifle pit, and, seeing that there was no position for the use of artillery there, he ordered his lieutenant to proceed with four of the guns to the rear and report to the first artillery officer he might meet; the fifth gun he retained, and placing it in the road between the rifle pits, he again opened fire upon the advancing and triumphant foe. The lieutenant took the four guns up the road and reported to Captain Best, who ordered him to take position on his right, where Dilger found him later. Dilger kept one gun with him, as it was all that he could use to advantage at the rifle pit, and this he planted in the middle of the road and opened a rapid fire to his front. While here he was supported by two companies of the brave Sixty-first Ohio, who stuck to him in the retreat and remained with him also at Fairview all night, when he took part in the cannonade. Buschbeck had ample time to recall his four regiments facing south on the Dowdall Farm and place them in the shallow and unfinished rifle pit facing west, long before Schurz's men, in battle before him, were forced back, and when General Steinwehr returned from escorting Barlow's Brigade below the Furnace, he found them behind the rifle pit and maintaining their position with firmness.

The position known as the Buschbeck line was as follows: The pit to the south of the Plank Road was occupied by the One Hundred and Fifty-fourth New York, Seventy-third and Twenty-seventh Pennsylvania, and by some of the rallied men of Devens' and Schurz's commands. The Plank Road was defended by Dilger and his one gun, supported by the two companies of the Sixty-first Ohio and some of Devens' Division. North of the road, the Twenty-ninth New York was first in line, and to the right the space was filled with fragments of Devens' Division and some of Schurz's men, and to the right of them, at the edge of the woods, were the Eighty-second Illinois and the Eighty-second Ohio, and in the woods farther to the right were the Fifty-eighth New York and the Twenty-sixth Wisconsin, of Schurz's Division. In the rear of the edge of the woods the One Hundred and Fifty-seventh New York was placed in reserve. The only piece of artillery in this line of defense was Dilger's single gun. Weidrick's Battery, which had been stationed just south of the Dowdall House, and in front of Buschbeck, had been withdrawn shortly before, with the loss of two guns, taken by the flank movement of the enemy passing to the south of the Talley House. The horses of one of these guns had been shot and the cannoneers of the other had been wounded. All of the reserve artillery had been ordered to retreat some time previously, as there was no opportunity to use it in the narrow space in rear of the rifle pit and the dense woods.—*See Map No. 6.*

In this last attempt to hold Jackson at bay, there were about four thousand to five thousand men only. The rest of the corps had gone up the road in retreat, or were left on the field of battle, or were three miles away with Barlow's Brigade, below the Furnace. Although parts of the corps had been resisting Jackson's attack for about an hour, no reinforcements had reached them. This third and final attempt, made by the remnants of the corps caught and wrecked in

detail, was along the shallow rifle pits which had been dug
in the morning by Barlow's Brigade, and which were unfinished when Barlow was ordered down into the woods below
the Furnace.　This line of earthworks was so slight that it
would protect the soldier only when kneeling or lying down.
It was constructed without provision for the use of artillery,
and when the pit was occupied by the infantry, all of the
artillery was ordered to the rear excepting Dilger's gun.
The scene at this moment was not assuring to the crushed
and overpowered Eleventh Corps.　Not a soldier or a gun
had been sent them in aid from the rest of the army, and in
fact Hooker had but just found out from the ambulance drivers and fugitives that the Eleventh Corps had been attacked.
The fields and the woods in front of them seemed to be
swarming with rebels in lines of battle four to eight deep,
and extending from the ravine south of the Dowdall Tavern
across the country northward, beyond the Hawkins Farm,
far into the woods.　Along the Pike and around the Talley
House were the batteries of Stuart's horse artillery in active play, and behind them could be seen a forest of bayonets
of A. P. Hill's Division, glistening in the rays of the setting
sun.　To the southward appeared great masses of infantry
and cavalry pouring out of the woods into the Plank Road
about half a mile distant, and hurrying forward to the battle
field, as though belated.　They were the men whom Colquitt,
by his strange fatuity, had kept back until their services were
not required.　They numbered seventeen regiments in all,
and made an imposing appearance as they debouched into
view with a dense array of bright bayonets.

　　The shallow rifle pit was completely filled with soldiers,
and more than it could properly hold.　The left part was occupied by the four regiments of Buschbeck who, as yet, had
not been in action, and were in perfect order, notwithstanding the tumult of the wrecks of Devens' Division passing by.
Three of the regiments were veterans, and mostly composed
of Germans or of German descent, and had been tried in
battle before.　The fourth regiment was an American regi-

ment, and under the command of Col. Patrick H. Jones. Hooker gave great praise to this brigade for its resistance, and it was the only drop of kindness he let fall in his bucket of abuse. Warren—Iago like—stated to Congress that they made no fight worth mentioning.

Along this line the contest raged for some time. Hooker states that it was an hour, but the actual fighting did not last over twenty minutes, probably. The front attacks of the enemy were repulsed, but when both flanks were turned by Iverson's, Nichols', Colquitt's and Ramseur's Brigades, and an enfilading fire from right and left flank reached the center of the line, the men slowly withdrew to the cover of the woods in their rear. Buschbeck's four regiments moved slowly back in perfect order, and, in complete control, halted in line of battle in the woods to check pursuit, but as none was pressed by the enemy, Buschbeck filed his columns into the road and marched slowly towards Chancellorsville. On the north side of the rifle pit, several of the regiments of Schurz's—the Eighty-second Illinois, Eighty-second Ohio, Twenty-sixth Wisconsin, Fifty-eighth New York, and the One Hundred and Fifty-seventh New York—retired in order into the woods north of the road, unmolested by the enemy. Dilger, with his single gun, retreated in the road, keeping the enemy out of his front by his rapid discharges of canister and solid shot. The two companies of the brave Irishmen of the Sixty-first Ohio still supported him, and besides these there were a number of officers of high rank, including both General Howard and General Schurz, who also wished to help the artillerymen who composed the rear guard of the routed corps.

With the forcing of the Buschbeck line, the impetus of the enemy seemed to be broken, as there was no pressing in pursuit whatever. Dilger slowly withdrew into the defile, keeping the road in front of him free with canister and solid shot, and was virtually the last man in the retreat. Shortly after reaching the woods, Dilger ceased firing, as there was no enemy within range to fire at. On the north side of the road, in the woods, all of that part of Schurz's Division which fought on the Hawkins Farm also withdrew in order and in good spirits. This body of troops halted on the Dirt Road, north of the position taken by Berry, and remained there in line of battle until called to the rear of the Chancellor House late in the evening. They were in fighting condition, and numbered about twelve to fifteen hundred men, and were the Twenty-sixth Wisconsin, the Eighty-second Illinois, Eighty-second Ohio, the Fifty-eighth and One Hundred and Fifty-seventh New York, and some of the Seventy-fifth Pennsylvania. Buschbeck's men were marched up the road in order to the Log Works built by Williams' Division of the Twelfth Corps, who, however, had left them and gone south with Sickles to attack the rear of Lee's "retreating" army. Here they halted, and were forming in line of battle when they were ordered by a staff officer to continue their march towards Chancellorsville. At this time there was no enemy in sight, unless it was some of the groups of foragers far down the road, but between them and Buschbeck was Dilger, with his single piece of artillery and his supports, retreating slowly and without the slightest molestation from the foe. On arriving at the Fairview field Buschbeck turned his brigade, together with the rallied soldiers of the broken regiments of Devens' and Schurz's Divisions, to the south of the road, and formed line of battle in the space in front of the batteries which Captain Best was then hastily placing in position in their rear, and between them and Chancellorsville. As soon as the brigade was in position, the adjutant was sent to the commander of the corps, on the crest of the hill in the rear, to inform him that the brigade was ready for duty, and to charge into the woods in their front, if required. Buschbeck and the men rallied with him were in position before Berry and his division arrived at the lines assumed by them on the north side of the road, and there they remained ready for action until the next morning, in front of Best's guns.

Buschbeck's Brigade numbered about one thousand men, and to these may be added, either on this line or close to the

6—B. C.

rear of Best's guns, one hundred and fifty men of McLean's Brigade under Colonel Lee ; one hundred and fifty of the Thirty-third Massachusetts, returning from picket on Hunting Run, under Colonel Hurst ; and detachments from the Sixty-first Ohio, Seventy-fourth Pennsylvania, Seventeenth Connecticut and other regiments, numbering in all about two thousand men, and perhaps more, making a total of quite thirty-five hundred to four thousand men of the corps halted in line of battle on the right and left of the Plank Road, ready to fight, and for which the corps has not received the slightest consideration.

Dilger, with his single gun, slowly retreated up the road until he met Captain Best, who informed him that the rest of his battery was on the left of his artillery and in good condition.   Dilger joined them and remained until morning, taking part in the artillery firing of the night.   Dilger's resolute action while retreating with his single gun, supported by the two companies of brave Irishmen of the Sixty-first Ohio, keeping the enemy at bay and the Plank Road free from active pursuit, forms one of the bright and pleasing episodes in this ill-fated campaign, but which has not received, even at this late day, the least notice whatever.

CHAPTER VIII.

Stonewall Jackson's Fatal Delay.

(See Map No. 7.)

JACKSON'S orders were at the onset to carry the position at or beyond the Talley Farm without halting, and it is clearly evident that if his command had been implicitly obeyed, the two divisions of Devens and Schurz would have been destroyed at the first blow. Colquitt's error, which kept back seventeen regiments on the right flank for forty to sixty minutes, was a fatal one. In half an hour Devens' Division of quite four thousand men, attacked in flank and rear and in detail, was completely crushed. In twenty minutes more Schurz's Division, attempting to form a second line of battle, was forced back past the Church to the Buschbeck line on the Dowdall field, five hundred yards or more in the rear. At 7 or 7.15, the battered wrecks of the Federal corps were driven out of the Buschbeck line into the woods eastward, and the way to the coveted position at the White House was now open to the victorious Confederates. For an hour and a half the nine thousand men of the Eleventh Corps, attacked in rear and flank, and in detail, without any assistance from the rest of the army, had endeavored to stay the impetuous march of Jackson's determined battalions, but had been hurled back into the forest, with a loss of eight guns, fifteen hundred killed and wounded, and about a thousand prisoners. The Federal army was now in extreme peril, for the important position at the White House was only two thousand yards distant, and the only force to oppose the Confederates advancing on the single avenue to it was the twelve hundred or fifteen hundred men of Schurz's Division, then retreating upon it, north of the Plank Road; for Buschbeck's Brigade and the fragments of the First and Third Divisions had passed up the Plank Road to Fairview, on the Chancellor plateau. Berry and Hayes, with their brigades, were hurrying to the Fairview fields, by Hooker's orders, who seemed to have overlooked the importance of guarding the Bullock Road, the direct avenue to his rear. Sickles at this time, with twenty thousand men, was still far below in the depths of the forest, and as yet unconscious of the fact that Jackson, whom he had been seeking in vain, was then directly in his rear, and had been pulverizing the Eleventh Corps for more than an hour and a half, and that his chances of escape were exceedingly small. Jackson ordered his men to push forward, but Colston and Rodes, who commanded the two front lines of battle, urged Jackson to halt, and represented to him that their men were too much exhausted by the long march of fifteen miles, the lack of food for the entire day, the difficulty of marching through the dense thickets, and the attack on the Eleventh Corps, to advance further, and they advised their chief to call a halt and reform.

General Jackson called a halt, but with great reluctance, for he believed, and with reason, too, that one more effort would place his men in command of the open field in the rear of the Chancellor House, and also of the only road by which a large part of the Third and Twelfth Corps could escape. Many years afterwards, General Colston stated in an article in the *Century Magazine* that the halt was not a mistake but a necessity, but it seems now to have been a fatal delay.

At this time the only force defending the Bullock Road leading to the White House was about twelve hundred or fifteen hundred men rallied by Schurz, and halted in the woods half a mile from the White House. Jackson had at this time for an immediate advance five brigades of Colston's and Rodes' Divisions in good condition, and the whole of Hill's Division, standing near the Church, and ready for an attack. The coveted position was clearly in the grasp of Jackson's forces. Fairview, on the Chancellor plateau, was not Jackson's objective point. The position of Jackson's men, at the time the halt was called, was as follows: Doles' Brigade, the foremost of Rodes' Division, halted in the woods on the eastern edge of the Dowdall Farm, south of the road. Colquitt and Ramseur's Brigades rested in the rear of the Dowdall Farm House. Paxton, with the five regiments of the Stonewall Brigade, was drawn up in line in front of the rifle pit on the field in front of the tavern. Iverson's and Nichols' Brigades had stopped in the woods on the north side of the road and near the Log Hut, where Colston summoned his broken regiments to reform. Stuart, with his cavalry, was near the Church, preparing to go with the Sixteenth North Carolina Infantry to guard the approach from the Ely Ford Road, and also to work around the rear of the Federal army in the direction of the United States Ford. The command to halt was not heard or heeded by a part of the rebel forces, and portions of three brigades, in desultory groups, slowly pushed up the road, or in the woods beside it, out of range of Dilger's gun, seeking for adventure or plunder. A part of this disorganized crowd drifted up as far as the Log Works of Williams' Division of the Twelfth Corps, and found there four companies of the Twenty-eighth New York Regiment behind the works, who had been left in charge of the baggage, and who thought it best to remain.

At this moment, while the rebels were demanding the surrender of the Federal soldiers left in the Log Works of Williams' Division, startling events occurred at Hazel Grove, to the south of it, and in the vista or road leading to it. The Grove is a small farm almost enclosed by dense forests, and lies southwest of the Chancellor House, and also of the Plank Road, about a mile distant. A narrow Dirt Road running through the forest for a mile connects it with the Plank Road. On the eastern and southern sides of the farm a small brook, known as Scott's Run, has worn away the soil and formed ravines of little depth on these borders. The northeastern corner slightly overlooks the Fairview plateau, in front of the Chancellor House, where Hooker placed many of his batteries in the battle of Sunday, May 3d, 1863.

The farm consists of but few acres of cleared land, but there was sufficient territory to enable Stuart to plant there early Sunday morning thirty or forty cannon, to enfilade the lines of battle on Fairview with a terrific fire, and in a short time to determine the fate of the campaign.

General Hooker testified before Congress, nearly two years after the event, that the bad conduct of the Eleventh Corps lost him the key to his position, and the battle. In answer to Hooker's remarks, it may be briefly stated that Hazel Grove was the position lost, and that the Eleventh Corps never were there, nor within a mile of it.

At Hazel Grove, and along the paths leading to it, were carelessly parked several of the batteries, wagons, and other material belonging to the force then at the Furnace under Sickles. At seven P. M. everything about Hazel Grove was in complete repose. No one seemed to be aware that a serious engagement had taken place at the Wilderness Church, two miles distant, and that danger was approaching.

Shortly before this period, Colonel Huey, of the Eighth Pennsylvania Cavalry, reported to General Pleasanton, whom he found some distance below the Hazel Grove Farm, on the road to the Welford Furnace, and not far from it, and then and there received orders from him to report to General Howard at the Dowdall Tavern. Colonel Huey states that there was nothing in the language or manner of General Pleasanton, when he gave the order, to lead him to suppose that a battle was in prospect, or that his services were soon to be required. Huey returned to Hazel Grove, and found his regiment in bivouac in the field southeast of the Hazel Grove House. He ordered his men to mount their horses and follow him. At this time the reserve ammunition train of the Third Corps, with seventy thousand rounds packed on mules, was parked in the Hazel Grove field, with many other trains and batteries. It was under the command of Col. Daniel Hall, and when he saw the Eighth Pennsylvania Cavalry proceeding leisurely towards the Plank Road, he ordered his train to follow the cavalry, intending to resume his former position behind the Chancellor House, where Berry, of the Third Corps, was then in bivouac.

As the cavalry and ammunition train wended their way among the batteries, wagons and troops halted in the open field, no messenger from the Eleventh Corps had reached the place to disturb the repose or give warning of an advancing enemy, and inform them that the wrecks of the corps had passed by them to the rear. It is also strange that the sounds of the distant conflict were not heard, or were too confused and indistinct to awaken suspicion. The noise of the battle did not seem to extend far. Sound has some remarkable characteristics, and in certain conditions of the atmosphere fails to refract or convey its waves to any considerable distance. The writer at one time noticed the batteries on Morris Island playing upon Sumter and Wagner, and heard no sounds of the explosions, although the guns were less than a third of a mile distant, yet the same artillery not long after awoke him at Beaufort, fifty miles away. The failure of fog signals has also been observed and studied in connection with this peculiarity.

McLaws, with his Confederate division, was waiting to hear the sounds of Jackson's guns before attacking Hancock with vigor. Posey and Wright, with their brigades concealed in the woods on Birney's flank, were listening for the same signal, but failed to hear definite sounds. Sickles, also, at the Welford Furnace, did not hear a sound of the fight which wrecked the Eleventh Corps, and was not aware of it until an hour or more after Jackson's men had driven the Federal troops back from the Dowdall Tavern.

But soon after the disappearance of Colonel Huey and his cavalry and the ammunition train, General Pleasanton arrived at Hazel Grove, and the scene rapidly changed. The field then presented a very animated sight, in which portions of the Eleventh Corps took very prominent parts, according to the testimony of some of the narrators.

Pleasanton at once took command, and in his report to Hooker brilliantly and graphically describes what appeared to his view :

"I immediately ordered the Eighth Pennsylvania Cavalry to proceed at a gallop, attack the rebels, and check them until we could get the artillery in position." [In fact the Eighth Pennsylvania Cavalry, with the reserve ammunition mule train of the Third Corps, with its seventy thousand rounds, had disappeared in the forest some time before.—*Compiler*.] "This service was splendidly performed by the Eighth, but with heavy loss, and I gained some fifteen minutes to bring Martin's Battery into position, reverse a battery of Sickles' Corps, detach some cavalry to stop runaways, and secure more guns from the retreating column.

"Every moment was invaluable. Fortunately I succeeded, before the enemy's columns showed themselves in the woods, in getting twenty-two pieces of artillery into position, double shotted with canister and bearing upon the direction the rebels were coming. To support this force I had two small squadrons of cavalry ready to charge upon any attempt to take the guns. My position was about three hundred and eighty yards from the Plank Road [the actual distance by measurement is sixteen hundred and fifty yards.—*Compiler*.] on the extreme left of the line of the Eleventh Corps, and as they recoiled from the fierce onset of the rebels through and over my guns, it was apparent we must soon meet the shock.

"It was now near the dusk of the evening, and in rear of the Eleventh Corps the rebels came on rapidly, but in silence, with that skill and adroitness they often display to gain their object. The only color visible was a Union flag with the center battalion. To clear up the doubt created by this flag my aid, Lieutenant Thompson, of the First New York Cavalry, rode to within one hundred yards of them, when they called out to him, "We are friends, come on," and he was induced to go fifty yards nearer, when their whole line opened with musketry, dropped the Union color, displayed eight or ten rebel battle flags, and commenced advancing. They were then not three hundred yards from the guns, and I gave the command to fire. This terrible discharge from twenty-two pieces at that distance staggered them, and threw the heads of their columns back on the woods, from which they opened a tremendous fire of musketry, bringing up fresh forces constantly and striving to advance as fast as they were swept back by our guns. The struggle continued nearly an hour.

"It was now dark, and the enemy's presence could only be ascertained by the flash of their muskets, from which a continuous stream of fire was seen nearly encircling us and gradually extending to our right to cut us off from the army. Finally this was checked by our guns, and the rebels withdrew. Several guns and caissons were recovered from the woods where they fought us."

Captain Martin, who commanded the Sixth New York Battery under Pleasanton, reports as follows :

"The scene before me was one of indescribable confusion. The Eleventh Corps was panic-stricken, and the pack trains, ambulances, artillery carriages, etc., belonging thereto, were rushing to and fro, many of the carriages without drivers or teamsters. Not more than two hundred and fifty yards from the battery there ran a line of fence, and behind this appeared a line of infantry. The fire of the enemy was very vigorous and well maintained. I trust that of my battery was equally so."

General Sickles reports of these events thus :

"Time was everything. The fugitives of the Eleventh Corps swarmed from the woods, and swept frantically over the cleared fields in which my artillery was parked. The exulting enemy at their heels mingled yells with their volleys, and in the confusion which followed it seemed as if cannon and caissons, dragoons, cannoniers and infantry could never be disentangled from the mass into which they were suddenly thrown. Fortunately there was only one obvious outlet for those panic-stricken hordes, after rushing over and between our guns, and this was through a ravine crossed in two or three places by the headwaters of Scott's Run. This was soon made impassable by the reckless crowd choking up the way. A few minutes was enough to restore comparative order and get our artillery in position.

"The enemy showing himself on the plain, Pleasanton met the shock at short range with the well-directed fire of twenty-two pieces double-shotted with canister. The heads of the columns were swept away to the woods, from which they opened a furious but ineffectual fire of musketry. Twice they attempted a flank movement, but the first was checked by our guns, and the second and most formidable was baffled by the advance of Whipple and Birney, who were coming up rapidly but in perfect order and forming in lines of brigades in rear of the artillery and on the flanks. My position was now secure in the adequate infantry support which had arrived. The loud cheers of our men as twilight closed the combat vainly challenged the enemy to renew the encounter."

Pleasanton, in his entertaining article published in the Century in 1888, a quarter of a century after the event, reiterates the statements of his early report, and enlarges on them. He states that Lieutenant Crosby, with his battery of the Fourth U. S. Artillery, was placed on the right of Martin's Battery. Not a gun of this battery nor of the Eleventh Corps was at Hazel Grove, but were at this time at Fairview, a mile away.

He estimates the attacking force of the infantry to be

five thousand muskets, and that his artillery fire was effective because he applied to it that principle of dynamics in which the angle of incidence is equal to the angle of reflection. The discharge fairly swept Jackson's men from the earth. He poured in the canister for about twenty minutes, "and the affair was over." He also enlarges upon the stampede at Hazel Grove of the Eleventh Corps, and says that "beef cattle, ambulances, mules, artillery wagons and horses became stuck in the mud, and others coming on crushed them down so that when the fight was over the pile of debris in that marsh was many feet high." This statement is utterly untrue and extremely unjust. None of the debris was formed by the Eleventh Corps, for their line of retreat was a mile or more directly north.

Pleasanton also says the Eleventh Corps had been encamped in the woods two hundred yards distant, whereas the nearest of the left flank of the Eleventh Corps was fully one thousand yards, and the right, under Von Gilsa, was more than three thousand yards distant by the nearest paths.

Lieutenant Thompson, the aid whom Pleasanton sent to the front to reconnoitre, in 1866 wrote that one man fired at him as he peered into the darkness to find out who were in front of him, and his narrative of how he turned, leading the rebel charge, and how he dodged the discharges of the Federal artillery, forms a very entertaining note in the Scribner series. He also states that the enemy were mowed down in heaps, that the roar of the artillery was continuous, and the execution terrific, etc.

Doubleday, in his work on Chancellorsville and Gettysburg, one of the Scribner series of Campaigns of the Civil War, published twenty years after, and regarded as semi-official, relates the story of Keenan and his charge as follows: He states that when Pleasanton arrived at Hazel Grove, he found "all hurrying furiously to the rear."

"There was but one way to delay Jackson; some force must be sacrificed, and Pleasanton ordered Maj. Peter Keenan, commanding the Eighth Pennsylvania Cavalry, to charge the ten thousand men in front with his four hundred. Keenan saw in a moment that if he threw his little force into that seeking mass of infantry, horses and men would go down on all sides, and there would be few left to tell the tale. A sad smile lit up his noble countenance as he said, 'General, I will do it.' At thirty-four years of age, literally impaled on the bayonets of the enemy, he laid down his life and saved the army from capture and his country from the unutterable degradation of the establishment of slavery in the Northern states. History will record the service rendered on that occasion as worthy to be classed with the sacrifices of Arnold Winckelried in Switzerland, and the Chevalier d'Assas in France."

Doubleday also states that "Pleasanton was enabled to clear a space in front of him, and twenty-two guns loaded with double canister were brought to bear upon the enemy. They came bursting over the parapet they had just taken with loud and continuous yells, and formed line of battle within three hundred yards. * * * He fired into their masses with all his guns at once. The discharge seemed fairly to blow them back over the works from which they had just emerged." Doubleday also alludes to two charges in succession which reached almost to the muzzles of Pleasanton's guns. He also refers to the severe enfilading fire of Archer's Brigade, which, in spite of Keenan's charge, had gained the woods and the Plank Road.

It is singular that Doubleday, with all the reports at his command, did not know, twenty years after the event, that Archer was at this time six miles or more away, on the Brock Road, and did not reach Hazel Grove until after daylight Sunday morning.

Furthermore General Tidball, in his recent excellent articles on the artillery service, relates how the fugitives of the Eleventh Corps, rushing through another battery of Birney's Division, then at the front, threw them into such confusion as to cause them to fall into the hands of the enemy. This battery I am unable to trace. Neither General Birney nor his Chief of Artillery mentions it. Tidball also describes the confusion at Hazel Grove, the heavy fire of musketry from the enemy, and how the batteries, entirely alone and unsupported, held the enemy in check, "completely and thoroughly checked by these batteries."

Furthermore he says: "Had it not been for the timely and gallant resistance offered by Huntington's twenty-two guns at Hazel Grove, which held the enemy in check until the Twelfth changed position, this corps too, would, have been taken in flank and rear, and would probably have shared the same fate as the Eleventh. It is difficult to estimate the value of the services of the guns at Hazel Grove."

The Comte de Paris, in his interesting work on the Civil War, copies Pleasanton's descriptions of his laudable work and also Keenan's cavalry charge. That Pleasanton stops the enemy advancing in good order, and in successive lines; that he dismounts the two guns brought up in the attack, and wounds Crutchfield of the Confederate artillery. Neither Crutchfield nor any of his guns were near Hazel Grove that night.

Major Stein, in his late work on the Army of the Potomac, almost thirty years after the event, repeats the romantic story of Keenan's charge, and endorses all of Pleasanton's exploits, and states that the carnage that followed the discharge of the double-shotted guns would have blanched the cheek of "the Lion-hearted."

Major General J. Watts de Peyster, a brilliant writer of the episodes of the war, lends his aid to immortalize the thrilling scenes, and writes in this manner: "The intrepid Pleasanton, with comprehensive, lightning-like glance, and a decision as instantaneous as the electric flash, gathered up his cavalry and hurled them upon the foe, until he could range his own rapidly collected guns upon a ridge, and then drove them back and saved the army. That this fearful disaster was averted is due to a feat of generalship and an exhibition of heroism to both of which the world can be challenged to produce superiors."

Pleasanton was asked by the Committee of Congress what produced the panic in the Eleventh Corps, and replied: "The combined effect upon their imagination of the sound of musketry, and the increasing yells of the rebels and their increasing artillery fire. It was a theatrical effect that Stonewall Jackson could produce better than any other man I have ever seen on the field of battle."

Pleasanton also informed the committee that he ordered the guns not to fire until he gave the word, as he wanted the effect of an immense shock. "There was an immense body of men, and I wanted the whole weight of the metal to check them." When he gave the order "the fire actually swept the men away. It seemed to blow those men in front clear over the parapet."

He also stated how he cleared behind him in a marsh the debris of the Eleventh Corps, piled up in great confusion. For this literary entertainment, Pleasanton was highly complimented, and the report reads : "Although a cavalry officer, he handled the artillery with exceeding great judgment and effectiveness. His skill, energy, daring and promptness upon this occasion contributed greatly to arrest the disaster which for a time threatened the whole army. His conduct upon this and many other occasions marks him as one of the ablest generals in our service, and as deserving of far higher consideration than from some cause he appears to have received."

These glowing accounts of military exploits performed at Hazel Grove, as narrated, when compared with the facts or what appear to be the facts, seem at variance, and far more worthy of a place among the tales of the late Baron Munchausen than the serious and truthful pages of the history of the Armies of the Potomac and of Northern Virginia.

It is too late for the authors of these false reports to make amends to the men of the Eleventh Corps, for the most of them are dead ; but it is not too late to correct the inscriptions in history wherein every deserving soldier receives his just reward, no matter whether he carrried a musket, with tattered uniform, or rode at the head of a column, adorned with sword and stars. The history of to-day should cover both with equal fairness, and it should also respect the valor of the Confederate soldier.

It may be safely affirmed that none of the fugitives

breaking out of the forest with guns, caissons, ambulances and horses, crowding upon the artillery of Pleasanton, were soldiers from the defeated Eleventh Corps. There may have been, sometime during the evening, a few of the pickets of the Seventy-fifth Pennsylvania, escaping from the forest south of the Dowdall Farm, seen crossing the southern border of Hazel Grove with guns on their shoulders. But in the disorderly torrent bursting out of the wood from the northwest, to the astonishment of Pleasanton, there was neither man nor beast, neither gun, caisson, nor material of any description, belonging to the abused Eleventh Corps. Furthermore, it may be asserted that no organization of Jackson's army approached Hazel Grove that night, or until daylight on Sunday morning. And that no Confederates attacked Pleasanton, except a handful of foragers, numbering from one hundred and fifty to two hundred men, who took to their heels as soon as the artillery fire permitted them to rise from cover. The survivors to-day declare that not one of the party was injured by the pyrotechnic display, and examination of the terrain and the cover it afforded strengthens the statement. Nearly all of Jackson's Corps, at this hour and at this moment, was halted near the Wilderness Church and about the Dowdall Farm. All had been ordered to halt there, and none went forward except the groups of disordered troops, who slowly drifted up the road in search of adventure or plunder as far as the Log Works built by Williams' Division of the Twelfth Corps, or to the western border of Hazel Grove.

It may also be stated that the story told by Pleasanton concerning the charge of the Eighth Pennsylvania Cavalry, in order to give him time to place his artillery in position, is a fabrication. Col. Pennoch Huey was the commander of the regiment, and he did not receive any order to charge. Furthermore, the regiment had disappeared in the woods on its way before Pleasanton reached Hazel Grove. As the regiment entered the forest, which extends for about a mile before the Plank Road is reached, it saw, halting by the road-

side, caissons, guns, carriages and other material belonging
to the troops who had gone down to the Furnace. A vista
about two hundred yards in length and twenty-five yards in
width was cleared beside the road, and afforded sufficient territory for the parking of this material, with men and animals.
As the cavalry passed this assemblage of troops and camp
followers, none of them seemed to be aware that a conflict
had taken place in the vicinity, or that the least danger was
impending. Not a straggler from the line of battle had even
then reached this secluded spot to give the alarm. And so
Huey and his men marched gaily along, with their swords in
their scabbards and their pistols in their holsters, closely followed by the Third Corps ammunition mule train. About
a third of a mile from the Plank Road a path turns off at the
left hand and enters the Plank Road to the westward near
the Dowdall Tavern. As Colonel Huey reached this narrow
road or path, he noticed some men in gray uniform moving
about in the twilight some distance from him, but he took
them to be some of our own scouts dressed in Confederate
gray, and passed on. Not a straggler nor a wounded soldier
from the routed Eleventh Corps had as yet appeared or
crossed the path the cavalry were marching on, and this fact
affords, or seems to afford, positive proof that the fugitives
described by Pleasanton could not have come from the Eleventh Corps.

The Eighth Pennsylvania Regiment marched completely
across the line of retreat of the beaten troops, and did not
meet one of them. They had passed up the Plank Road a
few moments before, and Dilger and his gun, with his rear
guard, were probably at this moment passing Bushbeck's line
of defense. Colonel Huey did not hear any shots fired at
this time, and the reason is this : Captain Dilger, after enter-
ing the woods with his gun and supports, stopped firing.
The enemy followed slowly at a respectful distance, and
neither the pursued nor the pursuers exchanged shots.

The Eighth Pennsylvania Cavalry, in column of twos,
passed on quietly until near the Plank Road, and then Col-

onel Huey saw, to his astonishment, groups of Confederates moving past him across the road toward the Chancellorsville House, while others were approaching his left flank in the woods. Huey saw that he had run into some part of the rebel army, and that it was too late to retreat, and his best chance was to break through the crowd in the road, gain the Plank Road, turn to the right, and fight his way to the Chancellor House. He instantly ordered his men to draw sabers and follow him at a gallop.

When Huey struck the Plank Road, he saw, to his dismay, a crowd of Confederates blocking the way on the right, while there were only a few in the road to the left, towards Dowdall Tavern. Huey led the column to the left, hoping to find some outlet of escape, but after he had passed about one hundred yards down the road he was met with a murderous volley from concealed troops in the woods. Major Keenan fell by his side, and Captain Arrowsmith, Captain Haddock, and about thirty others were struck down in the melee. Huey then turned the staggered column to the right of the road in the woods and passed along to the eastward, until he had flanked the Confederates in the road. He then struck the old mountain road, and led the men who followed him to the batteries in the road, where he met Captain Best placing the artillery in position, and requested him not to fire his guns down the road, as many of his men were still in the woods, trying to work their way out. The rear of the Eighth Pennsylvania Cavalry, hearing the attack on the head of the column, turned from the Hazel Grove road to the right and made their way through the woods and over or past the Log Works of the Twelfth Corps to the Fairview plateau, where they joined the rest of the regiment, supported the artillery, and acted as provost guard.

Such is the history of the charge of the Eighth Pennsylvania Cavalry. Colonel Huey, who was in command of the regiment, received no order from Pleasanton to charge, and gave none until he was enveloped by the enemy, a mile distant from Hazel Grove.

The ammunition train of the Third Corps, following the Eighth Pennsylvania Cavalry, was also fired into by the Georgia foragers coming up in the woods on their left flank. Col. Daniel Hall attempted to retreat to Hazel Grove, but a wild panic seized all parties in the vista, and the mule train soon became irretrievably mixed with the disorded mass of men, animals, guns and caissons, and dispersed. These were the runaways represented to have been fugitives of the Eleventh Corps.

Who were the men who attacked Hazel Grove and its twenty-two cannon so fiercely on Saturday evening, imperiling the safety of the Union army? There was an attack, for one man was killed and five wounded on the Union side, while engaged in this desperate combat at short range. The narratives mention immense masses of men in successive lines of battle, but the slaughter on the Union side does not indicate that the Confederates were well armed, if they were present in great force. After long inquiry among the survivors, and search among the archives of both armies, I can find but one report relating directly to Hazel Grove, and that is the one made by Lieutenant Colonel Winn, of the Fourth Georgia, written six days after the fight.

Winn states that when Doles' Brigade had halted at the edge of the woods beyond Dowdall's, "I ordered the battalion forward, and with the colors and left wing advanced through this thicket to a field, compelling the abandonment of one gun and two caissons, etc., etc., en route. The right wing of the regiment, taking direction from other regiments of the brigade, was halted on reaching the woods last mentioned. When I reached the field (which was the field in which the attack on the enemy was begun May 3d), I found two regiments of the enemy, with artillery, posted about three hundred yards obliquely to the left of the entrance of the road into the field. Here I ascertained that as senior officer present, I had with me about two hundred men of various commands. I formed line behind a slight rail barricade, formed by throwing down the fence. Just as the line was formed,

7—B. C.

the officer commanding the Federal troops, which were standing in line exhibiting no purpose to attack, rode toward me.
Though I ordered the men not to fire, when he got to within
one hundred yards of me two of the men excitedly fired at
him, whereupon he rode rapidly back to his command, and
immediately a terrible artillery and infantry fire was opened
upon us.   The men under my command gallantly returned
the fire until their small supply of ammunition was exhausted.   Shortly after the cessation of our firing, the enemy
ceased to fire, and my little force retired by right and left
flank to rejoin their respective commands."

Colonel Winn furthermore briefly states that "After re-
joining our brigade we bivouacked on the field until seven A. M.
May 3d."   No other Confederate troops approached Hazel
Grove that night, unless it was a small party under Colonel
Mercer, of the Twenty-first Georgia, of the same brigade.

Colonel Mercer says, in his report, written three days
after the event: "The brigade was ordered to halt and form
line in the edge of the field (Dowdall's).   This command not
having been heard, the colors and a portion of the Twenty-
first Georgia entered the thick pine woods in front and
advanced to within three hundred yards of a battery, which
opened fire and caused them to halt and protect themselves
by lying down, until a favorable opportunity was presented
for retiring."

The survivors of the attacking party declare that they
received no support; that Colonel Mercer and his small party
were not in sight or in support.   Colonel Mercer and his party
probably advanced to the pine woods, two or three hundred
yards to the right rear of where Colonel Winn was, but as
they were not in sight of Winn and his party, and took no
part in the attack, their whereabouts is not of much consequence.

General Stuart's Adjutant General states in his book
that Colonel Mercer supported the left of Colonel Winn
but this officer was not present at the time, having gone
with Stuart to Ely Ford, and did not return until midnight.

A staff officer of Doles' thinks this remark applies to the attack of May 3d, and not to that of May 2d.

The men in gray whom Colonel Huey saw in the by-path on the left of the Hazel Grove Road were probably Colonel Winn and his foragers, approaching the vista where the cannon, caissons, etc., were at rest. Bursting upon the men guarding this material with fierce yells and desultory firing, they stampeded them without difficulty. It was this crowd, routed by Winn, that burst out in disorder upon Hazel Grove, and for which the men of the Eleventh Corps have been given undue credit, as none of them took part in it. Winn's force was so feeble or so demoralized by its situation that it did not attempt to carry off the cannon or any of the material, which it had captured in the vista, fairly won, and could have easily removed. As to the numbers forming the attack, I believe Winn's estimate should be accepted, although some of the survivors think there was not over one hundred and fifty men engaged or present.

The incident recalls the remark General Pichegru made to his trembling followers: "Courage! Cowards look big in the dark." And so a hundred resolute men, dancing among the trees in the dusk of evening, firing at random and yelling lustily, might readily give rise to the belief that a large force was present. Braddock and his British regulars, in the woods at Fort Duquesne, thought the woods were filled with Indians, whereas in reality there were but few present.

The artillery at Hazel Grove comprised four batteries, one of which, Martin's, was under the direction of Pleasanton. The other three batteries belonged to the Third Corps, and were under the command of a cool, resolute officer, Maj. J. F. Huntington, whose capacity and firmness had been tested a year before, in the desperate fight of Port Republic. At the first sign of a disturbance, Huntington placed his batteries in position, and ordered them to fire into the woods when the rebel foragers fired at Lieutenant Thompson. He received no orders from Pleasanton or any one else, but managed his own affairs without interference, save the annoyance caused by the cavalry riding in disorder among his guns, and by the firing into his rear by the One Hundred and Tenth Pennsylvania Infantry. The casualties of these four batteries of twenty-two guns, fired into in front by the enemy and in rear by the supporting infantry, amounted to one man killed and five wounded. If the contest lasted about an hour, as Pleasanton states, this report of casualties would indicate that the Confederates were very poor r.arksmen, or that they were very few in number, or were destroyed without a return fire. Certainly some credit ought to be given to the infantry of the One Hundred and Tenth Pennsylvania, who poured a volley directly into the rear of these batteries !

CHAPTER IX.

At the Log Works—Twelfth Corps.

THE irregular groups of Colston's and Rodes' men halted at the Log Works constructed the day before by Williams' Division of the Twelfth Corps. These works were stout barricades of logs, with abattis on the western side, and extended from the ravines in front of Fairview westerly and northerly to about two hundred feet from the Plank Road and about sixty yards easterly of the entrance of the Dirt Road leading from Hazel Grove.

Along the line of these barricades, four companies of the Twenty-eighth New York and camp followers had been left to guard the baggage of Williams' Division of the Twelfth Corps, which had gone southward with Sickles in pursuit of General Lee. The Twenty-eighth New York reports that it deployed its men behind the works, and halted many of the stragglers of the Eleventh Corps, but that they fled at the first fire. General Williams, deriving information from the same source, and chagrined at the loss of his baggage and the conduct of his men, increases the number of halted stragglers to two thousand men, and states that they promptly receded at the first volley. It is certainly very doubtful if any of the Eleventh Corps men remained at this place after Buschbeck and his rear guard passed by, as they called in all fugitives, and so closely that none remained on the south side of the Plank Road to warn Colonel Huey and his cavalry of impending danger. Captain Dilger, with his rear guard, as he passed the Log Works, keeping the road free from close pursuit with his single gun, did not see any of the Eleventh Corps remaining near the works, but noticed a small and scattered body of infantry behind them, a short distance from the road, and appearing to have come up along the line from the southward. At this time the enemy were not within can-

ister range of Dilger's gun, and there was ample time for
the men of the Twenty-eighth New York to have escaped,
had they desired to do so, but they were ordered to remain in
place by their commanding officer.

A few moments later, Colston's and Rodes' foragers
came up and, getting into their rear, demanded their surrender. From the evidence thus far obtained, it is doubtful if
any resistance was made, or any volleys of musketry were fired
on either side. If there had been any resistance, Colonel
Huey and his men, then passing within one hundred yards,
would have heard the musketry. But they heard no sounds
of a conflict on their right flank. The official returns, also,
do not indicate that there was any fight whatever at these
works. The place was a fatal one to many of Knipe's Brigade, for a little later on in the evening three more of his
regiments became strangely entangled, confused and broken
up, with a loss to the brigade of about four hundred prisoners.

About seventy of the Twenty-eighth New York threw
down their arms and surrendered, while the rest retired
rapidly through the woods in the rear, joining in their flight
the broken cavalry, seeking escape, and the camp followers
left in the works. Near the western border of these woods,
the Thirteenth New Jersey, of the Twelfth Corps, had been
left in reserve, and when this demoralized crowd burst out
of the woods, shouting that the enemy were upon them, the
Thirteenth New Jersey promptly joined them. About this
time the frightened horde of fugitives whom Pleasanton has
so minutely described at Hazel Grove, together with groups
of cavalry that bothered the artillery of Huntington, and
guns, caissons, ambulances, beef cattle, mules, etc., came
tearing up the ravine with great force, but none of these
guns, caissons, ambulances, carriages or material of any kind
belonged to the Eleventh Corps, as is stated by Maj. J. F.
Huntington in the Century Papers, and as he was commander
of three of the batteries at Hazel Grove his statement is
authoritative.

They rushed past and through some of the regiments

of Knipe's and Ruger's Brigades of the Twelfth Corps, then rapidly returning to their old positions. The reinforced mob, as it rushed over the Fairview field to the Chancellor House, must have presented an alarming sight, and perhaps warranted the contemptuous statements of Captains Osborne and Winslow, of the artillery, who pictured them as, "aghast and terror-stricken, heads bare and panting for breath, they pleaded like infants at the mother's breast that we would let them pass to the rear unhindered."

These reports have been copied far and wide, and alluded to with much emphasis at times. In fact, it would seem as though the meetings of some of the New Jersey troops, even to recent dates, lacked inspiration until the Falstaffs had described the disgraceful rout, and heaped it all upon the unfortunate Eleventh Corps. These garlands were promptly assigned to the Eleventh Corps, and they have meekly worn them to the present day.—*See Map No. 6.*

Much has been said about the rout of the Eleventh Corps, and that it rushed past the Chancellor House with the force of a cyclone and the disorder of a blind stampede, and that in this disorderly mob the whole of the corps was included. Careful investigation seems to show that the advance of the routed part of the corps was much exaggerated, and also that the frantic and tumultuous crowd, fired into by Hooker's staff, and ridden down by the artillery and cavalry, was really that picturesque phalanx described by Pleasanton, which came from Hazel Grove, about a mile distant, and in which the Eleventh Corps took no part. The routed advance of the Eleventh Corps had three miles to run before reaching Chancellor's, and if they are the ones described, they must have possessed wonderful strength and endurance. In the stream of fugitives which passed the Chancellor House, or stopped in front and rear of it, there could not have been over three thousand men of the corps, or one-fourth of it, instead of the whole corps. The number of the corps was estimated at twelve thousand men, and deducting from it the three thousand men detached with Barlow, and not in the fight, the two thousand five hundred killed, wounded and missing, and the three thousand five hundred or four thousand rallied to the west of the Chancellor House, either on the field of Fairview or in the woods north of it, there remains twenty five hundred to three thousand to be accounted for in the routed portion at the Chancellor House.

Investigation seems to show that this historic emeute was mostly composed of men and camp followers of the Third and Twelfth Corps, and that none of the Eleventh were in it excepting perhaps a few of the pickets escaping from the south of Dowdall's. In fact, the retreating portion of the Eleventh Corps had passed the Chancellor House some time before, and were then being halted in rear of it and along the road leading to the White House. It can be shown that eight or nine thousand of the full strength of the corps, reckoned at twelve thousand men, were not at the Chancellor House in this rout, but were in line of battle, under Best's guns, or on the right flank of Berry, or left killed, wounded and prisoners on the Dowdall fields, or in the brigade of Barlow, in search of Lee, three to five miles south of Chancellor's. The remaining portion of three thousand or less men have been reckoned and described as the entire Eleventh Corps, and the whole corps denounced as cowardly Dutchmen, without caring to separate the native born Americans from the naturalized soldier of foreign birth. The closest scrutiny is invited to the causes and the actual conditions of the rout of this part of the Eleventh Corps, and attention is also called to the self laudations of the Fallstaffs who rushed forward to fill the gap, and hurled Jackson back into the woods where Jackson's Corps did not appear. There was no enemy in pursuit at this time. Nearly all of Jackson's men had halted at Dowdall's, two miles away. The cannon shot that fell among the trains of troops in this vicinity came from Hardaway's guns, on the Turnpike, southeast, and the Plank Road, south, about a mile distant. These batteries belonged to Anderson's and McLaws' Divisions, and were ordered to make this diversion in connection with Jackson's attack. Breathed's battery, with Jackson, was at the Dowdall Tavern, two miles distant, and their short range guns could not reach the Chancellor field, and did not try it.

It is quite impossible to give an estimate of the number of rebels who went forward to the Log Works. They were too much broken, disorganized and tired to form a line of battle, and after the capture or dispersion of the four companies of the Twenty-eighth New York, there were no Federal troops visible to attack. At this time General Rodes galloped up the Plank Road some distance, and satisfied himself that there was no line of battle this side of the Chancellorsville heights, Buschbeck and his men being concealed from view by the woods on the right, and Berry and his division not being in sight, or coming up in the woods on the left. Major Cobb, of the Forty-fourth Virginia, did the same, and sent the information to Jackson. While the prisoners and property of Williams' Division were being secured, the Fifth Connecticut and Forty-sixth New York came groping, in the gloom, along the Log Works, in search of their former position and their property. The rebel foragers promptly fired into them and demanded their surrender, and, after a slight resistance, about one hundred and fifty more prisoners were added to the list, while the rest promptly retired. The flash and reports of this musketry was probably that which attracted Pleasanton's attention, at Hazel Grove, one thousand yards or more to the southward. The Confederate foragers shortly returned to the rear, where the corps had halted, carrying with them many prisoners and some booty. The Log Works of General Williams' Division were then completely abandoned, although Rodes says his men did not leave them until relieved by Lane's Brigade; but Lane declares that none of Rodes' men were found by him in front. General Hill warned Lane not to fire into Rodes' men, as there might be some in front. But after forming the line, the regimental commanders, as well as Colonel Avery, commanding the skirmish line, informed Lane that they had seen none

of Rodes' men.   The Adjutant General of Lee's army states
that Rodes' men had retired some time before.   Lane is undoubtedly correct, for some of the Forty-sixth Pennsylvania
advanced and found the works deserted, and they remained
so until after the artillery fire of Captain Osborne had ceased,
when Lane advanced, which took place after eight P. M.

CHAPTER X.

The Wounding of Stonewall Jackson.

A T this time the position of the Federal troops was as follows : Pleasanton retained his position at Hazel Grove unmolested, with no Confederates nearer than Colston's line, attempting to reform at the Log Hut near the Plank Road, about half a mile from Dowdall's eastward, and more than a mile from the batteries at Hazel Grove. Behind Pleasanton, Whipple's Division was pressing forward, and Birney's was far in their rear. Berry's two brigades occupied the space from the Plank Road to, at or near the Bullock Road. Williams' Division of the Twelfth Corps had mostly returned, and was occupying the gap between Pleasanton's right and Berry's left. In the rear of this line stood Buschbeck, with his brigade and detachments, in front of Best's batteries. To the right of Berry, in the woods on the Bullock Road, stood the Twenty-sixth Wisconsin, Eighty-second Illinois, Eighty-second Ohio and One Hundred and Fifty-seventh New York, of Schurz's Division, and fragments of the other Eleventh Corps regiments, numbering in all, with Buschbeck's troops, more than three thousand men. In rear of Berry, Hays' Brigade of the Second Corps was moving to take position about four hundred yards distant in the rear.

Jackson was at the Dowdall Tavern, chafing under the delay, and ordered A. P. Hill to push his division to cover the front, and prepare for a night attack, while Colston and Rodes were reorganizing their disordered columns in the rear. General Hill then ordered Lane and his brigade to advance to the front, but before Lane put his troops in motion Crutchfield sent two Napoleons and one Parrot gun up the Plank Road about half a mile from Dowdall's, and opened fire upon the Federal batteries, supposed to be about twelve hundred yards distant, at eight P. M.   The Feueral artillery then in position or coming into position numbered forty-three guns, and from the batteries commanding the Plank Road Captain Osborne ordered eight or ten guns of his command to reply.   Lane had moved up to the rear of Crutchfield's guns, when the rapid return fire of Osborne's artillery raked his column in the road, and forced him to seek cover on the left side of it.   Lane refused to deploy until the artillery fire ceased, and asked General Hill to stop it.   Colonel Crutchfield, after a delay of about fifteen minutes, was ordered to stop firing, and Osborne ceasing to fire, Lane proceeded to form line of battle near the Log Works built by Williams' men, of the Twelth Corps.   Here he threw forward on the right and left of the Plank Road the entire Thirty-third North Carolina as skirmishers, and deployed the Seventh and Thirty-seventh North Carolina on the abattis side of the Log Works, on the right of the Plank Road, and placed the Eighteenth and Twenty-eighth North Carolina in line of battle on the left of the Plank Road a few yards in advance of the right wing, on the right of the Plank Road. Lane did not see the Log Works until after his men had been placed in front of them, and this is the reason why they were placed on the abattis side.   He did not throw any pickets in the direction of Hazel Grove, being in blissful ignorance of the "terrific struggle" that had taken place there shortly before, according to the statements made by Pleasanton.   In fact, Lane's right flank and rear were unguarded and open to an attack from Hazel Grove.   None of the Confederate leaders were aware of the imminent dangers that were lurking at Hazel Grove, and there was not a solitary picket on Lane's right to prevent Pleasanton from marching up the Dirt Road to McGowan's Brigade, resting in rear of Lane on the Plank Road, and inquiring the time of day.   The brigade was finally placed in position without any opposition whatever. Captain Braxton was stationed, with his two or three guns, in the road between the two wings of the brigade.   Neither Jackson, nor Hill, nor Lane was aware of Berry's line of battle in front, but supposed the infantry were in rear of the guns at Fairview. Instead of Berry's hurling Jackson's men back at the point of the bayonet, the evidence shows that Jackson's men did not know that Berry was in front of the Federal batteries.

The nearest position of Jackson's line of battle to that of the Federals was seven hundred yards west of Berry, with dense woods intervening. It was known to the Confederates that there was a strong line of skirmishers in front of them, and the ringing of axes later in the night indicated the construction of fortifications. Lane, in placing his regiments, had cautioned all of them to keep a sharp lookout for the enemy, as he was far in advance and alone, and that they must be in readiness to repel an attack. As soon as the line of battle was established, General Lane rode back to the road for his final orders, as he understood General Hill to say that he was to prepare for action. When Lane reached the road, it was too dark to distinguish persons, and he called out for General Hill, and the reply he got came from General Jackson, who recognized the voice of his old pupil, and called him to his side. Lane found Jackson at or near the meeting of the Hazel Grove and Bullock Roads, and in rear of the three guns placed on picket. Jackson was at that time alone, neither Hill nor any of his staff being visible. Lane reported for final orders, and Jackson, raising his arm in the direction of the enemy, exclaimed briefly : " Push right ahead, Lane ; right ahead !" Lane knew his old instructor too well to ask for any further instructions (he had been a student under Jackson at the Virginia Military Institute), and at once rode along his line to prepare for the advance, and he had reached the extreme right of his position and was about to give the signal, when Lieutenant Colonel Hill, one of his bravest officers, came to him and begged him not to give the order until he could ascertain what forces were moving on his right and rear, and whether they belonged to the army of Lee or Hooker. At this time distinct sounds of troops and trains could be heard in the woods, both in front and on the right flank, which was totally unprotected. In fact, neither Jackson nor Hill nor Lane had heard of the conflict as described by Pleasanton and Sickles, and were not aware of any danger impending from that quarter. General Lane was so ignorant of the presence of the enemy in that direction that he had not placed a single picket on the right of the Log Works, behind which his men were then standing, nor even on the Hazel Grove road in his flank and rear, and neither was he aware of the cannon, caissons, and trains of the Third Corps left in that road in the stampede caused by the Georgia foragers an hour or more previously. While General Lane and Colonel Hill were discussing the causes of the sounds in the woods on their right, a Federal officer came up along the Log Works from the right flank, waving a handkerchief and demanding to know what troops were in front of him. The officer proved to be Colonel Smith, of the One Hundred and Twenty-eighth Pennsylvania Regiment, which had come up from the expedition from the Furnace, and was trying to find in the darkness the baggage and former position of the regiment in the Log Works. He was promptly seized by some of the men of the Seventh North Carolina and brought before General Lane, who was then standing in the Log Works near by. After a moment's conversation with the prisoner, General Lane ordered Colonel Hill to send a squad of soldiers into the woods and ascertain how much of a force was then threatening their right flank and rear, concealed by the darkness of the night. Lieutenant Emack, of the Seventh North Carolina, was detailed, with four men, to advance into the forest whence Colonel Smith had emerged. About this time a Federal officer (undoubtedly General Knipe) rode up in the woods in front and called out for General Williams, the commander of the division. Sergeant Cowan, of the Thirty-third North Carolina, commanding that part of the skirmish line, ordered his men to fire upon the Federal officer, and instantly the nearest picket fired, followed by others of the skirmish line. The shots were promptly returned by the

Federal pickets, not far distant, and part of the Seventh North Carolina, standing in front of the Log Works, fired a volley in the direction of the Federal officer and, unthinkingly, into the rear of that portion of the Thirty-third North Carolina then drawn up as a skirmish line directly in their front. The picket fire became more animated, and rolled along both picket lines to the northward and past the Plank Road, and was increased by a volley from the Seventy-third New York, the left regiment of Berry's line of battle, stationed on the Plank Road, and also by a desultory fire from a part of the First Massachusetts Regiment, on the right of the Plank Road, which killed and wounded three of its own skirmishers.

This random firing took plack at 9.10, or 9.15, and is clearly the cause of the accident to General Jackson. When Lane left Jackson, he was in the road near where the Bullock Road comes into the Plank Road, and he was alone, and such was the distribution of his troops at this moment that a Federal scouting party could have come up the Hazel Grove Road and seized him as a prisoner of war. Even as late as nine P. M. it was totally unguarded, and Major Jed Hotchkiss, of Jackson's staff, rode down the road to the Hazel Grove field at this hour without meeting a solitary soldier of either army, and in fact he did not know that Lane's men were deployed between him and Chancellorsville, perhaps a hundred yards distant. General Hill and some of his staff soon joined Jackson, and then Jackson gave Hill his orders in the brief sentence: "Press them; cut them off from the United States Ford, Hill; press them." A. P. Hill replied that none of his staff were familiar with the country. Thereupon Jackson turned to Captain Boswell, who was well acquainted with all the roads and paths, and ordered him to report to Hill. Soon after, the party turned to the left, to the space in the forest where the Bullock and Mountain Roads came into the Plank Road, and were passing up the Mountain Road when a courier from General Stuart, who had gone to Ely Ford with his cavalry, rode up to Jackson and delivered a message. Jackson ordered the courier to wait for a reply. This cavalryman, named Dave Kyle, was born at the White House, in the rear of Chancellor's, and was perfectly acquainted with every path and road on the plateau of Chancellorsville, and it is by him that we are able to trace every footstep from this time until the fatal event. The Mountain Road is an old road, which comes out of the Plank Road about half a mile from Chancellor's, and runs parallel with and north of it from sixty to eighty yards distant, and again comes into it, together with the Bullock Road, opposite the road from Hazel Grove. Although long out of use, it is still distinctly visible to-day. It is certain that Jackson and his party passed along the Mountain Path, and not up the Plank Road, past the guns placed in battery. Furthermore, the two officers of the Eighteenth North Carolina Regiment, stationed on the Plank Road, have declared that Jackson did not pass by them, but turned off to the left of their rear, and passed out of view in the forest. Jackson was well aware that the Plank Road was swept by the fire of the Federal cannon at Fairview, and that the batteries were ready to open fire at the first sign of a movement by the enemy. Moreover, there was nothing to call him on the Plank Road, for Fairview was not his objective point, but the White House, and the path he was then upon led directly to it. For the first one hundred yards the Bullock and Mountain Roads are blended together, and up this roadway, about nine o'clock in the evening, the party of Confederate officers passed along, with their chieftain riding in the advance. About one hundred yards from the entrance of the paths into the Plank Road the party passed quietly through the ranks of the Eighteenth North Carolina Regiment, then drawn up in line of battle extending to the north for some distance, and awaiting for the signal of advance from General Lane. They passed so quietly through the Eighteenth Regiment that Major Barry, stationed on the left wing of the regiment, did not notice them, and was not informed of their passage. They continued slowly along the Mountain Road towards the Thirty-third North Carolina Regiment, then drawn up in a strong skirmish line, extending across the Plank Road into the forest some distance north of it, and from two hundred to three hundred yards in front of the Eighteenth North Carolina Regiment. They passed on, almost to the line of the Thirty-third North Carolina skirmishers, and halted. Jackson listened for a moment to the sounds coming from the Federal lines—the ringing of the axes in building the fortifications and the words of command being distinctly audible—and then turned his horse in silence and slowly retraced his steps back to the place where the Mountain, the Bullock, and the Hunting Roads, or paths, come together, about sixty to eighty yards from where the Eighteenth North Carolina Regiment was standing in the woods, and about sixty to seventy yards from where the Jackson monument now stands. Jackson then stopped, and, again turning his horse towards the Federal lines, was apparently listening to the sounds from the front, and for Lane's signal for the advance. Gen. A. P. Hill and his Adjutant General Colonel Palmer, again joined them. The group of horsemen gathered together in his rear, and all were standing still and in silence, when suddenly a single rifle shot rang out distinctly in the evening air, and at some distance south of the Plank Road. The fatal shot was that fired by the skirmishers of the Thirty-third North Carolina at the call of General Knipe. It was instantly replied to, and as the firing rolled along the line of the skirmishers of both armies, and was increased in volume by the volleys of the Seventy-third New York, part of the First Massachusetts (Federal), and a part of the Seventh North Carolina (rebel), both lines of battle became keenly on the alert. At this moment Colonel Purdie and the adjutant of the Eighteenth North Carolina had gone forward on the Plank Road about two hundred yards, to consult with Colonel Avery, of the Thirty-third North Carolina, near the old Vanwert Cabin, about the approach of the enemy on the right flank and rear, and while engaged in this conversation, the picket firing broke out in

8—B. C.

their front.   Purdie and his adjutant immediately turned and rushed with all their speed down the Plank Road toward their position at the head of the Eighteenth North Carolina Regiment.   The sounds of their footsteps startled the Confederate soldiers, already aroused by the roar of musketry in front, and as Major Barry, on the left of the Eighteenth, some distance in the woods, heard these sounds of rapid approach from the front, and suddenly saw a group of strange horsemen moving about among the shadows of the trees eighty yards in his front and to his right, he instantly gave the order to fire and repeat the firing.

The fire of the rifles of the North Carolina mountaineers was fearfully effective, and every one of that group of horsemen went down or disappeared before its fatal aim except Jackson.   The chieftain, although grievously wounded, kept his seat in the saddle, even when Old Sorrel, startled by the confusion around him, dashed across the path into an oak tree, whose branches nearly swept his rider to the ground.   A moment after the horse continued on toward the Plank Road, but finally stopped a few yards from it, where some of the officers who had escaped the destructive fire found him.   Tenderly lifting Jackson from the saddle, they laid the wounded chieftain under a pine tree.   Soon after Gen. A. P. Hill came to his side, and sent for aid, but as Jackson could walk, he was assisted to his feet, and taken to the Plank Road, and turned toward the Dowdall House.   As the party walked down the road the number was increased by the officers who desired to offer some assistance, and the enlarged group of men, both mounted and on foot, attracted the notice of Captain Osborne, who had charge of the two Federal guns placed at the foot of the hill on picket, about seven or eight hundred yards distant.   It was then bright moonlight, and objects could be seen a long distance on the broad road.   Osborne at once opened fire, and it was regarded by the batteries in the rear at Fairview as a signal that the enemy was advancing in force, and in a moment after, at 9.30 P. M., forty-three guns in all were directing a terrific fire down the Plank Road.   At this time the entire road below the Hazel Grove Road was filled with battalions of Confederate artillery and brigades of infantry, amounting to quite twenty thousand men, ready to take part in the advance movement. The Federal fire raked the road with fearful effect, and Jackson's bearers were struck down twice. It was in the midst of this tempest of bursting shell that Jackson delivered his last order to his army. It was to General Pender, whose column was being torn to pieces by the Federal shot and shell, and who expressed a doubt of his ability to hold his brigade in their present position under the murderous fire. The dying chieftain aroused himself, and exclaimed emphatically : "Pender, you must hold your ground!"

In the tumult and wild commotion which ensued, and which for a while threatened to break up the two exposed divisions of infantry, much damage was done to them and to the artillery battalions, and many men and officers were struck down, among them Colonel Crutchfield, Chief of Artillery, and Colonels Nichols and Mallory. The Fifty-fifth Virginia was involved in the melee, and thinking itself attacked, one of its wings poured a volley into an imaginary foe. Major Pegram fired a few shots from two of his guns over the heads of those around him, but as both of these parties were in rear of Lane's line of battle, and also McGowan's and Pender's Brigades, it is not easy to see how they attacked or repulsed the enemy, and especially as no Federal force advanced at this hour to attack anywhere along the line. All reports of fighting by various regiments of Jackson's Corps during the evening, excepting those of Lane's Brigade, are erroneous. Lane's and Pender's Brigades held the front line of battle until after Sickles' "midnight charge," and no infantry passed their lines that night. There was some desultory infantry firing at times, both by some of Lane's regiments (but only by the Eighteenth North Carolina, and part of the Seventh North Carolina), and some of the regiments in the rear of Lane, but they were random shots at imaginary foes, excepting the brief and feeble midnight attack from Hazel Grove. The skirmishers of the Thirty-third North Carolina, two hundred or three hundred yards in front of Lane, were compelled to rush forward to seek shelter when a part of Lane's line of battle fired its desultory volleys, and this rushing forward gave the impression that the rebels were making a charge, and caused some of the Federal regiments in Berry's and Williams' Divisions to fire into the woods to repel a threatened attack. Three times Colonel Avery re-established during the night his broken line of skirmishers. To the spectators near the Federal batteries at Fairview, the sharp musketry and the tall swearing and vociferation heard in the woods in front gave an impression that a severe fight was raging in the woods, but the lines of battle did not come within seven hundred yards of each other, excepting during the Hazel Grove episode.

In the meantime General Lane, at the extreme right of his brigade, was anxiously awaiting the return of the scouting party sent into the forest on his flank. In a few moments Lieutenant Emack, with his four North Carolina soldiers, returned with one hundred and fifty or more Federal soldiers of the One Hundred and Twenty-eighth Pennsylvania Regiment, who had become bewildered in the dark forest, and yielded to the summons of the Confederate officer. As the party came up to the·Log Works, where General Lane was standing, Colonel Smith refused to admit the surrender of his men, as a violation of the handkerchief of truce, and an earnest discussion arose over the question of right, when suddenly the artillery fire of the Federal batteries burst upon them, and to escape the tempest of destruction both Federals and rebels instantly sprang over to the shady side of the Log Works, and lay side by side in temporary brotherly love. But as soon as the Federal fire ceased, General Lane ordered the Federal soldiers to be conducted to the rear as prisoners of war. Shortly after, General Pender came to General Lane, still in the forest, and informed him of the accident to General Jackson, and also of the wounding of General Hill by the Federal artillery fire, and advised Lane not to advance.

The fatal shots came from the left wing of the Eighteenth North Carolina, and the whole brigade has been involved in the severe denunciations hurled upon them in this unfortunate affair.   When Mahone's Brigade of Virginians, in broad daylight, on the 6th of May, 1864, fired repeatedly into their own corps, killing General Jenkins and his aid Doby, and wounding General Longstreet and many others, nothing was said about it.   The mistake in daylight was more inexcusable than the error in the darkness of night. Barry ordered his men to fire, for he was not aware of anyone passing in his front except the pickets, and they were not mounted.   Major Barry was an officer cool and brave, and neither Jackson, nor Lane, nor Hill ever blamed him for his fearful error.   As to the charge of being panic-stricken, there is no evidence of it to be deduced from the particulars. On the contrary, there is much to be admired in the conduct of Lane's Brigade at this time.   The entire brigade had been warned by its commander to be on the alert, keenly on the alert, as they were in front of the Federal army, and without immediate support.   The charge that there was no picket line established is completely untrue, for the entire Thirty-third North Carolina Regiment was stretched across the Plank Road, above and below it, and far in advance of where Jackson stood when fired upon.   This brigade faced the Federal front in line of battle, and although twice exposed to the fire of forty-three cannon, it never faltered nor called for help, until its flank and rear were threatened by Sickles about midnight.   The history of this command, under its dauntless leader, throughout the war, and ending at Appomattox, will always be admired and respected by those who believe in American manhood.   And the student who seeks to discover a higher degree of courage and hardihood among the military organizations of either army will look over the true records of the war for a long time, if not in vain.   Investigation shows that the brigade was composed of young men, of the best stock the Old North State contained, and sent to represent it in that bulwark of secession, the Army of Northern Virginia. The records of the war show that it was in all of the principal battles of the Army of Northern Virginia, and that its blows were severe and its losses were frightful. In the battles around Richmond, in 1862, the brigade lost eight hundred men killed and wounded. At Chancellorsville it also lost nearly eight hundred men killed and wounded, and of its thirteen field officers, all but one were struck down. At Gettysburg it formed the left of Longstreet's charge, and although it had lost nearly forty per cent. in its three days' fighting, it marched off the field in excellent order when Pickett was routed, and took position in support of the rebel batteries, which some of the brigades of that charge did not do. This organization was among the last soldiers of Lee's army to recross the Potomac, after both Antietam and Gettysburg. North Carolina furnished more men than any other state of the Confederacy, and lost more in action than any of its sister states, and the records show, or seem to show, that her mountaineers struck many of the hardest blows the Army of the Potomac received from the Army of Northern Virginia

While Jackson was being carried down the road Gen. A. P. Hill returned to the front of the Eighteenth North Carolina, and was soon after wounded by a fragment of a Federal shell. At ten o'clock Captain Adams was sent to Ely Ford by Major Pendleton, of Jackson's staff, to recall General Stuart to take command of the army. Why Jackson felt impelled to take this step, and overlook the deserving claims of some of his able division commanders, is not yet clear. Rodes felt indignant at the want of confidence shown in him, and expresses his feeling of grievance briefly in his report of the battle. The others are silent. Stuart belonged to another arm of the service, was a stranger to the corps, and unknown personally to many of its officers. His Adjutant General complains of the lack of support received on his arrival, and states that not one of Jackson's staff, with the exception of Pendleton, reported to him that night.

Captain Adams started for Ely Ford about ten P. M., and

Stuart did not arrive until midnight, or after the midnight reconnaissance of Sickles, and in the meantime Jackson's victorious corps was adrift—almost as much adrift as the Army of the Potomac was when Hooker was disabled. For more than two hours no officer felt at liberty to take any decisive action, and the golden opportunity rapidly passed away. General Heth took command of Hill's Division, and declined to take any active steps. He ordered Lane to withdraw his two regiments from the left of the road to the right of the road, and keep quiet. Pender was placed in Lane's place on the left of the road, and bivouacked in the woods, eight hundred yards from Berry's line of battle, molested no one, and was not molested during the night.

The wounding of Jackson was a most fortunate circumstance for the Army of the Potomac at this moment, and it was certainly fraught with bitter disappointment to the Confederate cause. At nine o'clock the capture or destruction of a large part of Hooker's army seemed inevitable. Thirty minutes later all was changed by Jackson's carelessness or rashness. There was at this time great uncertainty and a feeling akin to panic prevailing among the Union forces around Chancellorsville, and it may be said truthfully that there was considerable of this feeling among the rebels themselves, though flushed with victory. It may be said, with due respect to both armies, that the bravest of men are liable to night terrors, not excepting Cæsar's or Napoleon's hardened veterans.

The advance of Lane's Brigade, even as late as ten P. M., attacking Berry's and Knipe's Brigades in front, while Pender and McGowan, with their brigades, slipped by the Federal right flank, leaving Heth's Brigade in reserve for Lane, would probably have resulted in serious disaster to the Federal army, then concentrated on the Chancellor plateau. The regiments of the Eleventh Corps, the Eighty-second Ohio, Eighty-second Illinois, Twenty-sixth Wisconsin, One Hundred and Fifty-seventh New York, and fragments of other regiments which remained halted on this road in line of battle for some time, had been withdrawn to the rear of the Chancellor House shortly before this hour, and no force had been sent to take their place.   Hays' Brigade rested on the Plank Road in rear of Berry.   Sykes and his regulars were far to the rear on the Ely or U. S. Ford Road, and apparently there was no force, no obstacle, to prevent Pender from marching directly to the field in the rear of Chancellor's.

Jackson undoubtedly felt at seven and at nine P. M. that he was "accompanied by the god of fortune and of war," and after his successful flanking movement directly in front of the Federal army, that nothing could be too absurd or too difficult for him to attempt.   At the hour of nine P. M. Jackson must have felt sure of success, for the field at the White House was about one thousand yards distant, with only the feeble remnants of the beaten Eleventh Corps and a regiment of Berry's Division to oppose him on the direct avenue of approach.   It is in evidence that while Lane's strong brigade was to engage the attention of the enemy at Fairview, Jackson intended to slip up the Bullock Road with Pender's, McGowan's, Heth's and other brigades, which were then close at hand and in readiness to advance, and this explains why Jackson and Hill were at the junction of the Bullock and Mountains Roads instead of being on the Plank Road.   The broad Plank Road in their rear was crowded for a long distance with several battalions of Confederate artillery and their ammunition trains, all ready to advance. The broken brigades of Colston's and Rodes' Divisions were also sufficiently reformed to support Hill's attack.   Williams, at this time, had returned to strengthen the Federal position at Fairview with his division of the Twelfth Corps, but the most of Sickles' force was at or below Hazel Grove, and Barlow's stout brigade was far below and lost in the darkness.   When we consider the position of the Federal army at Chancellorsville at this moment, and how many important battles have been won by trivial flank attacks—how Richepense, with a single brigade, ruined the Austrian army at Hohenlinden by a flank attack, etc.—we must admit that the Federal army was in great peril when Jackson arrived within one thousand yards of its vital point with more than twenty thousand men and fifty cannon, and the only obstacle in the way a handful of beaten soldiers of the wrecked Eleventh Corps, and a regiment of the Third Corps.

Jackson was absolutely fearless, like Admiral Nelson, and he had the power of imparting his intrepidity to those around him.   He was at the same time strangely reticent, abstruse, subtle and mysterious, and none of his officers were in his complete confidence.   It appears from what evidence now remains that his objective point was the White House in rear of Chancellor's, and once there, with the aid of the surrounding forest, which would serve as a fortress—a fortified camp, to which he could retire and from which he could emerge at will—he would have maintained his position with as great certainty as he did at Groveton the year previous. The audacity and experiences of the campaign of 1862 greatly strengthen this view.

CHAPTER XI.

Sickles' Famous "Midnight Charge."

A T Hazel Grove, nearly a mile to the south and right of the Plank Road, two divisions of the Third Corps, returning from the chase of Lee's forces far below the Furnace, were, on arrival, marshaled into columns of attack to retake the Dirt and Plank Roads, and to recover missing guns, caissons and the mule train. Birney's Division was selected for this difficult movement. Ward's Brigade formed the first line of assault, and Hayman's the second. On the left of this force the Dirt Road led to the Plank Road, and here were placed the Fortieth New York, Seventeenth Maine and Sixty-third Pennsylvania, and pushed forward by column of companies. On the right of this column the rest of the brigades, numbering eight regiments, moved in line of battle toward the Plank Road; but soon most of them inclined to the right, toward the position held by the Twelfth Corps.—*See Map No. 9.*

Sickles says that orders were given not to fire a gun until the Plank Road was reached; that the advance, in spite of a terrific fire of musketry and twenty guns at Dowdall's Tavern, was successfully executed; that the line of the Plank Road was regained; that Howard's rifle pits were reoccupied; that all of their guns, caissons, etc., were recovered; that two guns and three caissons of the enemy were captured, and that Jackson was then wounded; that the enemy, thrown into confusion by this attack on his right flank, then advanced on their left and center and attacked Berry's Division, but were repulsed. Sickles also states that the enemy were so completely surprised that they fell back, leaving the communications open.

The attacking column was formed with the Fortieth New York in the lead, with the Seventeenth Maine supporting, in column of companies, and the Sixty-third Pennsylvania as reserve. On the right of the Fortieth New York, the Third and Fourth Maine, the Thirty-eighth New York, and the Ninety-ninth Pennsylvania advanced in line of battle, followed by the First New York, the Third and Fifth Michigan, and the Thirty-seventh New York. The Fortieth New York, which was the famous Mozart Regiment, and of excellent reputation, proceeded with guns uncapped up the road or vista, which was wide at first, but soon became narrow, and on arriving at a point about five hundred yards from the Plank Road, found the Twenty-eighth North Carolina and the Eighteenth North Carolina barring the way and deployed in line of battle. These regiments stopped further progress with a tremendous volley, which threw the Fortieth New York in confusion upon the Seventeenth Maine, which in part, also broke and retreated. The rear companies of the Seventeenth Maine remained firm, and the regiment was soon reformed by Adjutant Roberts, and faced westerly instead of northerly, and here it remained unsupported, until Mc-Gowan's Brigade of South Carolinians was brought up to protect General Lane's flank, when General Ward called it back to the Hazel Grove field. The Seventeenth Maine, in returning, brought back with them the gun and three caissons which a part of the Third Corps had previously left in the vista. The line of battle on the right of the vista found its way impeded by the dense woods and the darkness of the night. The Third Maine Regiment ran into parts of the Eighteenth and Twenty-eighth North Carolina, and were driven back with the loss of several prisoners and their flag. The flag was captured by Captain Neven Clark's company, and afterwards burnt during the evacuation of Richmond. The rest of the assaulting force deviated to the right, and soon attacked portions of the Twelfth Corps, taking them to be Confederates.

Parts of Knipe's and Ruger's Brigades of the Twelfth Corps regarded the noisy crowd in front of them to be rebels, and returned the compliment with a severe fire of musketry and shell, and for a time the useless contest raged with great vigor with both parties. Some of the reports of this midnight encounter are missing, and their publication will throw much light upon its details. On the Federal side it was undoubtedly a mixed up mess, and some of the regiments complain of being fired into from the front and both flanks. Lane regarded the attack simply as a reconnaissance, as it was so easily repulsed by the Eighteenth, Twenty-eighth, and a part of the Thirty-third North Carolina Regiments. Just then the guns at Fairview opened again, and swept the Plank Road and its vicinity with a terrific fire. Had Birney's column succeeded in driving Lane from his position, the Federal fire from the forty-three guns would have prevented him from reaching the Plank Road. As soon as this artillery fire ceased Lane, finding that there was no force whatever defending his right flank, and that there was a wide gap between his right and Colston's line, reformed in the woods some distance to the westward, and went to General Heth and requested him to send some troops to take position on the right of the Twenty-eighth North Carolina, and protect his flank and rear from another attack from Hazel Grove. Lane led McGowan's Brigade into this position, and until this time—past midnight—there was no rebel force between Lane's Brigade and Colston's Division. Skirmishers were then thrown out before the new line, and they encountered the pickets of the Seventeenth Maine Regiment, with whom shots were exchanged. This ended all movements on the Confederate side that night, or until the arrival of Archer and his brigade of Tennesseeans, which was about two A. M. Sunday morning.

Investigation seems to show that Sickles and his forces did not succeed in reaching ground within a mile of Howard's earthworks, or even reach the Plank Road, and that his attack was easily repulsed by two regiments of Lane's Brigade, with trifling loss. It is not easy to see where the cannon shots that he encountered came from, as there were no guns stationed on the Dirt Road. Furthermore, it is extremely doubtful if twenty guns at Dowdall's Tavern, a mile away, opened fire at all. Many of them, at this time, were repairing damages received in the 9.30 cannonade from Best's Artillery. Another reason why they did not fire was because they could not throw their shot safely a mile through the woods wherein Colston's and Rodes' broken columns were reforming and taking position for the morning's attack. And another equally potent reason is the fact that the rebels did not know that Sickles was making the desperate attempt he describes. In fact, the Confederates were utterly unaware of the magnitude of Birney's attack until they read the glowing accounts of its prowess in the northern press, long after the event. The claim of wounding Jackson is weakened by the fact that he had been wounded two hours or more before, and was at this time miles distant. The guns and caissons he captured were his own, which had been left in the road when Winn and his foragers stampeded the Third Corps crowd left resting in the vista; but the mule train had long ago gone, to be credited to the disgrace of another corps. The redoubts claimed to have been captured were those constructed by Birney's Division of the Third Corps.

When Winn and his Georgians left in haste, after the cessation of Pleasanton's, or rather Huntington's, artillery fire, he neglected to take with him these guns, caissons, etc., and so they remained under the nose of Pleasanton for four hours, and no rebel within five hundred yards of them until after ten P. M. Birney not only failed to open the desired avenue of travel, but lost a number of men, of whom many were missing; it is a mystery where the missing went. The Eighteenth North Carolina captured but three, the Twenty-eighth North Carolina several, and the Thirty-third none.

The roads leading to the United States Ford have been reported as filled with stragglers of the Eleventh Corps, but General Meagher, who was in charge of the Provost Guard on the Ford Road, says they were not all Eleventh Corps men. Moreover, General Patrick, who was in charge of the Provost Guard at the United States Ford, was quoted at the mass meeting held in New York, June 2d, 1863, as saying that the stragglers arrested there were not Eleventh Corps men.   Birney lost the flag of one of his best regiments, a fine horse, several officers and men, and retired his troops the next morning through the swampy place leading to Fairview, where Pleasanton saw the great pile of debris of a corps that did not go within half a mile of it.

In relation to the attack on Berry, as described by Sickles, it may be said that Pender's Brigade was deployed in front of Berry, at the distance of eight hundred yards. The dense woods that intervened gave Pender's men a feeling of security, and they tried to sleep, and succeeded after the midnight cannonade ceased.   Pender's Brigade made no attack whatever on May 2d, 1863, but on the morning of the 3d of May, at seven A. M., it struck its first blow since the battle of Fredericksburg, and swept the First Brigade of the Third Corps out of its entrenchments without hesitation, and in quite as brief a space of time as when Rodes' rebel division overwhelmed Von Gilsa's Brigade (without entrenchments or supports) the evening before.   The reports of Berry and his men causing Jackson's Corps to halt are erroneous.   Berry did not go within a mile of the positions lost by the Eleventh Corps, and neither Colston nor Rodes, Lane nor Hill knew before 9.30 P. M. that Berry and his men were in the woods at the foot of the hill where the batteries were placed, four hundred yards in the rear.

The statement made that the First Corps, arriving late at night, occupied some of the positions abandoned by the Eleventh Corps, is erroneous.   The position to which the First Corps was led by Captain Candler, of Hooker's staff, was two miles or more distant from Buschbeck's line of battle, and more than three miles from the place where Von Gilsa attempted to fight.   None of the First Corps saw Dowdall's Tavern, excepting those carried there as prisoners of war.

Birney's Division of the Third Corps was one of the best in the Federal army, but this midnight adventure, so brilliantly described at the time, appears now to have been one of the most comical episodes in the history of the Army of the Potomac, and if the suppressed reports can be found this view may prove to be correct. At all events, after reading the reports of General Sickles at the time, and his statement a year afterwards to Congress—the brilliant array of gallant troops in the moonlight—the bold attack—the quick return of one of the columns, to be stopped by the bayonets of the Sixty-third Pennsylvania—the advance of the other column, deflecting to the right until it met General Slocum in person—certainly there is a slight occasion for a smile on the part of the reader. And this smile may be lengthened on reading the story of General De Trobriand, who was a participator, or the account left by Colonel Underwood, of the Thirty-third Massachusetts, who, returned from the depths of the Wilderness in time to witness and describe the ludicrous scene.

But all the comicality was not witnessed at Hazel Grove. When the woods resounded with the imprecations and the heavy tread of Birney's veterans, the men of the Twelfth Corps, under Knipe and Williams, were aroused by the approaching noises, and fired artillery and musketry into the darkness, causing severe loss to the Federal troops, according to the views of General Slocum, who had not been informed of the intended movement. The Twenty-seventh Indiana reports an attack with terrific yells, and the Third Wisconsin was fired into before and behind without a rebel appearing in sight. The Thirteenth New Jersey, wishing to take some part in the pyrotechnics, being in the second line of battle, fired into the Third Wisconsin, broke it up partly, and again for the second time during the evening took to its heels. In the meantime, the left half of Lane's Brigade, lying flat on their faces to escape the shot and shell of Best's artillery, wondered what was going on in their right front. No enemy appeared to challenge them, but the yells and strange noises indicated a breaking loose of pandemonium, and caused some trepidation to the superstitiously inclined. But even to this day, most of Lane's survivors are ignorant of what caused the circus in front and on the right flank.

At eight P. M. that evening there was a broad gap of

more than half a mile in width, extending from Green's Brigade of the Twelfth Corps northwest to the Confederate troops of Lane's Brigade, on and near the Plank Road. Through this gap and up its ravine the grand skedaddle, which Pleasanton and others have so elegantly described and erroneously credited to the Eleventh Corps, took place. Through this wide gap Williams' Division of the Twelfth Corps had no difficulty in squeezing, on returning from the front early in the evening, and it seemed broad enough for Sickles and his men to pass without attempting to open the Hazel Grove road. In fact, his troops finally reached the Fairview Plateau by this pathway in the ravine, and not a man of them went by way of the Plank Road. This broad gap remained open to the Federal arms until sunrise of the next morning, May 3d, when Hazel Grove and its approaches were seized and held by Archer's Brigade of Tennesseeans. A useless sacrifice of Lane's and Ramseur's Brigades of North Carolinians was made on Sunday morning, before Stuart recognized the vast importance of Archer's capture. Then about forty cannon were placed in battery in the field at Hazel Grove, which enfiladed the Federal batteries and redoubts at Fairview with a rapid and withering fire, and with the assistance of Hardaway's guns, to the south and east of Chancellorsville, rendered the plateau utterly untenable, deciding the fate of the campaign in about an hour. The inoffensive midnight charge of Sickles and Birney at the Hazel Grove Farm, and the terrific cannonade at the same time from the Federal batteries at Fairview, closed the evening's entertainment. Stuart arrived about this time, and, uncertain what to do in the absence of Hill and Jackson, and all the members of his staff but one, commanded rest and silence. The tired Confederates soon sank to sleep, and nothing disturbed the oppressive stillness of the evening air save the renewed songs of the startled whip-poor-wills and the subdued sounds of the Federal troops building barricades for the inevitable conflict of the next morning.

SUMMARY.

Where the Blame Properly Belongs.

THE findings of this inquiry show, or seem to show, that warnings of the massing of the enemy's forces on the flank and rear of the Eleventh Corps were sent at different times to the headquarters of the First Division and to the corps, but we have not found any evidence to show that they were forwarded to army headquarters at Chancellor's. Neither do we find any evidence to show that either Devens, Howard or Hooker took any measures after midday to ascertain if the right flank of the Army of the Potomac was free from danger. There is, however, abundant testimony to prove that General Devens, commanding the exposed flank, was warned again and again, by several of his officers, of imminent danger from the presence of a large force of the enemy massing on his flank and rear. But the commander of the First Division utterly refused to listen to the admonitions and the advice of his officers, and even after the attack was commenced, he declined to allow his regiments attacked or threatened in flank and in rear to change front while there was time to change. Furthermore, it appears that the resistance of this division, placed in such adverse circumstances and overwhelmed by a vastly superior force, was all that could reasonably be expected of it. To have remained fifteen minutes longer would have resulted in capture or destruction. The hurried retreat of some of the survivors of this division broke the formation of some of the best regiments of the Third Division—Schurz's—then drawn up in line of battle in the rear to receive the impending attack. Nevertheless, it appears that the rest of the Third Division, with many rallied from the wreck of the First Division, did make a stand, and resisted the enemy until overwhelmed and outflanked by superior numbers. It also appears that many of the men of the First (Devens') and the Third Divisions (Schurz's) did rally at the unfinished rifle pits of Barlow, and did resist with Buschbeck's Brigade, in the presence of more than twenty thousand men, until both flanks were turned and retreat or capture was inevitable.   It also appears that the retreat from this third and last attack was conducted in an orderly manner, and that Buschbeck's Brigade retired in complete order.   It seems that there was no active pursuit by the enemy at this time, and that the rear guard, with Dilger, and one gun in the road, and Busch-beck's Brigade in battle order, retreated unmolested down the road to Fairview, where Buschbeck's Brigade formed in line of battle in front of the Federal guns, and remained there until Sunday morning.

It also appears that a large number of the soldiers of the Third Division halted, by order of General Schurz, on the Bullock Road, north of the Plank Road, and protected for several hours that approach to the rear of the Chancellor House.   Beside these, there were several hundred of the Eleventh Corps men halted behind the batteries at Fair-view, where some of them remained during the night.   All these positions were taken before Berry's Division reached the position taken by it, about four hundred yards in advance of the Federal cannon and on the Plank Road.   The attack on the Eleventh Corps at Von Gilsa's position commenced at 5.30 P. M., and ceased at 7 or 7.15, when the Federal troops retreated from the Buschbeck line, and then Jackson ordered his tired and disordered battalions to halt at and around the Dowdall Tavern, two miles distant from the Chancellor House.   The statements that Berry's Division of the Third Corps, and that Huntington's guns at Hazel Grove, halted the victorious rebels, are erroneous ; for no line of battle of Jackson's army at the time, or during the night, approached within seven hundred to one thousand yards of Berry, with dense woods intervening.   And all the infantry that appeared in Pleasanton's front and in front of Huntington's guns was a group of foragers from Doles' Brigade, who promptly took to their heels without the loss of a man, when the artillery ceased firing, leaving behind them the cannon and caissons they had fairly won in the vista.

In fact, all the resistance Jackson's army met with on Saturday afternoon and evening, up to the time he was wounded—except the few cannon shots from Osborne's guns at Fairview at eight P. M.—was from the broken three divisions of the Eleventh Corps, numbering but nine thousand men, and attacked in flank and rear and overwhelmed in detail.   Analysis shows, or seems to show, that this resistance, in three attempts, was commendable under the circumstances, and that no other body of equal or even much larger numbers of troops of the Army of the Potomac could have held the flanked positions much longer and escaped complete destruction.   Furthermore, it appears that this resistance of the Eleventh Corps cost them nearly sixteen hundred men, killed and wounded, or more than five hundred more men than the British army lost at the bloody battle of Bunker Hill, and that it retarded the progress of Jackson's army for an hour and a half after it struck Von Gilsa, only about one mile distant from the last position assumed by the wrecks of the Eleventh Corps at the Buschbeck line, near the Dowdall Tavern.   This delay of one hour and a half of the enemy late in the afternoon, near sunset, was of extreme importance to the safety of the Army of the Potomac entrenched in front of Chancellor's, and especially of the twenty thousand men who had gone with Sickles down in the dense forests, two or three miles south of the Plank Road, in search of the "retreating" foe.

The investigation clearly shows that the story of the fearful panic and disordered retreat of men and animals, with cannon, etc., which startled Pleasanton at Hazel Grove, and was ascribed by him as belonging to the Eleventh Corps, was entirely misplaced, for it is proved that not one of the men, animals or vehicles seen in this picturesque tumult belonged to the Eleventh Corps.   Furthermore, it can be shown that the fearful panic which Hooker has described in front of the

Chancellor House and on Fairview was caused by and very largely composed of the troops of other corps, who came up from the southward and from Hazel Grove, where the Eleventh Corps had never been. In fact, the stragglers and wrecks of the Eleventh Corps had reached the rear or vicinity of the Chancellor House some time before these stampedes took place. And at the time of the panic, the rear guard and fragments of the crushed corps were then actually in line of battle behind Dilger's guns and the Federal batteries on Fairview, or with Buschbeck's Brigade in front of the batteries or in position on the Bullock Road, nearly a third of a mile north of the Plank Road, while Barlow's Brigade of nearly three thousand men of the Eleventh Corps were three or four miles south in the woods, searching for the enemy and for Birney's Division of Sickles' Corps, and unconscious of the disasters that had taken place in their rear. The abundant abuse heaped upon the members of the corps of a German name or descent does not appear to be at all justified by fact, and it can be shown that with few exceptions they fought as well as many other troops fought under similar conditions, and that the typical German organization known as Buschbeck's Brigade acted with great firmness, and retreated in perfect order in the face of the victorious enemy.

The investigation clearly proves that the disastrous results of the battle of Chancellorsville cannot be justly ascribed to the want of vigilance and soldierly conduct on the part of the rank and file of the Eleventh Corps. Furthermore, we may properly say that these unjust imputations and imprecations, which have been scattered far and wide over the land for the last thirty years, blighting the honor and embittering the life of ten thousand deserving soldiers, ought to have been righted long ago, and would have been if some of the West Point officers in command in the Army of the Potomac had shown common fairness, or if the War Department had ordered an impartial investigation, which was earnestly asked for by some of the officers of the corps.

LOSSES OF
THE CONTENDING FORCES

RESULTS OF THE CONFLICT.

Losses of the Contending Forces.

THE losses of the Eleventh Corps at Chancellorsville have been variously estimated, and given by the official records, as 2,412 killed, wounded and missing—1,438 killed and wounded and 974 missing. The statement of Howard of May 13, 1863, made the loss 2,508, which was the estimate given by Hooker to Congress two years afterward. It is evident, from the state records completed since the war, that the official estimate of loss was not accurately given, that the actual loss in killed and wounded was much greater than at first given, and that the entire loss of the corps on the 2d of May, 1863, was more than 2,600 men, of which 130 were officers killed and wounded. The official records of Ohio give to the four regiments of that state in Mc-Lean's Brigade a loss of 119 greater than is shown by the official returns at Washington. The official records show that but 9 men were killed in the 55th Ohio, but it is now shown that 27 men were killed or mortally wounded, and that the number reported as wounded was much too small. Many of those who were reported at first as missing are now known to have been killed. Surgeon Suckley, the Medical Director of the corps, remained at the Dowdall Tavern to look after the wounded. Suckley was an old army officer, and, being of a jovial disposition, had been a favorite with many or most of the rebel officers who had left the regular army to join the Southern cause. They were delighted to find their old comrade at the Dowdall Tavern, and treated him with great distinction, placing the Federal wounded under his charge, not only of his own corps but probably some of those of other corps wounded on Sunday, as he stated to one of his assistants that he had 1,100 wounded under his care, but did not state from what corps. Surgeon Suckley lost his horse in the melee about the Dowdall Farm, but General Stuart ordered a special search for the lost animal, and soon restored it to him. When Suckley was relieved from his duties and returned to his corps at Stafford Court House, he appeared in the full new uniform of a rebel colonel, having made an exchange of clothing during the hilarity of the last meeting with his old associates of the regular army then in the Army of Northern Virginia.

The losses of Jackson's forces in this contest of Saturday will never be accurately known, as nearly all of the regiments reckoned their losses collectively for the whole campaign. General Rodes, in mentioning his severe loss, intimates that quite a proportion of it occurred on the first day. General Colston also admits a loss. Some of the attacking regiments admit severe loss—the 12th Alabama 76 men, and the 10th Virginia about 50 killed and wounded, including some valuable officers.

Certainly the dense masses of Jackson's infantry must have lost many men during the canister fire of Dilger's Battery, even if they had escaped the musketry of the Federal infantry at the three successive lines of resistance. General Doles, whose brigade led the attack, states (p. 967): "In this engagement—Saturday—we lost many gallant men killed and wounded." We may form some estimate of their losses from he admitted casualties among the officers known to have fallen in the fight with the Eleventh Corps. And in this list we find the names of Colonels Cook, Hobson, Stalling and Warren ; Majors Bryan and Rowe ; also Captains Bisel, Credille, Allen, Green, Burnside, Phelan and Watkins.

The estimate of the casualties in the Confederate army in the whole campaign, as given in the official records, is believed to be much less than the actual loss. Many of the slightly wounded are not given, by Order No. 63 of General Lee. In Colston's return they are not estimated, and Rodes also omits them. Trivial scratches with the old soldier frequently proved to be serious or fatal wounds in a brief space of time. It was frequently stated in the South after Chancellorsville— and to the writer by competent authority—that the loss of the Army of Northern Virginia in that battle was enormous, and was not far from 17,000 men, but the official returns show only a loss of about 13,000 men, though in this return there are seven brigades which make no return of any missing. Longstreet, in his late work on the Army of Northern Virginia, states that " General Lee was actually so crippled by his victory that he was a full month restoring his army to condition to take the field."

It may be proper to note that in the return of the losses in Colston's Division, he gives his loss as 1,859 killed and wounded, without counting the slightly wounded. (Page 1008, Vol. XXV.)

Rodes also (page 949), in a foot-note to his list of killed and wounded, numbering 2,976, adds : "This list does not embrace the only slightly wounded." General Lee, in his Order No. 63 (Vol. XXV., Part II., page 798), forbids the mention of those wounded who are able to be placed on duty.

The North Carolinians lost in this battle 2,721 men killed and wounded. General Lane lost 739, Pender 693, Iverson 370, Ramseur 623, and two regiments of North Carolina troops lost 296 more. The Georgians in the brigades of Thomas, Doles and Colquitt lost 736 men. Virginia, in the four brigades of Heth, Paxton, Jones and three regiments of Colston, lost 1,532 men.

According to the official returns, the losses of the Eleventh Corps are as follows, but they are much larger according to later returns :

Von Gilsa's Brigade lost 133 men killed and wounded : 41st New York, killed and wounded, 30 ; 45th New York, killed and wounded, 32 ; 54th New York, killed and wounded, 25 ; 153d Pennsylvania, killed and wounded, 46.   Total loss of brigade, killed and wounded, 133 men.

McLean's Brigade : 17th Connecticut, killed and wounded, 42 ; 25th Ohio, 121 ; 55th Ohio, 96 ; 75th Ohio, 74 ; 107th Ohio, 59 killed and wounded.   Total loss of McLean's Brigade, killed and wounded, 393 men.

Buschbeck's Brigade : 29th New York, 57 ; 157th New York, 87 ; 27th Pennsylvania, 37 ; 73d Pennsylvania, 74.   Total loss of Buschbeck's Brigade, killed and wounded, 225 men.

Schimmelpfennig's Brigade : 82d Illinois, 107 ; 68th New York, 21 ; 157th New York, 79 ; 61st Ohio, 60 ; 74th Pennsylvania, 22.   Total loss of Schimmelpfennig's Brigade, killed and wounded, 289 men.

Kryzanowski's Brigade : 58th New York, 11 ; 119th New York, 78 ; 75th Pennsylvania—on picket—8 ; 26th Wisconsin, 158.   Total loss of Kryzanowski's Brigade, killed and wounded, 254 men.

The 82d Ohio, 56 ; batteries and staff, 39.   Total loss of corps, killed and wounded, 1,419 men, not including Barlow's Brigade, not in the battle.   Corrected accounts make the total loss as exceeding 1,500 killed and wounded men.

Official returns of the losses of Revere's Brigade, Third Corps, during the campaign : 70th New York, 15 ; 71st New York, 16 ; 72d New York, 42 ; 73d New York, 34 ; 74th New York, 25 ; 102d New York, 53. Total loss of Revere's Brigade, killed and wounded, 186 men.

Ward's Brigade of the Third Corps : 20th Indiana, 20 ; 3d Maine, 21 ; 4th Maine, 18 ; 38th New York, 18 ; 40th New York, 41 ; 99th Pennsylvania, 17.   Total loss of Ward's Brigade, killed and wounded, 135 men.

Hayman's Brigade, Third Corps : 17th Maine, 75 ; 3d Michigan, 53 ; 5th Michigan, 50 ; 1st New York, 21 ; 37th New York, 114.   Total loss of Hayman's Brigade, killed and wounded, 313 men.

Knipe's Brigade, Twelfth Corps : 5th Connecticut, 20 ; 28th New York, 7 ; 46th Pennsylvania, 18 ; 128th Pennsylvania, 13.   Total loss of Knipe's Brigade, killed and wounded, 58 men.

Devens' two brigades of nine regiments lost 526 men killed and wounded, while two brigades of eleven regiments of Birney's Division lost but 448 killed and wounded ; or, the two brigades of Revere and Ward, of twelve regiments, lost but 321 killed and wounded, while the two brigades of Schurz's Division of nine regiments lost 543 killed and wounded.

The entire Third Corps lost at the battles of Fair Oaks or Seven Pines but 1,154 men killed and wounded.   The Second Corps lost at the same time but 1,095 men killed and wounded.

At the battle of Williamsburg, where Hooker fought with his division, which Heintzleman said mustered 9,000 men, and where he fought more or less during the day, he lost but 1,215 men killed and wounded. The 9,000 men of the Eleventh Corps at Chancellorsville, attacked in flank and rear, lost in one hour and a half 1,500 or more men killed and wounded.

It has been stated that the men of the Eleventh Corps had not seen any hard fighting before it joined the Army of the Potomac, but the records seem to show that the First Corps, which afterwards formed the Eleventh, lost at the second battle of Bull Run 1,656 men killed and wounded out of the twenty regiments and nine batteries, while the Third Corps, out of fifty regiments and fifteen batteries, lost 3,448 men killed and wounded, and should have lost 4,140 men to have equaled the loss of the twenty regiments of the First Corps, estimating by regiments.

It has been said that the artillery of Devens' Division retired without firing a shot, but the evidence shows that the rebels were greeted with a severe fire from artillery somewhere from the Federal front, and as there were no guns stationed on the front line but the two on picket, the grape and canister must have come from the two guns of Dieckman, stationed in the angle of Von Gilsa's line, in the Turnpike, and from no others, as Dilger's Battery could not have come into action until his front was cleared of Devens' infantry, which was not until about half an hour afterwards. The other four guns of Dieckman's Battery, according to some accounts, ran away, and did not stop to take part in the action. Others say that the men ran away and left the guns in position, where they were taken by the enemy. But the accounts are so conflicting that the compiler is at loss what to accept, and the records are so incomplete that it is difficult to even form an opinion. It is certain, however, that the guns were placed in battery to command the Plank Road, and as there was no enemy appearing on the Plank Road, there was nothing for them to fire at, and in order to reach the enemy attacking on the Pike in their rear, they would have had to fire through the 17th Connecticut, who were drawn up to their right flank and rear. What became of these guns is a matter of much uncertainty to the compiler, and he does not surely know whether they remained where they were placed or were lost in the rush that followed the wrecking of Devens' Division. The report is lost, and the records of the Ordnance Department cannot solve the mystery. General Hunt, the Chief of Artillery of the Federal army, says that the Eleventh Corps lost but 8 guns and the rest of the army 6, or 14 in all. General Lee claims but 13, and his Chief of Ordinance reports only 13, and describes them. We know that Archer captured, on Sunday morning, 4 guns from the Third Corps, and later Jastram's Battery, of the same corps, lost another, or 5 guns in all. But who lost the sixth? Possibly the Eleventh lost 9 guns instead of 8. From the reports we are unable to solve the problem, and the Ordinance Department at Washington cannot decide the question. There is much confusion in the reports, and if we accept the reports of Jackson's army verbatim, we will find that they captured from the Eleventh Corps alone 24 guns, while General Lee claims but 13 in the campaign. One battery of the reserve artillery in the field north of the Dowdall House came into action when Schurz's line fell back from the western edge of the Hawkins Farm, half a mile north of Devens' men, but they could fire only solid shot or shell over the heads of the lines of infantry drawn up in front of them at a distance of more than half a mile on the Hawkins Farm and to the northwest of the little Church. The shallow rifle pit constructed in front of the reserve artillery left but little space for the artillery to manœuver, and the three batteries were withdrawn and sent to the rear before or when Bush-beck's line came into action. There was but one piece of artillery in action in the Bushbeck line, and that was Dilger's. There are conflict-ing accounts as to the condition of the artillery when it appeared at Fairview. Some, and, for instance, Hunt, the Chief of Artillery, and Warren, state that it came off in good conditon, and was used in the Best line at Fairview. There seems to be no reason why it should not arrive in good condition, as there was no pursuit in its rear, and the line of infantry along the Bushbeck rifle pit remained fighting some time after the guns were ordered to the rear. Dilger, retreating with his one gun, found the remains of his battery in line with Best's guns, and was com-plimented by Best on its condition.

The loss of material by the Army of the Potomac is a matter of interest to the student who seeks details of the campaign. General Ingalls called for the losses of knapsacks by the corps engaged, and the First Corps reported that the Third Brigade, mostly New Jersey men, threw away about one half of their knapsacks, estimate, 1,000 ; Second Division about 80. First Brigade, Third Division, 7 ; Second Brigade, Third Division, about 300 — 1,387. The Second Corps reports a loss of 2,195. Rusling, of the Third Corps, judges that the corps lost only 700 knapsacks, but as Revere reports a total loss of knapsacks by his bri-gade of six regiments—the First Massachusetts a loss of 157 more, and the Sixteenth Massachusetts all of theirs—the loss of the corps must have been 3,000 or more—say 3,000. The Fifth Corps reports a loss of 5,381 ; the Sixth Corps 8,787 ; the Eleventh Corps 6,009 ; the Twelfth Corps 4,614, making a total of 31,374 knapsacks lost by the Army of the Potomac.

In estimating the loss of the Eleventh Corps, it should be borne in mind that quite one-half of the whole loss was sustained by Barlow's Brigade, who deposited their knapsacks in the Dowdall Field when they went south two or three miles to support Birney below the Furnace, and did not return.

ADDENDA

NOTES, CORRESPONDENCE AND REMARKS.

General Lee not Surprised.

A S to the claim that Hooker surprised General Lee by his flank movement, by moving up the river, there is some doubt about it. Pleasanton states in Scribner's Magazine (Vol. III., p. 173), that he captured at Germania Ford an engineer officer of General Stuart's staff, with a big diary, in which it was stated that the first week in March a council of war had been held at General Stuart's headquarters, that Jackson, Hill, Ewell and Stuart were present, that the conference lasted five hours, and that it was there decided that in their opinion the next battle would take place at or near Chancellorsville. General Colston also has stated in his article in Scribner's Magazine that General Lee was not surprised by Hooker's movement, but expected the attack to come from the direction of the United States Ford. Longstreet states in· his late work that it was originally the intention of the Confederates, if attacked, to remain in their entrenchments around Fredericksburg until he could return with his force from south of Petersburg, and it was estimated that the 60,000 men entrenched were equal to Hooker's entire army.

Strength of the Two Armies.

The Army of the Potomac had on its rolls, the 30th of April, just before the advance movement, about 130,000 men, "for duty and equipped," exclusive of the Provost Guard. The exact number of soldiers under Hooker's command and actually present, May 1st, it is not easy now to determine, but it probably amounted to 120,000 men, or about double the strength of the Army of Northern Virginia.

A few days before the advance, President Lincoln visited Hooker and the army at Falmouth, and while in his tent alone with Noah Brooks, Lincoln took from his pocket a scrap of paper and handed it to Brooks. On this scrap were written these figures : " 216,718—146,000 —169,000," which Lincoln said represented the number on the rolls, the actual available force, and the last the strength to which the force might be increased.

Hooker assured Lincoln at the time that he was going straight to Richmond, if he lived, but his bravado impressed the President with very serious misgivings, and he exclaimed to one of his confidential friends: "It is about the worst thing I have seen since I have been down here." It is, perhaps, proper to state that of Hooker's force, the time of service of more than 20,000 men would expire in a few days, and that a marked discontent and insubordination had been rife among some of the regiments of one of the Northern States—so much so as to excite the fears of Franklin, Burnside, and others.

Longstreet gives the number of men in the Army of the Potomac available for line of battle as 113,838, as taken from Return Records (Vol. XXV., p. 320), and gives the number in the Confederate army as 59,681 as the effective aggregate for the month of March, and adds that possibly 1,000 more returned to the army during April.

NOTE NO. 3.

Discontent and Jealousy.

The feeling of discontent and jealousy among the higher officers of the army at this time was disgraceful, and the fact of such a condition is well established by many observers. In the article published in Scribner's Magazine (Vol. XIX.), by Henry J. Raymond, editor of the New York *Times*, who was well qualified to judge on the subject—having served on the staff of the French Emperor at Montebello and Solferino, in Italy—it is shown that there was an incredible want of patriotism among many of the officers high in command. Burnside stated to him that Generals Franklin, Smith, Hooker, Newton, Sturgis and Woodbury —all West Pointers—had done everything they could to thwart him in his movements; that Hooker was in the habit of abusing all in authority over him, to the scandal and the serious injury of the service; also that he (Hooker) had denounced him as incompetent, and the President and Government at Washington as imbecile and played out. Burnside stated to Raymond that he thought of removing several of these selfish officers, and that if Hooker resisted he would hang him before night. After Burnside was relieved, several of these officers were also relieved of their commands, or were sent away with the Ninth Corps. Raymond believed that the mass of the army was loyal and sound, and that the whole demoralization was with the officers. This unfortunate condition of things has been clearly proved by other authorities. General Walker, in his History of the Second Corps, gives much information on the subject at this period of the war. General Walker clearly states the condition of feeling in the army when he remarks that at the time, and later on, as Doubleday bluntly stated: "There always has been a great deal of favoritism in the Army of the Potomac." In fact, the army, up to the time of the Wilderness battles, was highly fermented with jealousy and rank suspicion. Birney, Howe and Pleasanton did not hesitate to say that they had no confidence in Meade as commander. Butterfield told the Committee of Congress (p. 83) that there was a conspiracy among the corps commanders against Hooker. Hancock said to the committee that the Eleventh Corps had never been considered a part of the original Army of the Potomac, and that not much dependence had been placed upon it. Hooker was urged after the battle by several officers of rank to break up the Eleventh Corps, and the reason why he did not do so was that gold was very high, the draft was coming on, and the question might precipitate an unpleasant subject upon the Administration. Walker also states (p. 10) that the Eleventh Corps had never been greatly depended upon in the plans of the commanding general, and that after the battle the troops of the corps were hardly regarded even as reserves. Hooker, in his letter to Lincoln of May 7, 1863, says that a glorious victory would have crowned his efforts but for one corps—meaning the Eleventh. Warren spoke the truth when he affirmed that the whole army needed reorganization.

NOTE NO. 4.

Characteristics of Jackson and Lee.

Jackson was singularly reticent, and his maxim was: "Mystery is the secret of success in war, as in all transactions of human life." None of his staff were informed of his intentions that night, but his laconic instructions to General Hill to press the enemy and cut them off from the United States Ford ; and the detailing of Captain Boswell, of his own staff, to show him (Hill) the way to the rear of the Chancellor House ; and the brief order to General Lane to attack, are sufficient evidence to show what Jackson's intentions were. Between Jackson and his able lieutenant, General A. P. Hill, the relations were somewhat strained, for Jackson had placed Hill under arrest two or three times during previous campaigns, and the good services of General Lee were required to adjust the difficulties. Hill was wounded by the Federal artillery half an hour before Captain Adams was sent for General Stuart, and we have no evidence that Jackson was prejudiced against Hill in this selection of his successor in command.

General Robert E. Lee stood in the old Federal army as one of the ablest, if not the ablest, officer in it, and his withdrawal from it at the call of his native state was regarded as a serious loss to the Union cause. Lee was admirably qualified, both by art and nature, as a leader of men. Envy was unknown to him and suspicion loathsome to his nature, and in his influence over the southern Hotspurs, he showed much of that admirable tact which distinguished the great Marlborough.

NOTE NO. 5.

The Cavalry, and Results.

Hooker expected much from his two cavalry expeditions under Averill and Stoneman, and he had ample reason to complain of the ridiculous results. Our cavalry exercised an important influence in several of our campaigns, and made victory possible. Appomattox would not have been known but for the cavalry. At Winchester the horsemen turned the tide of battle, and at Fisher's Hill the victory would have been far more decisive if Averill had led his horsemen to the attack of the routed enemy instead of ordering them into bivouac—which Sheridan resented with Averill's dismissal. It was a mere handful of resolute horsemen which dashed into the rear of Early's army, retreating from Cedar Creek with their spoils of the Federal army, and captured single handed more than forty pieces of cannon—one of the greatest feats in the war. Hannibal gained all his victories by his Numidian horse. Napoleon won many of his great battles with his heavy cavalry, and Marlborough decided with his German dragoons the famous battles of Blenheim, Ramillies, and Malplaquet.

NOTE NO. 6.

Sickles' Blunder.

Sickles, chafing under the sight of Jackson's men marching under his nose with utter indifference, obtained permission from Hooker to send Birney and his division down to the Furnace to harass the column, and a little later he took Williams' Division of the Twelfth Corps, and later the Barlow Brigade from the Eleventh Corps, both, according to Hooker, without his permission. Advancing without much opposition, he found the head of his column below the Welford House at the hour of seven P. M. The enemy had completely disappeared, and apparently there was nothing to oppose his troops between Hazel Grove and the Ohio River. Birney was preparing to bivouac at or below the Welford House, and Sickles told the Committee of Congress that he was about to attack the rear of Jackson with his whole force when an aid of Howard's told him that our men were retreating, which he would not believe, as he had heard no sounds of battle. Sickles was completely hypnotized with the idea that Lee was retreating, and urged Hooker to send him Berry's Division, which, however, was refused. Sickles sent for Pleasanton and his cavalry to assist, for everything indicated the most brilliant success. He felt very indignant at the officer who informed him of the rout of the Eleventh Corps, and was very much surprised when assured that Jackson was directly in his rear. Sickles stated to Congress that the cause of the failure of the campaign was due "to the giving way of the Eleventh Corps on Saturday,'' which was very true, and it is also true that there were no 9,000 men in the Army of the Potomac who could have stopped the overwhelming numbers of Jackson's army. Sickles further stated to Congress that he lost but one gun—stalled—stuck in the mud.

NOTE NO. 7.

Warnings of the Enemy's Movements.

Abundant evidence has been laid before the compiler to convince him that the picket line was fully established and on the alert. Captain Searles, of the Forty-first New York, has shown him the position he occupied that afternoon with a body of sharpshooters, quite a thousand yards in advance of Von Gilsa's line, on the Pike. On the right of Searles was another body of sharpshooters under Lieutenant Boecke, and warnings were sent back by them to the commanding officers in the rear several times. While retreating to the main line Searles lost one of his men by the Federal fire. There is abundant evidence to show that the line was extended completely around the exposed flank. The people at the Hawkins Farm brought in several wounded Federal soldiers who had been wounded as pickets in the woods, far to the flank and rear of Von Gilsa's line. The Signal Officer, Castle, states that he was stationed on the right of the Eleventh Corps, and reported all movements of the enemy to Howard at Locust Grove (Dowdall's). At 4.30 P. M. he reported an attack on the pickets. At five P. M. he states that the main force of the enemy swept down en masse. In less than fifteen minutes they were within forty rods of his position, and then he retreated to Locust Grove (Dowdall's), about two miles west of Chancellor's,

Acting Major Owen Rice, One Hundred and Fifty-third Pennsylvania Regiment, in command of a part of the picket line, sent to Von Gilsa warning of a great body of the enemy massing in his front, at 2.45 P. M. Von Gilsa told Rice the next day that he personally presented this dispatch to Howard, and was repulsed with taunts. (See page 379 of Vol. I. of the Loyal Legion of Ohio, 1888.) Von Gilsa, in 1864, requested that he and Rice be allowed to testify before the Committee on the Conduct of the War, but was refused (p. 379). Shortly before the attack the entire line of pickets was inspected by a staff officer, and found to be in place.

Col. J. C. Lee, of the Fifty-fifth Ohio, published an account of what he saw and did, in the *National Tribune* of March 19th, 1885. He affirmed that he sent out Captain Rollins to the picket line to ascertain the meaning of the movements of the enemy in his front, and that between eleven A. M. and four P. M. three messengers were sent by him to Colonel Lee, stating that artillery and infantry in heavy force were passing in front to the right flank of the Federal army. Colonel Lee took these scouts to Devens and McLean, and insisted that some action should be taken, but was rebuked. After this event more scouts were sent out, and brought back the information that a large body of the enemy were on our right flank, and apparently resting on their arms. Captain Culp, who was attached to the staff of General McLean, states that there is no proof on record that any attempt was made to ascertain the truth or falsity of the reports sent in from the picket line, and he doubts if any of them ever reached the headquarters of the corps.

Surgeon Robert Hubbard, of the Seventeenth Connecticut, a man of distinction and of strict integrity, was present at the Talley House, sometimes called the Hatch House, for several hours after noon, and has given the compiler much information of what occurred there during this time. He was present both times when Colonel Lee came to inform Devens of the massing of the enemy on his flank. The second time he came he brought a farmer and several scouts, who informed Devens that the rebels were advancing, but Devens refused to believe it, and said to Colonel Lee with decided emphasis, " You are frightened, sir !" Devens was at the time lying down on his back on a sofa nursing his leg, which had been injured by his horse running into a tree the day before. As Surgeon Hubbard left the house, and had crossed the road to the north side, one of the first cannon balls fired by the enemy struck the ground between him and the Talley House. Devens, according to Hubbard's statement, was then lying on the sofa in the farm house, and there is other evidence to show that this statement is correct.

NOTE NO. 8.

Further Warnings.

The warnings given at various times to the higher officers of the corps were numerous. Lieutenant Colonel Carmichael, of the One Hundred and Fifty-seventh New York, stated in writing in June that he and Colonel Lockman went on picket the night before the attack, heard Jackson's preparations, and went to corps headquarters and gave the information, and received as reply : " You are new troops, and more frightened than hurt." Major Schleiter, of the Seventy-fourth Pennsylvania, was ordered to reconnoitre at three P. M., and soon returned with the information that the enemy was massed for an attack, and was sent by General Schurz to report the same to Howard. He did so to his staff, and was told not to be alarmed. Schleiter heard the orders of the rebel officers as they massed their lines of battle, and in 1885 published an account of it in the *National Tribune.* Colonel Richardson, of the Twenty-fifth Ohio, brought in four scouts, and reported to Devens that the enemy was massing heavily a mile distant on the right and rear of the Hatch House—Talley's. Devens refused the information, and told General McLean to order him back to his regiment, according to the testimony of Captain Culp, who was present, and a member of McLean's staff. Colonel Friend, who was officer of the day of Devens' Division, reported to Devens that the enemy was massing on his right, and afterwards stated to Colonel Hurst that the commander was not in a condition to realize the danger. Friend then went to corps headquarters, and was insulted and warned not to bring on a panic, and to go back to his regiment. Friend returned to the picket line, and again at two P. M. went to corps headquarters, and was called a coward, and ordered to his regiment, with the remark that the enemy was retreating.

Col. J. C. Lee says in his article (*National Tribune* of March 19, 1885) that he showed General McLean, about ten A. M., Jackson's troops moving in the southeast towards our flank, and made a diagram of roads showing how our flank could be reached. Lee affirmed that Jackson was moving to our rear, and McLean promised to inform General Devens. Captain Rollins, commander of the picket line, was ordered to ascertain the meaning of this movement, and sent back between eleven A. M. and four P. M. three messengers to Lee, stating that artillery and infantry in heavy force were passing in front around to our right flank. Lee took these three scouts to McLean and Devens, and insisted that some action should be taken. Devens urged that he had no such information from army or corps headquarters, and said with impatience that "it was not worth while to be scared before we were hurt." After this event some more scouts were sent out, and soon returned, stating that a large body of the enemy were on our right flank, apparently resting. Colonel Richardson, of the Twenty-fifth Ohio, and Colonel Reily, of the Seventy-fifth Ohio, were informed of the facts, and made preparation to receive the attack. Shortly after, a squadron of cavalry went out, and soon returned, and the captain in command reported to Devens, in Lee's presence, that he could go but a little way, as he met a large body of infantry. Devens said impatiently : "I wish I could get some one who could make a reconnaissance for me." The Captain firmly replied : "General, I can go further, but I can't promise to return." Lee states that Von Gilsa and men were ready, but not expecting an attack in the rear.

NOTE NO. 9.

Colquitt's Blunder.

A few moments after the advance had commenced, Colquitt struck a strong, determined picket reserve, and noticed some cavalry on his right front, and conceived the singular idea that Sickles had moved his forces to the right, and was then threatening his flank. Why he should entertain this idea is very strange, as Stuart with his cavalry and the Stonewall Brigade of infantry were both on the Plank Road to his right, and guarding it from all attacks from that quarter. Besides this force, the brigades of Archer and Thomas were still in the rear, guarding the trains, and Colquitt ought to have known that Sickles could not have reached him without first disposing of these forces. This suspicion, unfounded as it was, can be credited indirectly to the movement below the Furnace, and it seems to be the only good that can be even distantly accredited to that brilliant expedition, excepting the capture of about 300 prisoners at a fearful cost. The men who made this resistance, which proved of such great importance to the Federal army, belonged of the Fifty-fifth Ohio, but the cavalry Colquitt saw were probably some of Stuart's, dressed in the United States uniform, who were halted at the Burton Farm, for no evidence can be found of any cavalry of ours stationed at that point. At all events, Colquitt was alarmed, and recalled the Sixth Georgia, which had quite reached the Talley Farm, and changed his brigade to front south. He also compelled Ramseur, with his brigade, to change front and meet the enemy. Ramseur did so reluctantly, and marched for some distance to the south without finding a solitary Yankee. On the Plank Road, Stuart's cavalry and the Stonewall Brigade of five regiments were compelled to remain quiet until Colquitt had unmasked the line of battle, as he had the right of way; and so for forty to sixty minutes, seventeen regiments were kept from performing that important part of the plan which Jackson had entrusted them with. When Colquitt and the forces that his fatuity had kept back arrived at Dowdall's, the wrecks of Devens' and Schurz's lines had escaped or were escaping, and the golden opportunity for complete victory had gone forever. There is certainly reason to believe that if Colquitt had followed his orders with the same alacrity the rest of his associates did, Devens' Division would have been captured almost to a man, and that Schurz's Division would have been rolled up before it could have fairly formed, and Jackson would have been in the field in the rear of Chancellor's House before Sickles knew of his attack. And it may be said, with some appearance of truth, that it was to Colquitt's want of comprehension, or to his stupidity, that Jackson's plans failed greatly in their intentions, and that indirectly the great soldier lost his life. Ramseur complains of Colquitt's action in his reports, but beyond this but little can be gleaned of what the Confederates thought of Colquitt. Apparently it was fortunate for Colquitt that Jackson did not live to demand the reasons of his delinquent and stupid subordinate. Colquitt was soon relieved and sent South, where he remained until near the end of the Petersburg campaign.

NOTE NO. 10.

The Federal Army in Extreme Danger.

At about seven P. M., or a few minutes after, Bushbeck's line of defense of the Eleventh Corps was flanked and forced, and the Union army was at this moment in imminent danger. The nearest support to the defeated corps, then retreating through the forest, was Berry's Division, two miles away, and then hurrying to take position in the edge of the forest on the right of Fairview. The center of the army had gone two or three miles south, with Sickles, below the Welford Furnace, to observe the forced flight of General Lee, then supposed to be retreating to Gordonsville. Lee and his men, however, had not fled, and the idea of flight had not been entertained by them. Their only thought, at this time, was to get at close quarters with the foe. Jackson and his seventy regiments had marched past the front with indifference, and at this moment, after a hot and dusty circuit of fifteen miles, was performing his part with energy and rapidity in the rear of the Eleventh Corps and on the flank of the Federal army. No one remained behind to further amuse Sickles, excepting some artillery of Brown's.

Opposite the Furnace, across the Run, however, concealed in the woods, Lee was ready to hurl Posey's and Wright's Brigades upon the exposed flank of Birney as soon as the guns of Jackson's attack were heard. Birney was preparing to bivouac, yet the unsupported wrecks of the Eleventh Corps had been vainly attempting to resist Jackson and his 30,000 men for an hour and a half, with a loss of quite 2,500 men. Sickles refused to credit the first officers who announced the defeat of the Eleventh Corps. Barlow and his brigade of 3,000 men—the reserve of the Eleventh Corps—had been taken from its proper position, and marched southward two miles distant, and halted in the dense forest, not far from Birney. Here it afterwards became lost, and escaped in the night with much difficulty. A little in the rear of Birney, Whipple's Division of eight regiments was halted, while on the other side of Scott's Run, to the eastward, in the dense woods, Williams' Division of thirteen regiments amused the active skirmishers of Anderson's Division of Lee's army.

NOTE NO. 11.

Colonel Candler's Statements.

Colonel Candler, formerly of the First Massachusetts, and one of Hooker's favorite aids, was much interested in the work of the compiler, and assisted him greatly in the investigations. And in fact all of the researches up to the time of the untimely death of this noble officer were freely exposed to his criticism, and in turn all the papers of Colonel Candler were generously confided to the writer, and were in his possession at the time of Candler's death.   In November, 1892, Colonel Candler stated to him that late on Saturday afternoon General Hooker, with his two aids, Candler and Russell, sat on the veranda of the Chancellor House, enjoying the summer evening, calm and sober.   Up to this time all had gone well.   Sickles was crowding the rear of the retreating foe, and Pleasanton had gone also with all of his cavalry to harass the retreating trains.   Now and then a shot came from the far distance, where the rebels on the Plank and the Pike Roads, on the left and south, were making a show of resistance, but nothing occurred to awaken the slightest anxiety among the officers resting at the Chancellor Tavern. Not a sound of the fighting at the Talley Farm, or even at the Wilderness Church, had reached them.   Not an officer from the attacked forces had come to them for aid, or to warn them of the impending danger, and so the hours passed until 6.15 to 6.30—and Colonel Candler was very positive that this was the exact time—when the sounds of distant cannonading came to their hearing, which they attributed to the movements of Birney and his forces.   They were all listening attentively, and speculating upon the results of the conflict, when Captain Russell stepped out in front and turned his glass in the direction of the Dowdall Tavern, far to the right.   A moment after he suddenly shouted to General Hooker: "My God, here they come!"   Hooker and his aids sprang upon their horses and rode some distance down the Plank Road before they reached the ambulances and fugitives from Devens' Division, and learned from them that the whole rebel army had broken loose upon the flank and rear of the Federal army.

NOTE NO. 12.

Williams' Log Works.

About half a mile from the Dowdall Tavern eastward, a line of Log Works stretched from near the Plank Road southward and eastward, connecting with the entrenchments of the Twelfth Corps at Fairview. They were strongly built, and commenced at a point about two hundred feet from the Plank Road, south of it, running parallel to the Hazel Grove Road for some distance, and then turned to the eastward, facing the Hazel Grove position.   They were intended to hold the entire division of Williams, of the Twelfth Corps, and when this division moved to join Sickles four companies of the Twenty-eight New York were left to guard the baggage and intrenchments, and were behind the Log Works a hundred yards or more south of the Plank Road when the wrecks of the Eleventh Corps retreated towards Chancellorsville.   The survivors of the Bushbeck line halted near these works, and were forming a line of battle to dispute Jackson's advance when they were ordered to Fairview by a staff officer, who rode up and stopped the attempt. The enemy were not in sight when the men of the Eleventh Corps filed into the road and marched again towards Chancellorsville, and the four companies of the Twenty-eighth New York could have escaped at that time, as Dilger and his rear guard were still between them and the enemy. After Dilger and his gun had passed by, calling on all stragglers to fall in with him, the acting adjutant of the Twenty-eighth New York rode to the Plank Road and, noticing groups of the rebels advancing in and beside the road, he galloped back a hundred or two yards south of the road and informed Colonel Cook of his danger, but Cook refused to retreat without orders, and a few moments after the rebels closed in on his front and right rear and demanded his surrender. The four companies of the Twenty-eighth made no resistance, but threw down their arms, and but three men made their escape. But other reports indicate that a larger part of this force did escape, and joined the rout with the Hazel Grove crowd. At this moment the Eighth Pennsylvania Cavalry were marching on the Hazel Grove Road in front of these Log Works, a hundred yards or more distant in the woods, and totally ignorant of the presence of the enemy or of any impending danger.

NOTE NO. 13.

Buschbeck's Final Position.

When Buschbeck came into position in front of where Captain Best was forming his battery, Berry's Division had not arrived to take position on the right of Buschbeck. Colonel Huey, of the Eighth Pennsylvania Cavalry, states that he found no infantry in his retreat on the north of the Plank Road, and Captain Carpenter, of the same regiment, says he got to Fairview Field some time before Berry came up. The information collected by General Underwood shows that Berry did not get into position until after Buschbeck had established his line and was ready with the rallied men of Schurz's Division on the Bullock Road, to repel the enemy if he advanced, which he did not until the next morning.

NOTE NO. 14.

The Hazel Grove and Fairview Stampedes.

The crowd which appeared at Fairview, coming from the southward, started from the vista at the time the Eighth Pennsylvania Cavalry were fired into by the rebel skirmishers. In this vista were halted one or two batteries, with their trains, pack trains, ambulances and material, mostly belonging to the brigades of the Third Corps which had gone south with Sickles in search of Jackson's army, and when Winn and his Georgian foragers suddenly fired into them without warning, the whole collection of men and animals broke into utter confusion and plunged headlong down the vista toward Hazel Grove. Here the mass of fugitives and material was largely increased by additions from the artillery, infantry and cavalry in bivouac at this farm, and at a high rate of speed sought safely in the direction of the Fairview Field, distant half a mile or more to the northeast. As the terrified mass of men, animals and material tore through the ravine leading to Fairview, it was increased in volume and energy by the men escaping from the Log Works of Williams' Division, and also by many members of the Twelfth Corps, just then returning from their support of Sickles near the Furnace. In the reports of the battle at this hour, much can be found to show the composition of this interesting movement, and also to prove that none of the berated Eleventh Corps were in it.

General Knipe, of the First Brigade of the Twelfth Corps, says (Vol. XXV., p. 686) that as he emerged from the swamp to approach his old position he met the Eleventh Corps falling back in disorder. The Eleventh Corps had fallen back to the rear some time before, most of them half an hour previously, and none of them did he meet at this place or time. Knipe further says: "A number of my men became mixed up with the fleeing troops, and were unable to join their comrades until I sent a staff officer to bring them forward." Colonel Quincy, of the Second Massachusetts, of the Third Brigade, Twelfth Corps, says (p. 714): "Some confusion and panic at this point." The Thirteenth New Jersey, of the same brigade, broke and joined the rabble. Colonel Diven, of the One Hundred and Seventh New York, of the same brigade (p. 718), admits that his regiment was also broken in fragments. A portion of this regiment rallied with the Twenty-seventh Indiana, and also two hundred of the One Hundred and Tenth Pennsylvania, of the Third Corps, which had left Hazel Grove at a high rate of speed, also came to the Twenty-seventh Indiana without a field officer, and stayed under the command of Colonel Cosgrove all night. There are many reports missing of the Third Corps and Twelfth Corps and the cavalry under Pleasanton, which, if brought to light, would clear up some of the obscurities attending the skedaddle from Hazel Grove up the ravine to Fairview, and they will undoubtedly add to the proof that the Eleventh Corps was not a part of it, but that the procession was composed almost entirely if not entirely, of men and material of others corps.

NOTE NO. 15.

Major Huntington's Views.

Extract from a letter from Maj. J. F. Huntington, who commanded three of the batteries at Hazel Grove, May 2, 1863:

As to the battle of Chancellorsville, allow me to say that in my opinion, no occurrence of the war has been more utterly and persistently misrepresented, to use a mild term, than has the behavior of the Eleventh Corps on the right, and, also, in a smaller way, that of the artillery at Hazel Grove, on Saturday evening. I presume there are many, even among those who think themselves pretty well up in war history, who believe that the right wing gave way before Jackson's onslaught without offering any resistance worth mentioning, and that the defeat of the Army of the Potomac was largely due to that fact. I trust and believe that Colonel Hamlin, in his forthcoming history, will do much to remove that groundless impression from the minds of the general public. There are those who, regarding the affair at Hazel Grove, still accept as gospel the apocrypha of Pleasanton, to the effect that on the approach of the enemy the artillery then fled in wild disorder, drivers cutting their traces, and all that sort of thing. When, suddenly Pleasanton appeared "*Deus ex machina*," and, as one version has it, cried in a voice of thunder : "Align those pieces!" Instantly the confusion ceased, the panic stricken cannoniers, gaining fresh courage, obeyed that extraordinary order. To enable them to do so, General Pleasanton had previously ordered the Eighth Pennsylvania Cavalry to make a charge that may well be called desperate, for it involved scaling a high fence into a dense wood where were the "seething ranks of a victorious enemy." There, as we are told by General Doubleday in his work on Chancellorsville and Gettysburg, fell Maj. Peter Keenan, "literally impaled on the bayonets of the enemy." That is a poetical description of the death of an officer who was killed by a musket ball about a mile from the spot in question. General Doubleday goes on to say : "Thus saving the army from destruction, and the country from the unutterable degradation of the establishment of slavery in the Northern States." The pages of history will be searched in vain for the record of another charge of a small regiment of cavalry that produced such stupendous results. After this glowing description, how tame and commonplace do the real facts seem! The fact is that the charge of the Eighth Pennsylvania was made far out of sight and hearing of Hazel Grove, and had no more bearing upon the defense of that position than it had upon the defense of Bunker Hill. That so far from having been ordered by General Pleasanton, he was ignorant that a charge had been made till informed of it by Colonel Huey, commanding the regiment, on Sunday morning ; that the guns at Hazel Grove, instead of having been rallied and aligned by a distinguished cavalry general, were put in battery within a few yards of the spot where they had previously been parked, under the direction of a humble captain of artillery, as it happened to be in the line of his duty as Division Chief of Artillery. Truly, it is easier to fight battles than it is to dig out lies about them after they have become fairly imbedded in history.

Yours truly and fraternally,

J. F. HUNTINGTON.

Major Huntington also stated in 1880, in the public press, that his batteries were ready for action before the enemy fired a shot, and concerning the assertion of General Pleasanton, he says that "A more impudent and unfounded claim was never made."

NOTE NO. 16.

Sickles' Midnight Charge.

General Sickles said to the committee of Congress that he charged Jackson entirely with the bayonet and drove him back to our original line, reoccupied Howard's rifle pits, recovered several pieces of artillery and some caissons abandoned during the day, killed Jackson in this attack, and hed the line until about four in the morning. He further stated in his report to Hooker (page 390) that "It is difficult to do justice to the brilliant execution of this movement by Birney and his splendid command. The night was very clear and still; the moon, nearly full, threw enough light in the woods to facilitate the advance and, against a terrific fire of musketry and artillery, some twenty pieces of which the enemy had massed in the opening (Dowdall's) where General Howard's headquarters had been established, the advance was successfully executed, the line and the Plank Road gained, and our breastworks reoccupied. All our guns and caissons and a portion of Whipple's mule train were recovered, besides two pieces of the enemy's artillery and three caissons captured." Furthermore, he states that after being thrown into hopeless confusion in front, the enemy advanced upon Berry's Division and was repulsed.

In reply to this erroneous statement, it may be said that Jackson's men were not driven back one foot by his charge ; that he did not come within two thousand yards of Howard's rifle pits, and that the guns he captured were those of his own corps which Winn and his handful of Georgians had stampeded in the vista three or four hours before; that Jackson had been wounded two hours before, and was then miles away in the rear; that instead of the enemy massing twenty guns and firing from the Dowdall Tavern, they did not fire a single shot, because there were two lines of battle then forming, of Colston's and Rodes' Divisions, between Hazel Grove and the Tavern. Furthermore, they did not fire a gun, because they were not aware of Sickles making an attack at this time, and did not learn of its magnitude until informed of it by the Northern papers long afterward. Moreover, it can be proved that instead of Berry's Division repulsing Jackson's forces, they did not—excepting skirmishers—come within eight hundred yards of him that night.

General Ward, of Birney's Division, states (Vol. XXV., page 429, Rebellion Records) that his brigade started about 11.30 P. M., supported by another brigade, and that the advance was a brilliant sight; that he soon drove the enemy out of his old barricades, taking them completely by surprise, leaving open our communications with the main army. In the meantime the Fortieth New York and Seventeenth Maine, advancing up the road — the vista — captured two field pieces and five caissons which had been taken by the enemy that afternoon. Colonel Hayman, who commanded the brigade in support of Ward, says he was ordered to charge with the bayonet, and after advancing some quarter of a mile carried the rifle pits—his own—encountering a terrible fire both from the front and both flanks, and from friend and foe. The Third and Fifth Michigan charged into the woods, and soon found that they had attacked the Twelfth Corps.—[*Report of Byron Pierce.*] The Third Michigan lost twenty-two wounded and missing, and the Fifth Michigan lost about thirty. The First New York were fired into, both flanks and front, and retired with a loss of five killed, eleven wounded, and one hundred and two missing.—[*Report of Colonel Leland.*] The Thirty-seventh New York advanced, but meeting with a warm reception, fell back to the starting point.—[*Major DeLacy.*] The Fortieth New York, supported by the Seventeeth Maine, were ordered to advance up the vista leading to the Plank Road and force a passage by the bayonet. They passed a short distance northward, when the Fortieth New York, known as the Mozart Regiment, approached the Twenty-eighth North Carolina, of Lane's Brigade, stretched across the way. The first volley of the Twenty-eighth North Carolina overthrew the Fortieth New York, marching in column of companies, and in retreating in confusion it upset the most of the Seventeenth Maine, marching in the rear. The Seventeenth Maine rallied, however, and were formed in line by Adjutant Roberts in the vista, but facing west instead of north, where Lane's men were awaiting them. Shortly afterward McGowan's Brigade took position on their right flank and front, and after the exchange of a few shots, General Ward recalled the regiment to Hazel Grove, to which it retired, taking a gun and two caissons left in the vista when Winn, with the Georgians, stampeded the forces left there in bivouac. Slocum, in his report, states that about midnight a portion of Birney's Division advanced to attack the enemy in front of Williams' Division, but as he had not been informed of the intent he mistook the movement to be an attack upon Williams' Division, and at once opened upon his threatened front with artillery. General Williams, taking the same view, also fired upon all who made their appearance in his front. Slocum also states that the losses suffered by our troops from our own fire must have been severe. General Ruger was not informed of Sickles' attack, but, anticipating it, ordered his brigade not to fire unless fired into. The Third Wisconsin was fired into from the front and also from the rear by the Thirteenth New Jersey, which soon afterwards took to its heels. Colonel Colgrove, of the Twenty-seventh Indiana, of the same brigade, says the rebels attacked him with terrific yells, but he repulsed them, yet at the same time Lieutenant Colonel Feshler, of the same regiment, reports "occasonal firing on the right of the regiment, but excepting stray shots there was none in front (page 713); and Colonel Quincy, of the Second Massachusetts, in the same line of battle, reports : "Our lines were not under fire until morning" (page 715).

In the work entitled "Michigan in the War," published in 1882, the reader may find, on page 242, the following account of the Michigan regiments in this charge of Sickles': "At midnight, participated in that bold, dashing, and successful bayonet charge on the enemy, which stands unsurpassed in this war."

NOTE NO. 17.

Abuse of the Eleventh Corps.

The blame of the disaster at Chancellorsville was thrown upon the Eleventh Corps, and chiefly upon the German regiments. The denunciation became extreme, and soon passed the bounds of decency. Some of the Northern papers were for shooting the whole corps, and the Germans were described as a worthless lot, and as coming from the ragged scum of a foreign and vicious population. The demands of the abused men to be heard in self-defense were refused. In the great public distress at this moment, when Lee was mustering his battalions to invade the North, the complaints and the wrongs of 10,000 men were of little consequence. The loyal Germans of New York held a mass meeting at the Cooper Institute a month afterwards, and protested in strong language against the unjust treatment of the soldiers of German descent. At this meeting it was stated on the authority of General Patrick, the Provost Marshal at the United States Ford, that none of the Eleventh Corps fled there that night, and General Meagher, who was the Provost Marshal at the White House, in the rear of Chancellor's, and who stopped the fugitives at that point, made a speech in defense of the Germans, and stated that in the crowd of fugitives his men arrested, there were but few Germans recognized by him. But no notice of this meeting or its demands was taken by the government, and, in consequence, the voluntary enlistment of the better class of Germans and other foreign nationalities almost entirely ceased.

After the battle the entire corps was denounced on all sides, and no one seemed to care to investigate and see if there were any circumstances to explain the disaster to the corps. Hooker and some of his staff joined in the abuse, and the whole corps, both Americans, Germans, French, Italians, Hungarians, Swiss, Irish and Welsh, were massed together as a worthless lot, and described as "Dutchmen." The Third Corps especially have made themselves conspicuous in the tirade, and have continued to do so up to recent times. Their regimental histories are full of abuse and denunciation of the Eleventh Corps and the prowess of their own in this battle. Their often-repeated falsehoods and self-laudation are remarkable when placed in view of the actual facts. It is useless to deny that the morale of the corps was seriously affected by the indifference, the hootings and the virulent invectives of its associates. The terms of reproach lavishly and unjustly hurled upon them from all sides became household words in the land, and linger yet. Nowhere were words of comfort offered to them, or the hand of friendship extended, save the solitary instance of a New York battalion presenting arms to some of the dejected wrecks of the corps marching past on Sunday morning.

To the earnest appeals of some of the officers to be heard in defense of their soldiers, the War Department and Congress declined to listen. West Point was in serious danger, a victim was needed, and as the chief of Hooker's staff has truly said, the Eleventh Corps was made the scapegoat. For thirty years these unjust imputations have been scattered over the world wherever military records are read, blighting the honorable reputation of an entire corps and embittering the life of many a gallant soldier. Nothing affects the soldier like ridicule or scorn, and in time it bends the bravest heart and wrecks the strongest resolution. It has the same destroying power, whether it attacks the patriot soldier like G. K. Warren, or the traitor like Benedict Arnold. Human nature bends and blights before its infernal influence.

In looking over the articles printed in the reports of Congress, in the encyclopædias, and various popular magazines throughout the country, concerning the particulars of the battle of Chancellorsville, we are forcibly reminded of the strange remark of the English wit and writer, Sir Horace Walpole, when he said : '' Read me anything but history, for I know that is false.'' So when we read in the report of Congress how Pleasanton, under great inspiration, placed twenty-two guns in battery and blew the exultant and advancing masses of Jackson's army into fragments and out of the ramparts abandoned by the Eleventh Corps, and saved the Army of the Potomac from capture or destruction ; when we read in the same report the testimony of Birney and Warren, to the effect that the Eleventh Corps made no defense, but ran away ; when we read that both Hooker and Sickles laid the blame of the disaster to the Eleventh Corps, because that corps did not, single-handed, and without the aid of a gun or a man from the rest of the Army of the Potomac, resist and annihilate Jackson's vastly superior forces, three times its numbers ; when we read in the encyclopædias that Berry's splendid division, after the rout of the Eleventh Corps, rushed to the front and plunged with the bayonet into the immense masses of the advancing foe and, after a bloody struggle, hurled them back into the forest again and again, defeated and dismayed ; when we read these and many other similar articles scattered over the land, and compare them with the actual facts, we can then estimate the force, the truth and the significance of Walpole's remark, and must then admit the justice of the objection of the Confederate soldier to the acceptance of military history composed in this reckless and ridiculous manner.

The evidence seems to show that none of Jackson's forces approached the guns of Pleasanton at Hazel Grove that night excepting a few foragers of Doles' Brigade, who promptly fled without the loss of a man when the guns ceased firing. The evidence also decidedly shows that Berry's Division, instead of hurling Jackson back into the forest and stopping his advance, did not really see Jackson's line of battle until the next morning. And instead of the Eleventh Corps running away at the first fire, the evidence shows that it resisted and retarded Jackson's men for more than an hour and a half, without the aid of a man or a gun from the reserves of the Army of the Potomac, and that all the resistance Jackson's men met with up to eight P. M.—nearly an hour after the halt had been ordered—was from the men of the Eleventh Corps, fighting and wrecked in detail.

The contemptuous statement of General Sickles to Congress, that if the Eleventh Corps had held its ground, victory would have followed, is, on reflection, the highest praise that could possibly be bestowed upon the nine thousand men of the Eleventh Corps in action. In other words, if the nine thousand men of the Eleventh Corps, though attacked in rear, had whipped Jackson's army, thirty thousand strong, all would have been glorious, and the Army of the Potomac would not have been attacked in front by the same force on the next day, and would have escaped defeat and humiliation. This is the plain logic of it.

The abuse heaped upon the Eleventh Corps after Chancellorsville seems almost incredible, as we investigate the actual condition of things as they existed at that time. It is apparent that much of this abuse originated with the Third Corps, and it is also still more painfully true that the calumnies and falsehoods have been kept alive and circulated since that time by the Falstaffs and the historians of their regimental and other organizations.

NOTE NO. 18.

Examples of Calumny and Falsehood.

For brief examples we will offer but two from the great number extant: The historian of the Eleventh New Jersey stated at their May meeting, 1885, and without contradiction, that the Eleventh Corps fled like frightened hares before the yelping hounds, and that their division (Berry's) checked the enemy, and moreover the Eleventh Corps lost the battle. Captain Blake, of the Eleventh Massachusetts, of the same brigade, indulges in the following outrageous falsehoods in his history of his regiment, page 178: In the attack "a spectacle of shameful cowardice was witnessed, which can be rarely paralleled in the history of civilized warfare. The corps, composed mainly of Germans, was stationed behind strong earthworks, and broke a few minutes after four P. M.;" that "the Germans basely fled without receiving a volley, and rushed pell-mell by thousands upon the road to the ford. Officers of other corps made themselves speechless by striving to rally the Flying Dutchman, who was no longer an illusion but a despicable reality," etc. "The Germans thought to escape the censure which the whole army justly bestowed upon them by tearing the badges from their caps—for the crescent was recognized as the insignia of a poltroon."

For another example we will take a description from the authorized work published by the State of New Jersey [J. Y. Foster, editor], relating to the Thirteenth Regiment of that state, in the Twelfth Corps, to show how little care was taken by its editor to relate the truth : "The Thirteenth New Jersey bravely and steadily obeyed the order to stand firm as the masses of fugitives swept down from the woods, behaving admirably throughout. So immovable was our line, and so terrible the fire of Best's guns (not the Third Corps, as represented in cotemporary accounts), that the headlong advance of the enemy was speedily checked; that the division, with Hooker, Sickles and Berry at the head, moved at double-quick, with a shout, amid the booming of cannon and crackle of musketry, upon the rebels, slowly driving them from the ground lost by the Eleventh Corps in the morning, and recovering several abandoned guns and caissons. Repeatedly during the night he renewed the contest—again repulsed with great slaughter. In both of these combats the fighting was grand, of the most desperate character, and the scene was grand and almost fearful in its sublimity."

For the truth of this narrative the reader is respectfully referred to the reports of the commander of this regiment, who plainly states that the regiment broke before the enemy came in sight and joined the historic skedaddle, credit for which has largely been bestowed upon the Eleventh Corps. Furthermore, on reading the report of Ruger's Brigade of the Twelfth Corps, it appears that this same regiment, when Sickles made his brilliant midnight charge, again becoming animated, fired into the Third Wisconsin Regiment, thirty paces in front of them, and broke up the right wing of the regiment, and again took to its heels. At the time there was no enemy attacking. It is proper, however, to say that the Thirteenth New Jersey, although behaving very strangely on Saturday night, did on Sunday morning fight with gallantry, and is deserving of the strongest praise. Investigation will also show that there was no fighting in front of that regiment, save the Sickles episode, and that no guns or grounds lost by the Eleventh Corps were recovered by any body of troops that night or at any other time.

General De Trobriand, in his interesting memoirs, gives a correct view of the feelings of the Army of the Potomac at this time, when he says : "The Eleventh Corps was the object of a general hue and cry, nobody stopping to ask if there were not some extenuating circumstances —so quickly does injustice germinate in adversity." The Eleventh Corps was then considered as lawful dumping ground for errors and mistakes, and all kinds of burdens and humiliations were heaped upon it, varying in degree from the grand accusation of not having destroyed

Jackson's much larger army, to the lesser and meaner one of stealing the Third Corps' beef. After the battle, there was no one in authority found brave enough, generous enough, or just enough, to say a word in justice or in kindness concerning the corps, and since that time but two of the high officers of the Army of the Potomac — Couch and Doubleday — have dared to speak a word kindly and openly in its favor.

Howard, at the midnight conference held by Hooker and his corps officers on Sunday night, stated to the conference that "the situation was due to the bad conduct of his corps, or words to that effect," according to the report of the meeting as given by General Couch. This unfortunate and unjust remark was accepted by Hooker and repeated by him at the hearing before the Committee on the Conduct of the War, two years afterwards, and it has since been accepted far and wide as an official statement. It now appears that the fault lay not with the troops, but in the fault of the position, for which the rank and file of the corps are not in the least responsible. Eminent officers of Jackson's Corps freely state to-day that they did not consider that the corps was wrecked from any fault of its own, but from the inexcusable fault of its position, in which the bravest troops in the world could not have resisted, without certain destruction, longer than did the Eleventh Corps. The simple fact that it took Jackson's men one hour and a half to march one mile and a-quarter after the attack began, is positive evidence of serious resistance. Longstreet's column of assault at Gettysburg, under Pettigrew and Pickett, numbering quite fifteen thousand men, marched the same distance and was wrecked in thirty minutes.

The loss of the campaign was due to some cause, and that cause has been generally assigned to the want of resistance of the Eleventh Corps. Howard, its commander, so stated in the midnight conference, and Hooker repeated the statement in his report to Congress. Since then it has been spread broadcast over the world, to the detriment of the unfortunate corps. There surely was a cause for the defeat of an army by another army of greatly inferior strength. There was a cause and a responsibility for the disaster, and as the French historian well says : "Responsibility cannot exist without a name."

Hooker, it seems, was anxious to have Howard take command of the corps, and in his letter to Stanton he plainly shows the reasons why he does so. It is chiefly the desire to get rid of Schurz, then in temporary command. And it is not hazarding much of an opinion in saying that the letter, hatched in a spirit of dislike, was the cause of much disappointment and disgust. Hooker had a dislike of the corps, but why is not known. The men of the corps were fond of him, and freely filled him up with their best vintages when he made them a visit; but he disliked the corps nevertheless. Sickles said he did to Congress, and there is other proof. The look of sardonic disdain which he wore when he said to Howard: "I give you the Eleventh Corps, which you know is the best in the army," betrayed the feelings and the sincerity of the man. Hooker's sending Devens to the corps to displace one of its veterans settled his fate. Both of these appointments were of Hooker's own seeking, and the responsibility rests with him. Officers testified to Congress that the Army of the Potomac had no confidence in the corps when it came to join it at Fredericksburg, and there is much evidence to show the existence of this objection, but no evidence to show any real cause for it.

Hooker denounced the corps freely, and said in California as late as 1872 that the corps left guns, knapsacks and everything, and ran like a herd of buffaloes, and that some of his staff rode among them and shot a number of them, to prevent extension of the panic. He evidently had forgotten the battle at Williamsburg, where he had nine thousand men under his command—according to Heintzelman—and where he gained the name of fighting Joe Hooker, but yet in spite of all the so-called terrific fighting there during the day, he did not lose as many men killed and wounded as the despised nine thousand men of the Eleventh Corps lost in an hour and a half at Chancellorsville when attacked in flank and rear.

Hooker's hatred of Howard was so strong that he did not discriminate between the men of the corps and the principal object of his disgust. His statement of his staff shooting fugitives is not sustained. Colonel Candler denied it in toto, and showed that he and Captains Russell, Dahlgren and Moore were away on duty, and knew nothing of such action. As near as could be ascertained, this barbarous and untrue story arose from one of the Falstaffs loitering around headquarters. And as for the cavalry stopping fugitives of the Eleventh Corps, it appears that they had nearly all reached or passed the Chancellor House before the cavalry arrived on the scene, and the skedaddlers the cavalry stopped were from the Hazel Grove crowd, and not members of the Eleventh Corps.

Hooker was one of the old, stalwart regulars who believed in the immortality of West Point, and did not realize or admit that the soldier, like the poet, is born and not made by a course of academical study. He also, like many of the veteran regulars, both North and South, believed in strong potations and stronger expletives. His positive and profane assertion to his followers of certain victory, and his defiance of the God of battles to prevent him was certainly improper and unworthy of the soldier and the man. Hooker, when his mind was clear, was a superior man in tact and popular diplomacy. His personal accomplishments and his military bearing gave him prestige with those of his soldiers who were wont to measure the qualifications of their heroes by their stature. His management of the army after the demoralizing and useless slaughter at Fredericksburg, the courage and harmony which he infused into his men, and the celerity and promptness with which he moved a large part of his army across the river into the enemy's territory, certainly stamp him as a soldier of energy and skill. But on Saturday evening Hooker underwent a great change ; his mind seemed paralyzed by the rout of the Eleventh Corps, and despondency took the place of the hopes which he so defiantly proclaimed shortly before.

General Hooker, on assuming command, asked for the assignment of Gen. C. P. Stone as his Chief of Staff but the War Department refused, and sent Gen. Daniel Butterfield instead. Butterfield was a man of great energy and sagacity, and probably much of the improved condition of the army after Hooker took command was really due to the efforts of the Chief of Staff rather than to the officer in command, who has received the praise due another.

NOTE NO. 19.

General Birney's Statements.

General Birney stated to Congress a year after the battle that he sent Graham's Brigade to Howard to strengthen the Eleventh Corps on Friday afternoon, the day before the battle, but that Howard refused it. Investigation seems to show that this statement was an afterthought, and mostly gratuitous. Graham arrived near the Chancellor House about noon, and then received orders to picket Hunting Run, near Dowdall's. At or about the same time Howard received orders to follow Slocum and the Twelfth Corps, and support it in the movement towards Fredericksburg, so that at the time Graham received his orders to move to the Dowdall Tavern, there was no one left there to guard that part of the Federal line. The Eleventh Corps had not proceeded far on its way when it was ordered to return to its former position, and it arrived there before Graham reached the position assigned to him. At this time the flank movement of Jackson was not contemplated, and all of the rebel infantry was east of Sykes, then more than a mile east of the Chancellor House. There were no rebels near the position of the Eleventh Corps at this time ; the scouting parties testing the flanks and positions of their opponents did not reach the Plank Road in front of Talley's until late in the afternoon or at dusk. The nearest rebel infantry was, at this time, that of Posey's and Wright's Brigades, which flanked Slocum near Aldrich's, between three and four P. M.

Birney also stated to the committee of Congress at this time, that the Eleventh Corps suffered no loss in the battle except in prisoners, as it ran away ; and he also distinctly states that the disaster of the campaign was due to the bad conduct of the Eleventh Corps. Why this excellent officer of the Third Corps should deliberately state these false-hoods a year after the battle is incomprehensible. A little investigation or inquiry would have shown him that the nine thousand men of the

Eleventh Corps, while attempting to hold Jackson's army at bay until reinforcements from the reserves could reach them—and which never came—lost in one hour and a half more men killed and wounded than the whole Third Corps lost in the seven days' battles around Richmond, or in the severe fighting of the two days' struggle at Fair Oaks or Seven Pines. And it appears, or seems to appear, that the neglected Eleventh Corps, attacked in flank and rear, lost out of its nine thousand men more, comparatively, than the splendid Third Corps of double the number, or eighteen thousand men, lost on Sunday morning, when attacked in front, protected by defenses and the fire of thirty cannon, and assisted by parts of the Second and the Twelfth Corps. To have equaled the loss of the Eleventh Corps, comparatively, which Hooker stated to Congress, two years after the battle, was twenty-five hundred men, and which inquiry shows to be correct, the Third Corps, with twice the number of men, should have lost quite five thousand men. Hooker stated the loss of the Third Corps to have been 4,039 in the entire campaign, but inquiry shows that it was about 4,123, and from this estimate some two or three hundred must be subtracted as the loss of the previous day and evening, making a total loss of less than four thousand men on Sunday.

The Eleventh Corps have no objection to critical comparisons of regiments or brigades in this battle with those of the Third Corps on Saturday night, or even on Sunday morning, position and all circumstances to be considered in the comparisons.

The writer has no desire to play the part of the harsh censor, or to mingle sarcasm with the sting of truth, but he must say that the details of the midnight charge of Birney's Division, or the resistance of Berry's Division Sunday morning, offer no well-founded evidence for claims of superior action, but the evidence seems to show that Von Gilsa, with his thousand men, without support, stood the assaults of Rodes' and Colston's Divisions quite as long as the front line of Berry's Division did before Pender's Brigade on Sunday morning. Von Gilsa had but two guns to protect him, while Revere had more than twenty cannon, well protected, to cover his flank and rear. The minutes of the Revere court martial do not furnish any pleasant reading to the Federal soldier, although the New York *Herald* of May 10, 1863, says: "They [Revere's Brigade] fought like tigers wherever placed, and never wavered."

Only a few weeks after Birney made these remarkable and unjust statements, he found himself in temporary command of the grand old Second Corps, which had at one time over forty-six thousand soldiers on its rolls, and which seems from its history to have been the "*Legio Fulminans*" of the Army of the Potomac; and at this time—June 22d, 1864—he was attacked in flank, and lost four guns and seventeen hundred men. His position appears to have been much stronger than that of the Eleventh Corps at Chancellorsville, and Barlow, who commanded the assaulted division, reported that whole regiments surrendered to an inferior force. Later in August, the same corps was again tapped on the flank, and lost nine guns and twenty-three hundred men, and yet the corps was not savagely denounced for these disasters, as was the Eleventh at Chancellorsville. There is abundant evidence in the history of the Army of the Potomac to show that flight and confusion happened to some of the strongest corps when attacked in flank or in rear. Lieutenant General Hill, of the Confederate army, in his paper on Chickamauga, declares that American troops will not stand flank and rear attacks.

General Sickles, nearly a year after the battle, went before Congress and unblushingly laid the defeat of the campaign to the flight of the Eleventh Corps. He lauds his own movements surprisingly, and among other false statements, he said that he lost but one gun —stalled—and nc prisoners, but gratuitously adds that the Eleventh Corps lost heavily in prisoners, and that the Twelfth Corps was partially engaged. The facts seem to be that the stalled gun was pulled out by Bowman's men and restored to Huntington, and that Jackson's men went off with four or five of Sickles' cannon, and that he lost over a thousand men as prisoners, or more than the Eleventh Corps lost. And instead of the Twelfth Corps being partially engaged, the records indicate that it was severely engaged, and that the most of it fought with great distinction. Moreover, he describes events which did not take place, but which appear to his advantage, and he is silent on the remarkable rout of his favorite troops when Pender attacked them early on Sunday morning, and which placed the artillery on Fairview and the Twelfth Corps on its left in extreme jeopardy. He also defends the wild-goose movement below the Furnace, which took quite twenty thousand men out of the center of the army and left the Eleventh Corps in the air without support, and two miles distant from the nearest troops. Yet Sickles stated that the flight of the Eleventh Corps left a long gap in the line. Where that gap was it is now difficult to ascertain, as there were no Federal troops this side of the Rapidan, and Jackson's battalions filled the space between the river and Chancellorsville.

NOTE NO. 20.

Sickles and Warren.

Major General Underwood, who was in Barlow's Brigade at this time, made a study of the battle, and who in 1881 published a work on its events, is very plain in his statements concerning the part Sickles took in this unfortunate affair, and he distinctly states : "No one was more responsible than he for leaving that corps (Eleventh) utterly isolated and beyond the power of help when the attack came ; and if he was in a critical position when Jackson passed around his right and rear, what of the Eleventh Corps, which he left alone with half his number of men? The movement which he made was of his own planning. He pursuaded Hooker to let him make it, and begged for one division after another until he had three, and wanted another, and had sent to him all the cavalry which Hooker had, and dreadfully needed, too, elsewhere. His ill-timed movement, away from the main body, on his own account, did as much as any one thing to produce the result."

Furthermore, Underwood states that Hooker told him that he never authorized Sickles to take Williams' Division from the Twelfth Corps, or Barlow's Brigade from the Eleventh Corps. But if he did not permit Sickles to do this, how came Moore, of his staff, down at the Dowdall Tavern, demanding Barlow's Brigade, and leading it in person down to Sickles, at or below the Furnace? It is very difficult to decide how much of Hooker's statements on these subject should receive credence, for in investigating his remarks, his reports and his correspondence since the battle, it is certainly charitable to believe that Hooker's head was severely injured at the Chancellor House, as well as his back.

General Warren went before Congress a year after the battle and testified that the Eleventh Corps made no fight worth mentioning, that the infantry deserted the artillery, and that the enemy's infantry hardly made any attack on that part of the front where he was, which must have been at the Dowdall Tavern. It is evident that Warren did not stop long to assist, or he would have seen that the infantry remained in the rifle pit at Dowdall's some time after the artillery had been withdrawn, excepting the one gun of Dilger's. He would also have noticed that the infantry, in the presence of an overwhelming force of the enemy, did make considerable defense on the Hawkins Farm and then on the Buschbeck line, which Hooker highly praised. He also stated contemptuously that the first he saw of the rout of the Eleventh Corps was ambulances, mules, etc. What else did he expect to see? These impedimenta were ordered off the field soon after the attack, as there was but one road for retreat, and when the immense forces of the enemy were unmasked it was apparent to all that retreat was inevitable. What Warren met and saw, as he rode down the road, cannot fairly be placed to the discredit of the corps. If so, what corps is free from the same contemptuous imputation?

He also stated that the First Corps came up and took the position of the Eleventh Corps at dark, and also that the fire of Pleasanton's and Sickles' guns soon stopped Jackson's progress and killed him. He also sent a dispatch to Sedgwick at midnight on Sunday, that all was snug at Chancellorsville, that the lines were contracted a little, and the last assault was repelled with ease. The accuracy of Warren's remarks and his knowledge of affairs may be estimated by the facts that the guns of Pleasanton and Sickles did not stop Jackson, because Jackson stopped before the guns were fired, and nearly all of his corps had halted at Dowdall's Tavern, out of range and sight of the Federal artillery ; that the First Corps did not come into position until after midnight, and then they were three miles away from the position lost by the Eleventh Corps ; that when he sent the dispatch to Sedgwick, Hooker's army had been penned up and badly defeated, with a loss of thirteen guns and many thousand prisoners.

This deceptive and dangerous dispatch to Sedgwick may be excused, perhaps, in war, but it was false, and Warren was aware of it. Warren's actions in this battle awakened the suspicions of Hooker's friends, and it is stated on good authority that Warren asked Hooker for the return of his reports to correct them, and that they were not changed for Hooker's benefit. Furthermore, it is stated that Warren recalled letters written after the battle and destroyed them, for some reason not now known. Hooker, in July, asked Seth Williams, the Adjutant General of the Army of the Potomac, to send him the reports of the battle of Chancellorsville, and Williams replied that he would send him on that day—July 28th 1863—by Lieutenant Taylor, all the reports received at date, and would send Warren's report, with map, as soon as received. Warren's report, although dated May 12th, 1863, was not then in the hands of Williams on July 28th, and its absence is certainly singular. The map joined to the report, and as published by the War Department, is erroneous, and highly injurious to Hooker's defense. The broad open fields shown by the map did not exist then, nor do they appear to-day. It is evident from Williams' letter that all the reports were not then sent in—nearly three months after the battle—and it is also evident that the present absence of these reports in the national archives cannot entirely be laid to Hooker. The absence of these important reports is a serious loss to the student of our military history, and it is certainly suggestive of gross negligence or malevolence somewhere. More than two-thirds of the reports of the Eleventh Corps are not to be found, and although rewards have been offered and diligent search made for them during the past five years, not one of them has been brought to light. Many other reports of other corps are also missing, and their absence evidently indicates a wise selection on the part of the abstractor.

The remarks Warren made before Congress concerning Sickles and the composition of the Third Corps, seemingly in derogation, and his disgruntled views in general of affairs and men, are not calculated to increase the respect the student may have for his abilities or his candor. West Point is clearly his Mecca, whence all good and perfect things must come. The Third Corps, notwithstanding Warren's malicious views, was certainly an admirable corps, and contained some of the best personnel to be found in the Army of the Potomac, even if some of its regiments did perform comical movements at times. The bravest men sometimes have moments of discretion, as happened to the intrepid

Frederick the Great, when he took to his heels at Mollwitz and rode twenty miles before he was overtaken by the messenger of the dauntless Schwerin, who had stuck to the field, and finally won the battle.

If the powerful Third Corps, entrenched behind strong works, protected by the fire of thirty cannon and firmly supported by other troops of the Second and Twelfth Corps, numbering altogether quite thirty thousand men, could not resist Jackson's forces without the inspiring presence of Jackson, why expect the depleted Eleventh Corps to destroy them with Jackson in command, when attacked under great disadvantage, and when it could not muster over five thousand men to form line of battle, either at the Church, or later at the rifle pits? All fair-minded soldiers will at once see that the remark: "If the Eleventh Corps had stood firm, the campaign would have ended in a great victory," is a very comical observation. And it must be apparent to any one who will examine the situation and the circumstances of the attack, that the resistance of the troops of the Eleventh Corps, under these circumstances, was all that could be reasonably expected of them.

The story General Doubleday relates of Von Gilsa going to Howard for aid, and being told that he must trust in the Lord, as he had no reinforcements to send him, is clearly erroneous, for the reason that Howard was not at the Dowdall House, and had not returned from the Furnace when Von Gilsa was attacked; also, that Von Gilsa had not time to ride back to headquarters—more than a mile distant—to call for aid; also, because Von Gilsa knew that it was perfectly useless to call for aid, either from Devens or Howard.

Upon close investigation, it appears that the offense of the Eleventh Corps was chiefly that it did not, single-handed, pulverize Jackson and his greatly superior army for their presumption in attacking the Eleventh in the rear and far away from any support; that it did not change front and fortify without permission from its superior officers; that it did have in its ranks many volunteers of German birth or of other nationalities who had offered their services in defense of the government; that it did also contain a number of naturalized officers of foreign birth, highly educated in military affairs, and whose abilities could have been easily demonstrated in competitive comparison with many of those who claimed superior knowledge of the arts of war, and who lost no opportunity to exhibit their dislike and their jealousy. These were the potent reasons. It is quite certain that the composition of the corps had much to do with the fierce and unrelenting denunciations hurled upon it by those really at fault, and who sought to escape censure by declaring the men of the Eleventh Corps as the scapegoats, and whose amazing self-conceit and shameless selfishness prevented them from exercising the common dictates of fairness and humanity. For some of these shortsighted men history has in store a terrible indictment, and time does not always soften the vengeance of her pen.

Justice and words of commendation will come too late for many thousands who have been mustered out by death, and with the conviction that they had been deeply wronged by the authorities at Washington and their fellow soldiers, and it will be of little moment to many of the survivors, whom long continued abuse has steeled to indifference. But it is not too late to correct the inscriptions in our national history, and Hooker spoke the public mind when he wrote to his aid, Colonel Candler, in 1878: "In my judgment it is never too late to correct an error."

In military life, trivial incidents, improperly related and exaggerated, gather force rapidly, and may enhance worthless characters, and as rapidly impair or destroy worthy reputations. Falsehoods in military affairs seem to travel faster, cling closer, and sting deeper than in any other profession. Often repeated, they assume form, and become almost as stubborn as facts.

NOTE NO. 21.

Abuse of the Germans.

The German portion of the corps so savagely denounced for alleged cowardice appears, on investigation, to have fought well wherever they had a fair chance. Von Gilsa's Brigade certainly could not have fought, or attempted to fight, much longer than it did, attacked in the rear. The next German regiments Jackson's men approached were the Twenty-sixth Wisconsin, the Eighty-second Illinois, and the Fifty-eighth New York, and there is no question that they fought desperately, retreated in battle order north of the road, and halted in line of battle on the right of Berry's position. The next German regiment in Schurz's line was the Seventy-fourth Pennsylvania, one of the best in the whole corps, but it was disabled in the rush of Devens' broken division, and could not be collected together in battle order, yet it seems to have done about as well as the American regiment next to it, the Sixty-first Ohio, a most admirable regiment. The Sixty-eighth and One Hundred and Nineteenth New York Regiments, next in line, seem to have made a creditable fight. The Seventy-fifth Pennsylvania, on picket south of the Dowdall Tavern, with only one hundred and eighty men, certainly could not be expected to stand its ground and resist the seventeen regiments Colquitt let loose upon it. The remaining three German regiments were in Buschbeck's Brigade, fought steadily, retreated in perfect battle order, and won applause from every one except Warren.

Of the three German batteries, Dilger's, Dieckman's and Weidrick's, no fault can be justly found. Dilger and Weidrick stood to their guns as long as their positions were tenable. The two guns of Dieckman, on picket, were served as long as they could be worked, with a loss of thirteen men to the section. The other four guns at the Talley House were in a faulty position, and had no opportunity whatever to fight, the enemy being completely in their rear, and flight or surrender were the only alternatives. The investigator fails to find cause for blaming the Germans in the battle of Chancellorsville. On the contrary, he finds much worthy of praise, and that the denunciations against them are extremely unfair and unjust, and arose from ignorance, from malice or from prejudice.

NOTE NO. 22.

Berry's Division not in Action.

Although the histories of the war teem with glowing accounts of how Berry's Division stopped the advance of Jackson's Corps, and, as Hooker affirms, hurled Jackson's men back at the point of the bayonet, the compiler is unable to find any evidence that Jackson's men approached nearer than seven hundred yards—except pickets—to Berry's line of battle. Up to ten P. M. the nearest rebels were those of Lane's Brigade, seven to eight hundred yards in front of Berry, with a dense forest intervening. After ten P. M. Lane's left wing was withdrawn to the south of the road, and Pender's Brigade took the vacant place north of the road, and he says that his skirmishers were thrown out and remained until Sunday morning, and that there was no fighting, and no firing except artillery shelling.—(Page 935.)

General Revere, of the Second Brigade of Berry's Division, and in the front line, reported (page 461) that he was ordered to charge with the bayonet on arriving at the front, but there was no enemy in front to charge except pickets. Captain Poland, Chief of Staff, placed the troops in position by order of General Berry, and reports at nine P. M. that the enemy was distant three hundred yards in front, and does not mention any fighting whatever. Colonel Burns, of the Seventy-third New York, on the left of the Plank Road, reports that he repulsed two attacks of the enemy, but as Lane's men were behind the Log Works of Williams, a thousand yards distant, and from which they did not move until Sunday morning, it is very evident that Burns mistook the picket firing for that of a line of battle. With the exception of the First Massachusetts, none of all the regiments of Berry's Division report any fighting during the night or in the evening, when they advanced to check Jackson's victorious columns, which did not appear until Sunday morning. This regiment reports two men killed and one wounded during the evening, and it seems that those were shot when a part of the regiment fired into its own skirmishers.

NOTE NO. 23.

General Couch's Statements, Etc.

Couch's statements concerning affairs at Chancellorsville are not

very favorable to Hooker. He assured Couch that he had Lee just where
he wanted him, and that Lee must fight him on his own ground; but
Couch then believed the battle would be lost. Afterwards he informed
Couch that Lee was in full retreat, and that he had sent Sickles to capture his artillery. Couch states that at the midnight meeting of the
4th of May, Howard was for fight, admitting that the situation was due
to the bad conduct of his corps—the Eleventh. General Couch has since
the battle affirmed that no corps surprised as the Eleventh was at this
time could have held its ground under similar circumstances.

When Sickles started on his expedition south of the Furnace, General Hooker was adverse to commencing the attack, and his last words
were: "Don't bring on a fight, Sickles." Pleasanton states that the
Eleventh Corps was in a miserable position, and he testified that Hooker
sent for him and told him that Lee was retreating to Gordonsville, and
he wanted him to follow the rebels up and do all the damage possible.
Generals Warren and Hancock both testified to Congress that it was
generally supposed in the army that General Lee's army was running
away. Hooker also stated to the same committee that his telegram to
Sedgwick was based upon a report sent in from General Sickles that the
enemy was flying. When Sickles asked for his Third Division he also
asked that Pleasanton and his cavalry be sent to him, that his forces were
in position, and he was about to open his attack in full force.

NOTE NO. 24.

Report of Major General Carl Schurz, U. S. Army.

STAFFORD COURT HOUSE, *May 12, 1863.*

* * * In closing this report, I beg leave to make one addi-
tional remark. The Eleventh Corps, and, by error or malice, especially
the Third Division, has been held up to the whole country as a band of
cowards. My division has been made responsible for the defeat of the
Eleventh Corps, and the Eleventh Corps for the failure of the campaign.
Preposterous as this is, yet we have been overwhelmed by the army and
the press with abuse and insult beyond measure. We have borne as
much as human nature can endure. I am far from saying that on May 2,
everybody did his duty to the best of his power. But one thing I will
say, because I know it: These men are not cowards. I have seen most
of them fight before this, and they fought as bravely as any. I am also
far from saying that it would have been quite impossible to do better in
the position the corps occupied on May 2nd; but I have seen with my
own eyes troops who now affect to look down upon the Eleventh Corps
with sovereign contempt behave much worse under circumstances far
less trying.

Being charged with such an enormous responsibility as the failure of a campaign involves, it would seem to me that every commander in this corps has a right to a fair investigation of his conduct, and of the circumstances surrounding him and his command on that occasion. I would, therefore, most respectfully and most urgently ask for permission to publish this report. Every statement contained therein is strictly truthful, to the best of my information. If I have erred in any particular, my errors can easily be corrected. But if what I say is true, I deem it due to myself and those who serve under me that the country should know it.

I am, General, most respectfully, your obedient servant,

C. SCHURZ,

Major-General, Comdg. Third Div. Eleventh Army Corps.

MAJ. GEN. O. O. HOWARD,

Commanding Eleventh Army Corps.

Schurz Objects to a Transfer.

May 21, 1863.

General — The arrangement spoken of between yourself and the Secretary of War with regard to my transfer to another army is not acceptable under present circumstances. You remember that about seven weeks ago I expressed a desire to leave with my troops, for the reason that I anticipated difficulties which would be apt to impair the efficiency of the corps. The disaster which befell us on the 2nd of May has brought about a state of things which seems to justify my apprehensions in a much larger measure than I expected; nevertheless, it is now impossible for me and my troops to agree to an arrangement which formerly we would have been happy to accept.

My reasons are these : I have been most outrageously slandered by the press. Ridiculous as it may seem, my division has been made responsible for the defeat of the corps ; my officers and men have been called cowards. If we go now, will it not have the appearance as if we were shaken off by the Army of the Potomac? Would it not, to a certainty, confirm the slanders circulated about me? Would it not seem as if I voluntarily accepted the responsibility for the disaster of May 2nd? To such an arrangement, under such circumstances, I can never consent.

I have asked for one of two things : Either the publication of my official report, or a court of inquiry, so that the true facts may come to light, and the responsibility for the disaster be fairly apportioned. For this, and nothing else, have I asked, and I shall urge this with all possible energy. Although under all other circumstances I should be willing to go to some other theater of war, under these circumstances I am satisfied with my command as it is and where it is. I consider it a duty to myself and my men to stand right here until the mist that hangs over the events of the 2nd of May is cleared up.

Besides, I had a conversation with General Hooker, in the course of which this subject was incidentally touched, and he pronounced himself decidedly opposed to my going, either with or without my troops.

I am, General, most respectfully, yours,

C. SCHURZ,

MAJOR-GENERAL O. O. HOWARD,   *Major-General.*
Headquarters Eleventh Corps.

Schurz Wanted His Report Published.

CAMP NEAR STAFFORD COURT-HOUSE,
May 18, 1863.

HON. E. M. STANTON, *Secretary of War.*

Sir—I would respectfully ask for permission to publish my report on the part taken by my division in the action of the 2nd of May. My reasons for making this request are the following : The conduct of the Eleventh Corps, and especially of my division, has been so outrageously and so persistently misrepresented by the press throughout the country, and officers, as well as men, have had and still have to suffer so much abuse and insult at the hands of the rest of the army, that they would seem to have a right to have a true statement of the circumstances of the case laid before the people, so that they may hope to be judged by their true merits.

It is a very hard thing for soldiers to be universally stigmatized as cowards, and is apt to demoralize them more than a defeat. Without claiming for the officers and men of my command anything that is not due to them, I would respectfully represent that, in my humble opinion, it would be but just, and greatly for the benefit of the morale of the men, that the country should be made to understand the disastrous occurrence of the 2nd of May in its true character.

If the publication of my report should seem inexpedient to you, I would respectfully ask for a court of inquiry, to publicly investigate the circumstances surrounding my command on the 2nd of May, and the causes of its defeat.

I am, sir, most respectfully, your obedient servant,

C. SCHURZ,
Major-General, Comdg. Third Div. Eleventh Army Corps.

HEADQUARTERS ELEVENTH ARMY CORPS,
May 18, 1863.

Respectfully forwarded.

O. O. HOWARD,
Major-General, Commanding.

HEADQUARTERS ARMY OF THE POTOMAC,
May 18, 1863.

Respectfully forwarded.   I hope soon to be able to transmit all the reports of the recent battles, and meanwhile I cannot approve of the publication of an isolated report.

JOSEPH HOOKER,
Major-General, Commanding.

A Court of Inquiry Asked For.

CAMP NEAR BROOKE'S STATION, VA., *May 30, 1863.*

HON. E. M. STANTON, *Secretary of War.*

Sir—To my application for permission to publish my report of the part taken by my division in the battle of Chancellorsville, I received, through the Adjutant General, the reply that "It is contrary to orders to publish the reports of battles except through the proper official channels."

In accordance with this, I would, for the reasons enumerated in my letter of the 18th instant, respectfully request you to publish my report when it reaches the War Department through the proper channels.

I would also most respectfully repeat my request that if the publication of my report should seem inexpedient to you, a court of inquiry be granted me, for the purpose of publicly investigating the circumstances surrounding my command on the 2nd of May, the causes of its defeat, and my conduct on that occasion.

I am, sir, most respectfully, your obedient servant,

C. SCHURZ,
Major-General, Comdg. Third Div. Eleventh Army Corps.

(Indorsements.)

HEADQUARTERS ELEVENTH ARMY CORPS, *May 30, 1863.*

Respectfully forwarded.   With reference to the court of inquiry asked for, I recommend that the request be granted.   I do not know of any charges against General Schurz from an official quarter, but I do not shrink from a thorough investigation of all the circumstances connected with the disaster of May 2nd.

O. O. HOWARD,
Major-General, Commanding.

HEADQUARTERS ARMY OF THE POTOMAC, *June 1, 1863.*

Respectfully forwarded to the Adjutant General of the army.

JOSEPH HOOKER,
Major-General, Commanding.

June 4, 1863.

Publication of partial reports not approved till the general commanding has time to make his report.

W. H. HALLECK,
General-in-Chief.

[Hooker never made any official report, and Halleck has stated that he never received any official information, either of his plans or their execution.—COMPILER.]

General Shimmelpfennig's Protest.

HEADQUARTERS FIRST BRIGADE, THIRD DIVISION,

ELEVENTH ARMY CORPS, *May 10, 1863.*

General—The officers and men of this brigade of your division, filled with indignation, come to me with newspapers in their hands, and ask if such be the rewards they may expect for the sufferings they have endured and the bravery they have displayed. The most infamous falsehoods have been circulated through the papers in regard to the conduct of the troops of your division in the battle of the 2nd instant. It would seem as if a nest of vipers had but waited for an auspicious moment to spit out their poisonous slanders upon this heretofore honored corps. Little would I heed it were these reports but emanations from the prurient imaginations of those who live by dipping their pens in the blood of the slain, instead of standing up for their country, sword and musket in hand ; but they are dated "Headquarters of General Hooker," and they are signed by responsible names.

*   *   *   *   *   *   *   *   *

General, I am an old soldier. To this hour I have been proud to command the brave men of this brigade ; but I am sure that unless these infamous falsehoods be retracted and reparation made, their good-will and soldierly spirit will be broken, and I shall no longer be at the head of the same brave men whom I have had heretofore the honor to lead. In the name of truth and common honesty, in the name of the good cause of our country, I ask, therefore, for satisfaction. If our superior officers be not sufficiently in possession of the facts, I demand an investigation ; if they are, I demand that the miserable penny-a-liners who have slandered the division be excluded, by a public order, from our lines, and that the names of the originators of these slanders be made known to me and my brigade, that they may be held responsible for their acts.

Respectfully,

A. SCHIMMELPFENNIG,

MAJ. GEN, CARL SCHURZ,   *Brigadier-General, Commanding.*
Commanding Division.

RESOLUTIONS

RESOLUTIONS.

WHEREAS, Doubts have heretofore existed as to the conduct of the Eleventh Army Corps of the Army of the Potomac in the battle of Chancellorsville, on the evening of May 2nd, 1863; and

Whereas, Colonel A. C. Hamlin, of Bangor, Maine, the historian of said corps, after long years of careful research, has demonstrated by his history of said corps, now ready for publication, that it was free from fault in said battle, when meeting the flower of the Confederate army, under its most able and distinguished commander, Lieutenant General Stonewall Jackson, who came down upon the right flank of the Eleventh Corps with more fearful odds than was ever known in any battle of the Civil War; and

Whereas, The soldiers of said Eleventh Corps gallantly and desperately met said charge, and stood up bravely against it, but had no chance for victory, and were forced to retire, completely outflanked and outgeneraled by overwhelming numbers; and

Whereas, Their commanders sought to conceal their incapacity by causing reflections to be cast upon the soldierly conduct of the members of said Eleventh Corps; and

Whereas, Colonel Hamlin has fully vindicated the honor and courage of the soldiers of said Eleventh Corps, as appears at length in his able history of said battle; now therefore be it

Resolved, By the Society of the Officers and Soldiers of said Eleventh Army Corps, at its annual meeting, held in the city of New York on the 19th day of December, 1895, as follows, to wit:

1. That the earnest and hearty thanks of this society are hereby unanimously tendered to Colonel A. C. Hamlin, the historian of said corps, for the able manner in which he

(175)

has so fully vindicated the honor and soldierly courage of the Eleventh Corps in the battle of Chancellorsville, on May 2nd, 1863.

2. That we unanimously express our admiration for the untiring efforts of Colonel Hamlin, who, without reward or compensation, but from a sense of duty and affection for his comrades, has, after years of labor, made plain the true history of the conduct of the Eleventh Corps in the battle of Chancellorsville, and has demonstrated beyond question that its conduct was that of gallant soldiers doing their full duty upon the field of battle.

3. That we especially commend the literary ability of Colonel Hamlin in the preparation of this work, and recommend that every surviving officer and soldier of the Eleventh Corps procure a copy thereof as soon as the necessary funds for its publication have been raised.

4. *Resolved*, That a copy of these resolutions be transmitted to Colonel Hamlin by the secretary of this society.

EXPLANATION OF MAPS

NUMBERS 1 TO 9, INCLUSIVE

EXPLANATION OF MAPS.

MAP NO. 1.

Position of Federal Troops Saturday Morning.

MAP No. 1 represents the position of the Federal troops at eight o'clock Saturday morning, May 2d, 1863. All the roads and by-paths in the forest and the railroad cut were filled with Jackson's men and fighting trains, marching rapidly to the west, to the rear and flank of the Eleventh Corps.

MAP NO. 2.

Position of Both Armies at 5 p. m.

This map shows the positions of the two armies at the hour of five o'clock Saturday afternoon, May 2d, 1863. Jackson's line of battle stretched more than a mile to the rear of the unprotected Eleventh Corps, most of the regiments of which faced south, instead of to the west to meet the enemy. Birney's Division, with Barlow's Brigade of the Eleventh Corps, were marching south in search of Jackson, while Whipple's and Williams' Divisions were threatening Anderson's Division of General Lee's army. The Third Corps works at Hazel Grove were abandoned, and the Log Works of the Twelfth Corps, Williams' Division, had but four companies of the Twenty-eighth New York to protect them. There was no suspicion of Jackson's position at this time at the Federal headquarters at the Chancellor House.

MAP NO. 3.

Jackson's Attack.

This map shows the positions at 5.30 to 5.45 P. M. Jackson had enveloped Von Gilsa's men. Colquitt had halted and ordered his brigade to face to the south. Birney, with his division of the Third Corps, was still marching to the south in search of Jackson, while Barlow's Brigade of the Eleventh Corps marched in the same direction, protecting the right flank of the column. The positions of the regiments of the Eleventh Corps were unchanged, mostly facing south, except the Twenty-fifth and Seventy-fifth Ohio, in reserve at the Talley Farm, which were then changing front without orders. Williams' and Whipple's Divisions were still in front of Anderson's Division of Lee's army, and at the Chancellor House there were, as yet, no suspicions of danger.

(179)

MAP NO. 4.

Jackson's Progress.

This map shows the positions at 5.45 to 6.10 P. M. Von Gilsa's Brigade had been wrecked, and alone the Seventy-fifth Ohio, with some of the men from Von Gilsa's line, two hundred yards west of the Dirt Road, were attempting to hold back several brigades of the enemy, who enveloped them on three sides. The left wing of Jackson's force was about to attack the right of Schurz's Division, whose left was attempting to change front in the rush of Devens' routed men. Barlow and Birney were still marching south, unconscious of Jackson's attack. Whipple and Williams, with their powerful divisions, were yet amusing the skirmishers of Anderson's Division, and at the Chancellor House all was serene. Hooker and two of his staff were seated on the veranda enjoying the summer evening, unconscious of the fact that Jackson had been destroying Devens' Division, less than three miles distant. Colquitt had turned his brigade, without orders, to the south, and, with Ramseur's Brigade, was vainly seeking Federal troops, while Paxton and Lee, with nine regiments, were obliged to remain passive spectators of the fight in front of them; seventeen regiments withheld by Colquitt's folly.

MAP NO. 5.

The Attack on Schurz's Division.

This map represents the positions at 6.10 to 6.30 P. M. Devens' Division had been destroyed, and Schurz's Division, with the rallied men of Devens, was making a stand. Colquitt had found out his error, and had turned his brigade again to march to the support of Jackson's right flank, but too late. Seventeen rebel regiments detained from the first and second attacks. Barlow and Birney were still marching south, unconscious of the massacre in their rear. Hooker is at last aware of the presence of the enemy, but Whipple and Williams still amuse Anderson, near the Furnace. All serene at Hazel Grove, where there are three regiments of cavalry, one regiment of infantry and four batteries, with trains in bivouac, unconscious of the fighting only a mile and a half away.

MAP NO. 6.

The Attack on Buschbeck.

Map of positions at 6.30 to 7 or 7.15 P. M. The Buschbeck line, or the third position of the Eleventh Corps, attacked and flanked by Jackson's men, Colquitt, Ramseur and Paxton having joined the attacking force. Barlow and Birney are still hunting for Jackson below the Railroad Cut. Williams warned by Slocum to retire. Berry ordered to advance. At Hazel Grove all is serene, the Eighth Pennsylvania

Cavalry starting to join Howard at Dowdall's. Batteries and regiments
of cavalry and infantry in bivouac, and unaware of danger. Anderson
and McLaws still unaware of Jackson's attack, and ready to press their
front as soon as they were sure of it.

MAP NO. 7.

Jackson's Army Halting at Dowdall's.

This map represents the positions at 7.15 to 7.45 P. M. Jackson's
Corps had all halted at Dowdall's, with the exception of the men who
had gone forward without orders as far as the Log Works of Williams'
Division, or the vista, near Hazel Grove. The Eighth Pennsylvania
Cavalry, with the ammunition mule train of the Third Corps, had passed
out of Hazel Grove, and the head of the column had run into the groups
of rebel foragers near the Plank Road. The dotted line shows the
route of the cavalry, and where Huey and survivors came out into the
Plank Road, and before Berry had reached his position. Buschbeck had
already taken his position in front of the batteries which Captain Best
was endeavoring to form into line, and which he held until the next
morning. To the north of the Plank Road the wrecks of the right of
Schurz's Division had formed a line of defense on the Bullock Road,
which they maintained for some time. The foragers under Winn
stampeded the trains, batteries and men resting in the vista leading from
Hazel Grove, and the frightened crowd, as it sped over the field of
Hazel Grove, was increased from the organizations halted there, and as
the stream of frantic fugitives (not of the Eleventh Corps) hurried up
the ravine, it gathered in some of Williams' Division of the Twelfth
Corps, then hurrying back to their former position, including the Thirteenth New Jersey entire, with groups of men from the Twenty-eighth
New York, and others from the Log Works of Williams. As the mass of
men, animals, vehicles, cavalry, infantry and camp followers rushed up
the Fairview field towards Chancellor's it presented a scene never to
be forgotten. It has been described as the rout of the Eleventh Corps,
when there were none of the corps in it. The wrecks of the Eleventh
Corps long before this event had passed up the Plank Road, or to the
north of it, to the vicinity of Chancellor's. Birney was still below the
Furnace, hunting for Jackson, while Barlow had disappeared far below
the railroad. Stuart and the rebel cavalry were starting with a regiment
of infantry for Ely Ford and the rear of Hooker's army. Anderson and
McLaws were yet ignorant of the success or the position of Jackson's
forces, and did not press their opponents as vigorously as the plan of
attack intended.

MAP NO. 8.

Jackson's Forces Reforming.

Time, nine to ten P. M. Stuart and one regiment of infantry had gone to Ely Ford. Jackson's forces were halted or reforming at or near the Dowdall fields. Lane's Brigade had deployed in front, with Pender in column, some distance in the rear. McGowan was at the Log Hut, farther in the rear, and Heth's Brigade to the west of them. Colquitt, Ramseur and Paxton were ready to move forward, while the broad road was crowded with battalions of artillery. Both Rodes' and Colston's Divisions were formed, ready to assist Hill's Division. Lane's right flank and rear were totally unprotected, as he was unaware of the enemy at Hazel Grove. The dotted lines show where Jackson went after parting with Lane, and where he was when shot. The monument to Jackson stands at the junction of the Dirt and the Plank Roads, sixty yards, more or less, south of the place where he was fired upon. Buschbeck's Brigade of the Eleventh Corps was still in position in front of Best's guns, and the rallied parts of Schurz's Division were on the Bullock Road, to the right of Berry's men. Sickles and Birney were returning to Hazel Grove, while Barlow was trying to find his way back in the darkness and tangled paths of the forest.

MAP NO. 9.

Position of both Armies at the Midnight Charge.

Time, ten P. M. to twelve midnight. Jackson's army in position. Lane, by command of Heth, had withdrawn the two regiments from the north of the Plank Road, and deflected his right to cover the road coming from Hazel Grove, in time to meet the reconnaissance of the left of Birney's Division—known as the Midnight Charge. Barlow found his way out of the woods, and arrived at Hazel Grove just in time to witness the rapid return of many of Birney's Division when fired into by Lane's North Carolinians. Buschbeck's Brigade of the Eleventh Corps was still in position in front of the Federal batteries. The rallied parts of Schurz's Division, on the Bullock Road, had been withdrawn. The dotted lines represent the Federal artillery fire, both at 9 30 P. M., after the wounding of Jackson, and also at the time when Birney made his midnight charge.

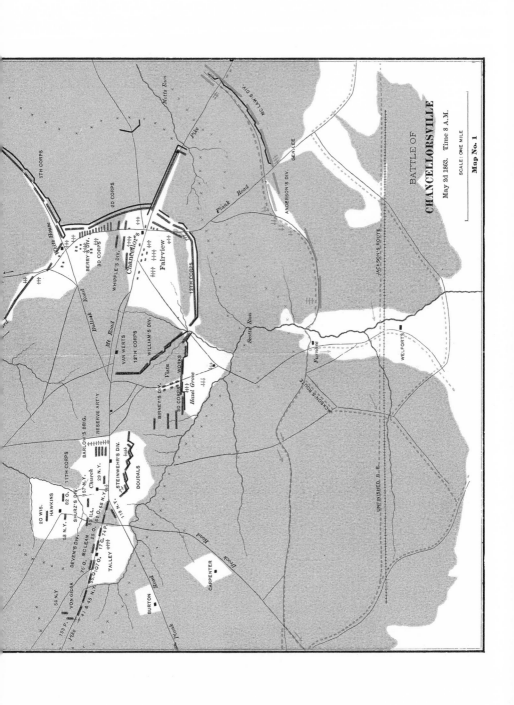

BATTLE OF

CHANCELLORSVILLE

May 2d 1863.   Time 8 A.M.

SCALE: ONE MILE

Map No. 1

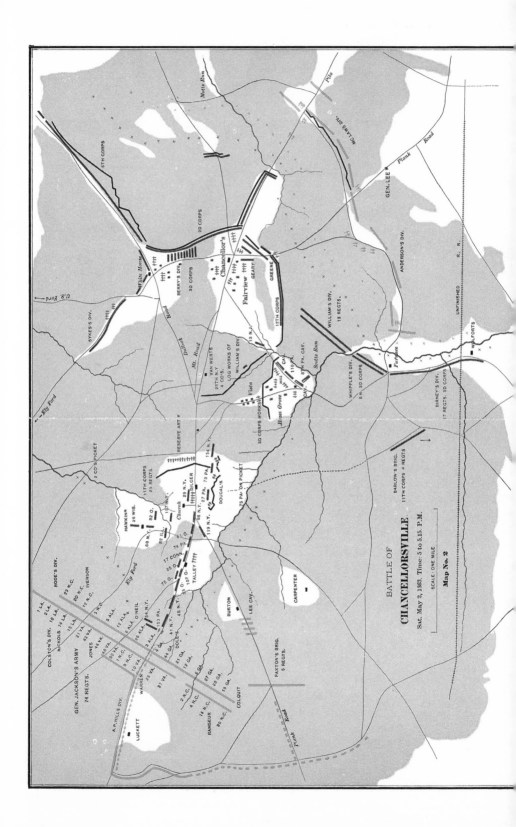

BATTLE OF

CHANCELLORSVILLE.

Sat. May 2, 1863. Time: 5 to 5.15. P.M.

SCALE: ONE MILE

Map No. 2

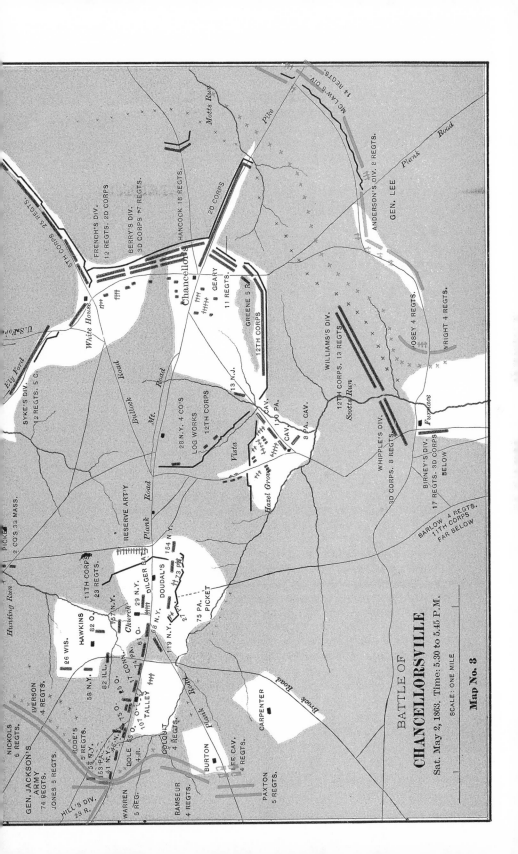

BATTLE OF
CHANCELLORSVILLE

Sat. May 2, 1863, Time: 5.30 to 5.45 P.M.

SCALE: ONE MILE

Map No. 3

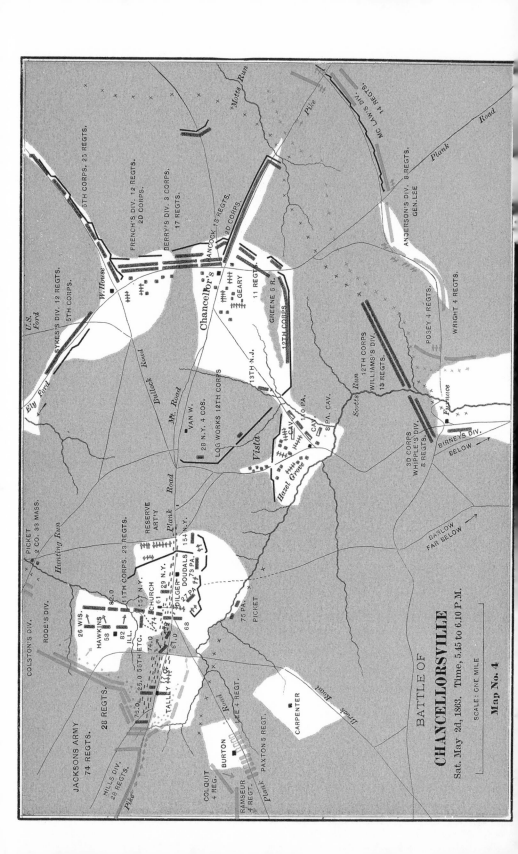

BATTLE OF
CHANCELLORSVILLE
Sat. May 2d, 1863. Time, 5.45 to 6.10 P.M.

SCALE: ONE MILE

Map No. 4

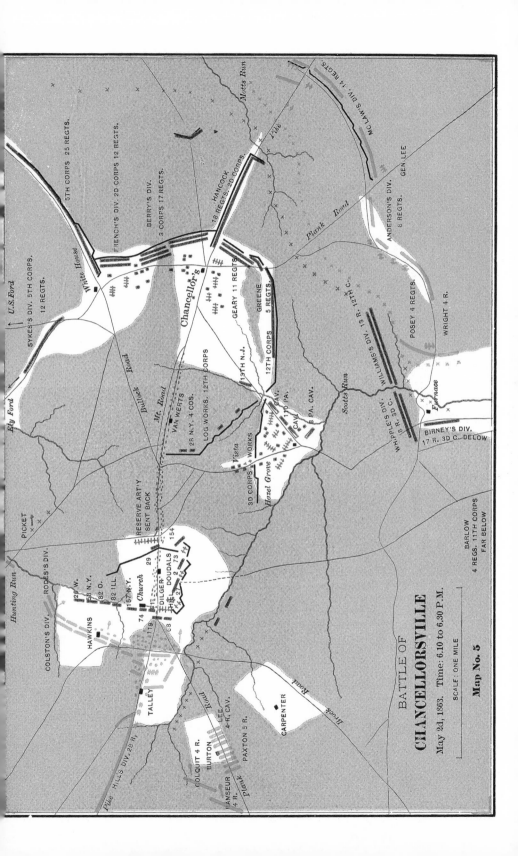

BATTLE OF

CHANCELLORSVILLE

May 2d, 1863. Time: 6.10 to 6.30 P.M.

SCALE: ONE MILE

Map No. 5

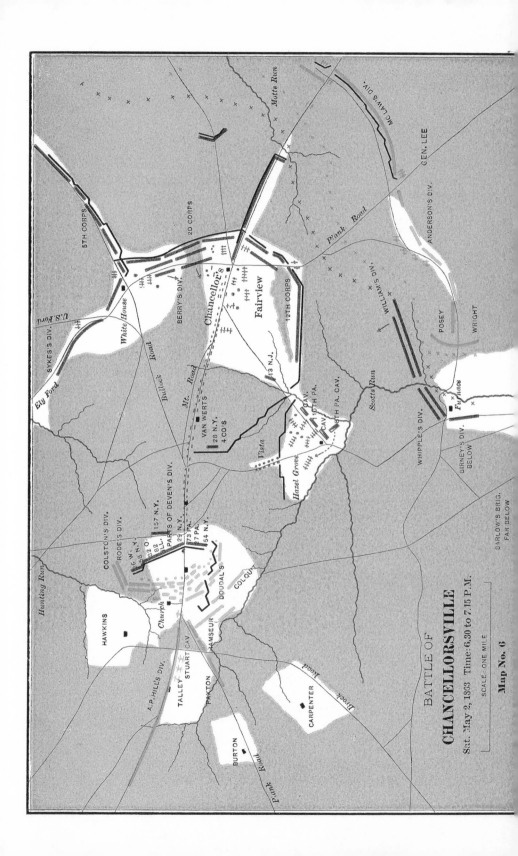

BATTLE OF
CHANCELLORSVILLE

Sat. May 2, 1863 Time: 6.30 to 7.15 P.M.

SCALE: ONE MILE

Map No. 6

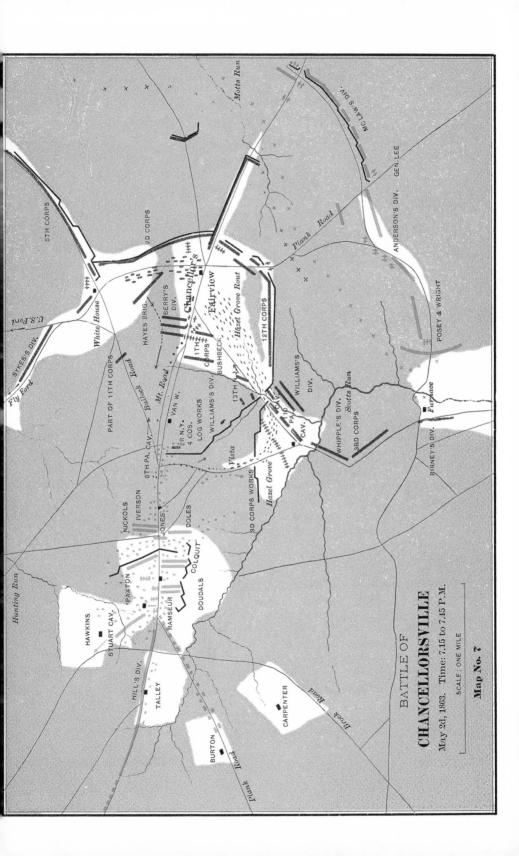

BATTLE OF

CHANCELLORSVILLE

May 2d, 1863. Time: 7.15 to 7.45 P.M.

SCALE: ONE MILE

Map No. 7

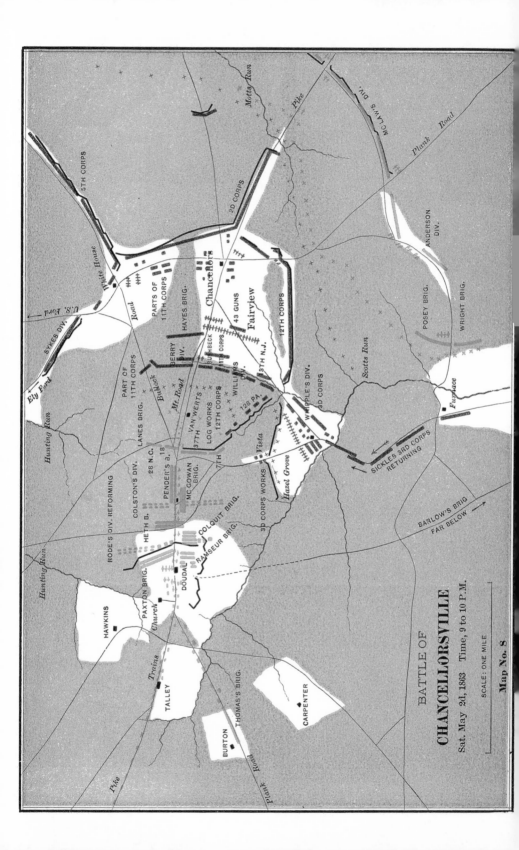

BATTLE OF
CHANCELLORSVILLE
Sat. May 2d, 1863   Time, 9 to 10 P.M.

SCALE: ONE MILE

Map No. 8

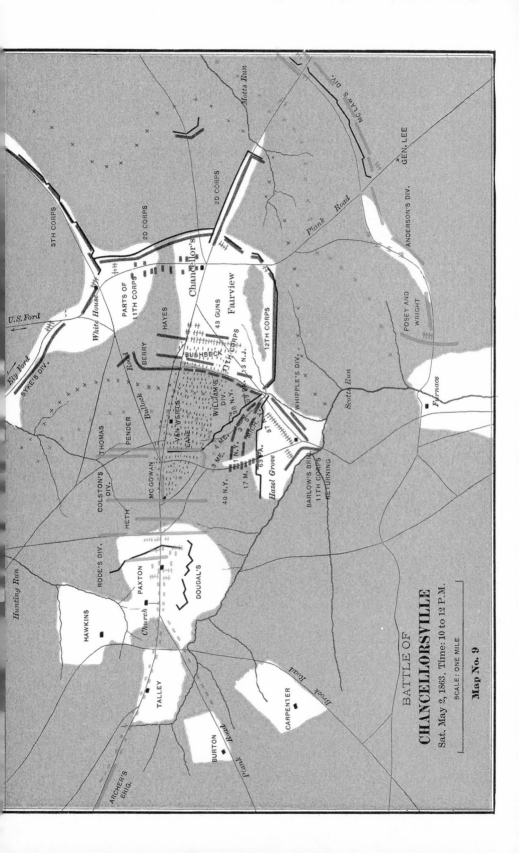

BATTLE OF
CHANCELLORSVILLE
Sat. May 2, 1863, Time: 10 to 12 P.M.

SCALE: ONE MILE

Map No. 9

INDEX

INDEX.

A.

(185)

188   INDEX.

H.

W.

ERRATA.

A careful reading of the printed sheets of "The Battle of Chancellorsville" by a keen-eyed friend of the author has brought to light some errors in compilation and typography, which are corrected as indicated below :

Page 5, 10th line from bottom, should read "May 3d," instead of "May 2d."

" 39, 18th line, should read "Peissner," instead of Peisner."

" 40, 19th line, and page 62, 18th line, should read "Reily," instead of "Riley."

" 41, 23d line, should read "Amsberg," instead of "Arnsberg."

" 42, 9th line, should read "Brückner," instead of "Bruenecker."

" 46, 5th line, and page 172, at foot, should read "Schimmelfennig," instead of "Schimmelpfennig."

" 51, 24th line, should read "cavalry," instead of "calvary."

" 55, 2d line from bottom, should read "Battery I, First Ohio," instead of "Independent Battery I, of Ohio."

" 88, 17th line, should read "Stine," instead of "Stein."

" 101, 19th line, should read "Forty-sixth Pennsylvania," instead of "Forty-sixth New York."

" 124, top line, should read "Greene's," instead of "Green's."

" 131, 14th line, should read "35 men were killed and wounded," instead of "27 men," etc.

" 133, 25th line, at end, should read "120th New York," instead of "102d New York."

" 139, 4th line, should read "Germanna Ford," instead of "Germania Ford.'

" 153, 6th line, from bottom should read "Fesler," instead of "Feshler."